MW00817305

BACKPACKING
the KELTY WAY

Most Perigee Books are available at special quantity discounts for bulk purchases for sales promotions, premiums, fund-raising, or educational use. Special books, or book excerpts, can also be created to fit specific needs.

For details, write Special Markets, The Berkley Publishing Group, 375 Hudson Street, New York, New York 10014.

BACKPACKING
the KELTY WAY

Nena Kelty and
Steve Boga

A Perigee Book

A Perigee Book
Published by The Berkley Publishing Group
A division of Penguin Putnam Inc.
375 Hudson Street
New York, New York 10014

Copyright © 2000 by Nena Kelty and Steve Boga
Book design by Tiffany Kukec
Cover design by Miguel Santana

Front cover photograph credits (clockwise, starting from the top): Rick Ridgeway/Adventure Photo & Film, Rick Ridgeway/Adventure Photo & Film, Brian Bailey/Adventure Photo & Film, Dennis Welsh/Adventure Photo & Film, Rick Ridgeway/Adventure Photo & Film, Scott Spiker/Adventure Photo & Film, Rick Ridgeway/Adventure Photo & Film, Greg Epperson/Adventure Photo & Film, Dennis Welsh/Adventure Photo & Film, Rick Ridgeway/Adventure Photo & Film, Rick Ridgeway/Adventure Photo & Film, Gary Brettnacher/Adventure Photo & Film

Interior photographs credits: Tracy Reid (pg. x), Tom McMakin (pg. 16), Carl Siechert (pg. 20, 127, 131, 361), Chris Brown (pg. 27), Rick Ridgeway (pg. 65, 129, 131, 133, 134, 349, 359), Dick Kelty (pg. 126), and John Kelty (pg. 350)

All photographs and illustrations not specifically credited are provided courtesy of the Kelty family.

Interior illustrations credits: Jade Lew (pg. 3, 281, 284); John Kelty (pg. 52, 64, 212, 213, 222, 317)

All rights reserved. This book, or parts thereof,
may not be reproduced in any form without permission.

First edition: April 2000

Published simultaneously in Canada.

The Penguin Putnam Inc. World Wide Web site address is
http://www.penguinputnam.com

Library of Congress Cataloging-in-Publication Data

Kelty, Nena.
   Backpacking the Kelty way / Nena Kelty and Steve Boga.—1st ed.
      p. cm.
   Includes index.
   ISBN 0-399-52585-8
   1. Backpacking—United States.   2. Hiking—United States.   I. Boga, Steve, 1947–
II. Title.
GV199.4.K45 2000

                                                                              99-058103

Printed in the United States of America

10   9   8   7   6   5   4   3   2   1

To Dick
whose vision and accomplishments
were the inspiration for this book

CONTENTS

FOREWORD

IN 1942, if a fortune-teller had predicted that within ten years I would be hiking the Sierra Nevada Mountains in California with a pack on my back, I would have scoffed at the notion. At the time, I was dancing at the London Palladium in the musical show *Happy and Glorious*.

It was a glamorous life—working with England's top talent, meeting visiting movie stars. But when Dick Kelty came along with his winning ways, swept me off my feet, and said, "Let me take you away from all this," I gave it up willingly. From that moment on, my life changed dramatically: I married, emigrated to America, and started to raise a family.

It was in the early fifties, after we had settled down in California and Dick was busy developing the Kelty Pack, that I first backpacked. Although excited by the prospect of visiting the High Sierra, mountains I'd seen only on calendars, I was dubious. Hike up and down mountains, carry my food and lodging on my back, sleep on the ground—on my vacation? But my fears were unfounded. The stunning beauty of pristine streams, azure lakes, and craggy rocks shaped like castles, the realization of how little equipment I needed to see it all, even the physical effort of hiking—it all gave me a sense of freedom and joy I'd never known before.

Dick and I took many trips into the High Sierra with friends and, later, with our children. For Dick, the Sierra were heaven on earth. He felt little need to venture farther. But I had seen little of America, and so when my geologist friend, Margaret Cox, asked if I wanted to join her on a hike to the bottom of Grand Canyon, I jumped at the chance.

Dick Kelty

Photo by Tracy Reid

The first day we drove to Williams, Arizona, where we spent the night. Getting an early start the next morning, we drove fifty-nine miles to Grand Canyon Village and parked the car. It was snowing, which surprised me. How would this affect our plans? Margaret, familiar with weather vagaries in the area, assured me that we would soon be enjoying nice weather. Confidence partially restored, I shouldered my backpack and started off behind her down Bright Angel Trail. Margaret's forecast came true. We were soon out of snow, and the day grew warmer. At a rest shelter, we read warnings on a bulletin board: "Be sure to carry plenty of water, there is no water on the trail!" Another offered "Drag-out—$20." We hoped we had enough water and wouldn't have to be dragged out. It sounded both painful and embarrassing. A mule train passed us about halfway down the seven-and-a-half-mile trail. The men in the group seemed embarrassed to see two women on foot while they traveled in "luxury." Although we hiked by choice, I began to wonder why. The relentless downhill punished my knees, and I lost count of how many aspirin I swallowed.

Finally we reached the bottom, tired but pleased with ourselves. We dropped our packs and walked over to Phantom Ranch, a tiny hotel built just beyond the campground at the end of the trail. It was now hot and we downed plenty of water, then strolled over to talk to the geologist who lived in a mobile home near the hotel. His job was to measure the silt in the Colorado River. He did this by hauling himself in a cage along a wire stretched across the river and dipping a measuring cylinder into the water. His reports were used to determine how much water would be released daily from Hoover Dam.

The next day a leisurely hike took us to Indian Garden Campground. Margaret was concerned about the rocks near where we were supposed to sleep. "Grand Canyon is home to the deadliest scorpion in the world and it lives around rocks," she said. "We'd better not sleep on the ground. We'll have to sleep on the picnic tables."

It was quite a night. I kept dozing off, only to wake with a start and grab the edge of the table, petrified that I was falling off. Around midnight we were surprised to hear voices. A whole family, including small children, strolled into the campground. As far as we could tell, they carried nothing with them—no food, water, or sleeping bags. Suddenly a young girl pulled down her jeans and relieved herself not more than ten feet from us. She obviously didn't realize the mounds on the picnic tables were actually two groggy, goggle-eyed hikers. After much chattering, the family strolled out of camp, seemingly without a care in the world.

Finally, dawn broke and it was time to leave. We found the Kaibab Trail and started the steep climb out. Uphill was strenuous but a lot easier on the knees than downhill. Feeling adventurous and carefree, we hitched a ride back to our car. Margaret and I had such a good time that we immediately planned our next trip—to Havasupai Indian Reservation. But next time, we would take our young daughters.

Later I began to wonder if my fellow backpackers knew about the pioneers who had created the gear that made it possible for them to enjoy the wilderness in relative comfort. Someone should write backpacking's history and techniques before it's all lost, I thought. It had to be more than a book about the development of the Kelty Pack. Over the years, I had collected newspaper articles and photographs related to the growth of backpacking. Maybe I should write it, I thought. But I procrastinated, until too many years had passed since I had last backpacked. I wanted a cowriter who could bring modern experiences and expertise to the project. I found him in Steve Boga, an accomplished writer and author of several books on outdoor sports. We forged an alliance both enjoyable and productive. This book is the result.

I owe debts of gratitude to many people: to the old-timers, including the early owners of Kelty Packs for their support through the years; to Rick Ridgeway, who generously provided not only photographs, but plenty of advice and encouragement; and to the many backpacking friends who contributed anecdotes, stories, pictures, and drawings. Their enthusiasm has been most appreciated.

But most of all, I owe a big "Thank you!" to Dick, not only for introducing me to backpacking, but for the integrity and dedication to service he offered his customers. It was an honor to play a small part in his revolutionary impact on the modern backpack.

—Nena Kelty

PREFACE

Let me enjoy the Earth no less
Because the all-enacting Might
That fashioned forth its loveliness
Had aims other than my delight.

—Thomas Hardy

RECENT years have seen a backpacking boom, a true growth spurt. Consider the evidence:

- The number of backpackers jumped 72.2 percent between 1982 and 1995, making this the third-fastest-growing outdoor activity, behind only bird-watching and hiking.

- About 49 million Americans went backpacking/wilderness camping in 1992. That's up from 42.3 million in 1988.

- The number of visitor hours spent camping on Bureau of Land Management territory increased 13 percent between 1989 and 1991.

- In 1992 camping or backpacking was the most popular participation activity in seven states (Arizona, Idaho, Nevada, Oregon, Utah, Washington, and Kansas), compared with only three states in 1991.

- Sales of backpacks made a dramatic leap in 1990 to six million units, up from four million the previous year.

And for those of you who think of backpacking as the same basic routine—race to the trailhead, hike from point A to point B, admire the sunset, then crawl into the tent to rest up for the hike back to point A—there are a host of camping trips designed to yank the most jaded backcountry hiker out of his rut. There are educational trips, historical trips, and trips that make you a part of a trail crew or a scientific expedition.

Some of these wild-hare excursions are even more offbeat. Three of our favorites:

- *Hunting for Mammoths.* The remains of two mastodons and a nearly complete skeleton of a mammoth were unearthed above nine thousand feet in Utah's Manti-LaSal National Forest. Now you can hunt mammoths with a shovel and a backpack. Contact: Earthwatch, 680 Mount Auburn St., P.O. Box 403, Watertown, MA 02272; (617) 926-8200.

- *Moose and Wolves of Isle Royale.* Collecting moose bones is an important part of the research being conducted in an attempt to provide data on the survival of moose and wolves in Michigan's Isle Royale National Park. Teams of volunteers join Dr. Rolf Peterson from Michigan Technological University in his ongoing study of the predator-prey relationship between wolves and moose. "This is not a routine backpacking trip," Peterson warns. "It will be necessary to go over or under fallen trees, work your way through thick woody shrubs, travel through thick vegetation when you can't see your feet, and negotiate bogs and numerous wetlands." All that while carrying a pack full of moose bones. Contact: Earthwatch, 680 Mount Auburn St., P.O. Box 403, Watertown, MA 02272; (617) 926-8200.

- *Backpacking in the Buff.* Groups of like-minded people in local hiking and nudist clubs organize discreet gatherings in secluded backcountry sites that offer privacy and freedom from clothing. From the mountains to the sea, these are trips that put your whole body in touch with nature. Contact: Clothing Optional Vacations, (800) 252-6833.

Chapter One

HISTORY OF
BACKPACKING

ACKPACKING for recreation is relatively new. Merriam-Webster, the dictionary people, date the first known oral use of the noun to 1914; the verb had to wait until 1927. In 1973, after appearing twelve times in print, noun and verb met the criterion for inclusion in the eighth edition of *Webster's New Collegiate Dictionary*.

A startling discovery in September 1991 taught us that if back-packing is not an old sport, it is at least an old activity. Two German alpinists on holiday in the Alps discovered a body partially buried in the Similaun Glacier on the Austrian/Italian border. It proved to be 5,300-year-old "Ice Man." Lying next to him was a larch and hazel-wood frame with a leather pouch—a primitive backpack. Traces of grain found in the pouch convinced scientists that Ice Man did not live in that area but hiked there to gather food.

The first recorded evidence of someone hiking for fun dates to 1543. Conrad Gesner, a botanist, bibliographer, and professor of phi-losophy in Zurich, Switzerland, wrote to a friend that he hiked in the mountains "for the sake of bodily exercise and the delight of the spirit." As the mountains were widely seen as homes to demons, drag-ons, and evil spirits, Gesner demonstrated a love of mountains unu-sual for the time.

In the sixteenth and seventeenth centuries, a few spirited men in Spain, France, and Italy began to explore their local mountains. And in the nineteenth century, spearheaded mostly by the British during the reign of Queen Victoria, the golden age of mountain climbing began. Well-financed sportsmen pushed exploration into unknown areas, especially in the Alps, greatly advancing survival techniques in thin, cold air.

In North America, the attitude toward hiking and backpacking also began to change in the nineteenth century, when the mountain men discovered the wild, beautiful backcountry of the United States. The era spawned writers who were capable of inspiring others to follow.

In the East, Henry David Thoreau, a mid-nineteenth-century naturalist, professional surveyor, and lover of wild country, wrote of his hikes in New England and New York. When exploring mountains, he usually hired an Indian guide, who would sometimes combine the trip with a little moose hunting. Out West, Clarence King, a participant in the Geological Survey of California in 1863–66, was the first to climb the Sierra Nevada range and write about it. He wrote of the moody grandeur of the mountains, sparking interest in other ranges.

The next wilderness preacher was John Muir. He spent the summer of 1869, and many summers thereafter, tramping through the Sierra. For the rest of his life, his love of the granite grandeur, especially in Yosemite, never diminished. A naturalist, mountaineer, and pioneer conservationist, Muir founded the Sierra Club, serving as president from 1892 to 1914. More than anyone, he aroused the American public to the need to preserve our unique wilderness beauty.

The Tumpline

The writings of these pioneers make little mention of the equipment they used. By 1796, Europeans, newly arrived in the United States, had noticed Algonquin Indians hauling goods with a unique device called a tumpline, a sling formed by a strap slung over the forehead or chest to help support a pack on the back. The Abnakis, an Indian tribe in Maine and southern Quebec, had a similar device, called the madumbi pack strap. Thoreau, in *The Maine Woods*, recommends an "India-rubber knapsack for carrying personal goods." John Muir traveled so light—blanket, biscuits, and coffee—that a cloth sack was enough for him.

During World War II, creative minds tackled the problem of how thousands of foot soldiers could carry huge loads on their backs. The necessary piece of equipment had to be rugged, cheap, and durable; comfort was a low priority. The result was the army packboard, a piece of plywood shaped into a shallow U. On it was mounted a wide canvas band that rested against the back. A heavy canvas bag was lashed to the packboard with a cord that passed around metal hooks mounted along the sides of the vertical struts. With no belly strap, the load rested entirely on the shoulders.

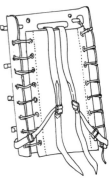

Army Packboard

After the war, this pack was sold in army surplus stores. But by 1950 only one backpack had been commercially developed for recreational hiking— the Trapper Nelson, sold through Sears Roebuck and Company. Like the army backpack, it was of simple design, with straight wooden side rails connected by several horizontal curved wooden slats. Attached to the frame was a large, deep canvas bag. One or two canvas bands mounted on the frame kept the load away from the wearer's back. The apparatus was heavy, uncomfortable, and available in one size only.

Trapper Nelson

In the early 1950s, backpack design had plenty of room for improvement. Seeing a hole and hoping to fill it, an innovative young man working in his garage in Glendale, California, revolutionized the industry with his unique design: the Kelty Pack.

Adirondack Pack Basket, Duluth Pack, Norwegian Fram or
Ski Pack, Yukon Pack

Dick Kelty's First Trip to the Sierra

Dick Kelty was born in Duluth, Minnesota, the youngest of three boys. He grew up in Glendale, California, having traveled west by train with his family in 1922.

While his father, Clifford, began work as plant superintendent of Owen's Parks, a large Los Angeles lumber company, Dick, his two brothers, Phil and Doug, and his mother, Eliza, settled down to a new life.

After about three years, Clifford, who hailed from Wisconsin, was itching to resume one of his favorite pastimes—fishing. He'd heard about great fishing near the town of Lee Vining, just east of Yosemite National Park. But how to get there? Driving in those days was an adventure in itself. The road north was paved for only about a hundred miles, as far as Mojave, and the remaining 250 miles were either oiled or gravel.

The first step was to buy a car—a brand-new Star touring car complete with canvas top and isinglass side curtains. It was risky in those days to make such a long drive alone, and so Clifford invited along another adventurous family: Rose and Bill Tannahill and their sons, Myron and Everett. Preparations for the trip began in earnest.

Clifford packed the car with the usual camping gear: tent, cots, blankets, stove, food, and fishing gear. He added two spare tires and accoutrements, including jack, inner tubes, tire irons, patching kit, and pump. Finally, he squeezed in two canvas water bags, a bag of tools, extra fan belts, some baling wire, and, just in case there was an opportunity for hunting, his .22 rifle. The car was so crammed, both inside and in the luggage racks on the running boards, that it was impossible to open the doors. Everyone had to climb over the doors to get in or out. The Tannahills equipped their Buick in a similar manner, and so early one morning in June 1925, the Kelty and Tannahill families set off for their first glimpse of the Sierra Nevada.

By the time they reached Mojave, they had to contend with the end of the paved road and the scorching heat of the Mojave Desert. Without air-conditioning, the heat was oppressive and enervating.

Road signs were few and far between. They encountered so little traffic that when they did see another car, everyone waved as if greeting a long-lost friend. Most of the time they could only guess which way to turn. In Red Rock Canyon, they guessed wrong. Arriving at a fork in the road, they noted that what few cars there were all turned left, and so they followed. Unfortunately, they hit a dead end at an aqueduct. The other cars belonged to the workers on the aqueduct. The Keltys and Tannahills had to turn around and retrace ten miles, no small distance in those days. As they left Red Rock Canyon, the country started to change. Evidence of volcanic action grabbed everyone's attention, and the boys received a lesson from their fathers on how the terrain had developed. They could see for themselves the old lava flows and cinder cones.

On the first night, they set up camp near Little Lake, glad to be able to get out of the cars and stretch their legs. As the families were settling down for the night, two visitors suddenly appeared in their camp. Introducing themselves as guards from the aqueduct, they asked the families what they were doing there. Clifford responded that they were on their way to Lee Vining and were just staying one night at Little Lake. The guards explained that they had to check on strangers because the year before, irate farmers, upset that "their" water had been diverted to Los Angeles, had dynamited the aqueduct. Assured that the families meant no harm, the guards went on their way. For the next seventy years, the aqueduct would be a bone of contention between the city of Los Angeles and the farmers of Owens Valley who believed their water was being stolen by a foreign power.

Their fears were justified: The depletion of water would eventually cripple profitable farming.

Early next morning, with dew still on the ground, they started off again. The stench of crude oil, used to keep the dust down on the roads, plagued their nostrils. Even today, whenever Dick revisits that smell, he waxes nostalgic. He'll sigh and say, "Oh, that takes me back to those early trips up the Owens Valley."

They were not far from Little Lake when an unbelievable sight unfolded before them: a two-mile stretch of concrete road, eight feet wide, with numerous turnouts! It was an experimental road built by the California Department of Transportation to determine how well concrete would endure the punishment of cars. It was a welcome, though all too brief, respite from oiled roads, and a luxury compared to what lay ahead. Before the day was out, they would blow two tires, validating Clifford's foresight.

The next big challenge was Sherwin Grade, just north of Bishop. For the cars of those days, driving up that steep, twisting, single-lane road was like climbing Mount Everest. Without synchro-mesh gears, the sound of metal grinding against metal was deafening. Before reaching the steepest part, near Paradise, both families stopped to let their engines cool down and to check the tires. Everything seemed fine, so they started up again. Just before reaching Tom's Place, a gas station and restaurant that still stands today despite being bypassed by Highway 395, the Kelty car developed a problem—steam was pouring from under the hood. Luckily they had stopped by a creek, and so the boys scrambled down the banks and brought back buckets of water to cool the engine.

After the car had cooled down, the travelers made a devastating discovery. The cast-iron support for the fan belt had cracked, preventing the fan from cooling the engine. Ever a resourceful man, Clifford fashioned a new support, using the eighteen-gauge baling wire he presciently had brought.

As they moved north, the scenery became even more dramatic. The jaw-dropping snow-capped peaks of the Sierra Nevada scratched the western sky, and the barren White Mountains, home of the bristlecone pine and little else, rose in the east. The contrast was enthralling, and no one was asking, "Are we there yet?"

Tannahill and Kelty families at Tioga Pass, 1925, and their Star Touring Car

The families finally reached Lee Vining and set up camp. They had the place to themselves. In fact, during their visits in the ensuing years, only one other couple ever camped there. Dick remembers, "The only other person we met in the area was an old man who lived in a crude shack by a small dam near Lee Vining Creek. He liked to entertain all of us boys by carving a chain out of a single piece of wood. No one knew for sure why he lived there, but it was generally assumed that he was a caretaker for the dam."

After they set up camp, Clifford took the car to the nearest garage. The joint he had rigged with wire had to be brazed, and he needed to replace two tires. He bought the tires, the work was successful, and the joint was once again a solid piece.

Eliza, who had been a good sport about the adventuring, suggested they do something that she and Rose would enjoy. "You fellows have your fishing," she said. "I think every other day the families should do something together, see more of the country." Everyone agreed, with various degrees of enthusiasm. Because of her insistence, the families made short side trips to the old mining towns of Lundy and Bodie, which were virtually unchanged since their abandonment thirty years before. They drove into Yosemite National Park on old Tioga Road, a steep, twisting, hair-raising experience back then. When they reached the park entrance, the ranger asked if they had any guns in the car. Clifford told him he had a .22 rifle. "I'll just take that and put a seal on it," the ranger said. "Shooting is not allowed in the park. If another ranger stops you, he'll want to check to see if the seal has been broken and the rifle fired."

Tannahill and Kelty boys fishing

Both families were in awe of the high-altitude mix of granite and grass at Tuolumne Meadows. A long swim in the Tuolumne River before they left to go back to camp provided a perfect ending to the day. Lee Vining proved to be a good base camp for these outings.

But fishing was what the men and boys had come for. Bill Tannahill took the prize one day with a record nine-pound trout out of Grant's Lake. Unfortunately, Dick's eleven-year-old brother, Phil, could only brag about the fish he caught, as he ate them before he could offer them into evidence. It happened the day the dads dropped Phil and Myron off at Rush Creek to go fishing. As they drove away, Clifford shouted, "We'll pick you up at five o'clock!"

The boys had a great day of fishing, but by five o'clock they were ready to return to camp. No fathers were in sight, so they stretched out on the grass and compared fish. Soon, the sun went down behind the mountains and it started to get chilly. "We'd better start a fire," said Phil. That cut the chill, but now they were hungry and a little scared. They decided to cook their fish. After eating, they were just as alone as ever. By now they were scared and mad. Would they have to spend the night there? they wondered. Finally, at about eight o'clock, the fathers appeared. "I was so mad at them," says Phil, "that I can't remember to this day what reason they gave for being late."

After two and a half weeks, it was time for the Keltys and Tannahills to go home. Before they could leave, however, the authorities told them that foot-and-mouth disease had broken out in Inyo County. To prevent further spread of this dread disease, Clifford and Bill had to drive their cars slowly through a shallow trough filled with antiseptic liquid designed to kill any of the highly infectious virus that might be on the tires.

The Keltys and Tannahills arrived home full of wonder, thrilled by the prospect of future trips to the beautiful mountains up north. Although six-year-old Dick Kelty didn't realize it at the time, his father had introduced him to what would become his favorite place on earth—the beautiful Sierra Nevada. Decades later, all three boys could vividly recall details of their first trip to the Sierra.

■ Ireland in the 1940s

Glendale, nestled at the base of the Verdugo Mountains and often called the bedroom community of Los Angeles, was the ideal place to raise a family in the twenties and thirties. Dick enjoyed a happy childhood and did well in school. He recalls, "I was not a joiner of clubs and not interested in team sports, although I did go out for track. My favorite activity was hiking. I hiked every chance I got, mostly in the Verdugo Mountains with friends and in the Sierra with the family."

After graduation from high school, he followed his brother Doug to the Curtis-Wright Aviation School in Glendale. After completing that course, he was able to get a job at Northrup, which was then in Inglewood. About six months later, he took another job at Lockheed in Burbank, where he assembled aircraft parts for Hudson bombers destined for Great Britain. "Although I enjoyed the work," he says, "I didn't think I'd be doing it for the rest of my life."

In 1942, the Lockheed Overseas Corporation offered some of its workers a two-year contract to work in Northern Ireland. It was an attractive offer with good pay, and Dick accepted. By July, he and 150 other men were on their way to Europe. When they arrived in New York, the men were assigned to three different ships all headed for Halifax, Nova Scotia, where they would join a convoy before crossing the Atlantic Ocean. After nine days at sea, they reached Liverpool, where they were told that Langford Lodge, their final destination in Ireland, was not yet ready to accommodate so many people. A new, unoccupied facility, built for munitions workers near Manchester, became their home for the next few weeks.

When the men finally got the go-ahead, they took a train north to Stranraer, where they caught the ferry to Belfast. Their final destination—Langford Lodge, formerly a private estate—was located on the shores of Lake Neagh. Though beautiful, it was mostly inaccessible due to the thick growth of rhododendron around it. Dick's first impression of Ireland was "green grass and mud—and lots of both. It was the kind of mud that would suck your boots off." On arrival, the men discovered that preparations were not complete and that much needed to be done before the base would be operational. Dick was put in charge of a crew of local workers and told to build a stretch of road. "For two months we did everything from digging ditches to installing electrical wiring and heaters, anything to get the base up and running," he says.

Most of Dick's time at Langford was spent modifying B17s and B24s for use in the war in Europe and Africa. He also worked on P38s destined for African operations and C47s that would drop parachutists. Eventually, he became the liaison between Lockheed and the Army Air Force base at Wharton, in northern England.

Dick and I met when he was on one of his trips to Wharton. I was appearing with my father and my brother Raf in a show at the Winter Gardens Theatre in Blackpool. My dad was a comedian, and Raf and I supported him with dancing and music. It was a week before my twenty-first birthday, and Raf, nineteen, was awaiting orders from the Royal Marines. The night I met Dick, I was actually on a date with an officer in the Army Air Force. Plans for a dance at the base fell through, and so my date invited me to the officers' mess for a rum Coke, the exotic drink of the forties. Dick was there, the only one in "civvies," and I wondered who that good-looking guy was. He had an easygoing, relaxed manner, and I was immediately attracted to him. The next night, Dick came to the show with some friends. Backstage, all the girls in the show were agog over the grinning, enthusiastic Yanks in the front row. After that, Dick and I began to date and soon fell in love. Because life was so uncertain, we decided we would wait until after the war to marry.

The base in Ireland closed in 1944. Dick had the option of going home or joining the U.S. Navy and staying in England. He opted for the latter, and so, in the unlikely spot of Londonderry, Ireland, he enlisted. He recalls, "I stayed there for two weeks, spending most of my time playing cards with the other guys. We couldn't understand why we weren't being assigned. Finally, the mystery was solved when we learned of the invasion of Europe. All travel not directly connected with the invasion ceased." The navy eventually gave Dick a rating of Aviation Machinist Mate Second Class, and as soon as travel was allowed, sent him to another unlikely spot—Dunkeswell, Exeter, a little village in southern England. His assignment was to run an office that kept track of all the service records of the navy's planes. After so much work on planes, Dick had hoped for a different kind of challenge. "I found the work dull and unproductive," he says. "Quadruple copies of every sheet of paper were required, yet when I was finally sent back to the States eighteen months later, all those papers were destroyed and the planes they pertained to scrapped."

Soon after he returned to the United States, Dick received his discharge. The war ended, and he made plans to return to England for our wedding, which took place on April 1, 1946, in Wimbledon, Surrey.

In August, after several delays, mostly due to my six-week isolation in a hospital for diphtheria, we left on what seemed to me to be a journey to the ends of the earth. When we arrived in Glendale, we hunted for a place to live, with no luck. Apartments were scarce after the war. Moreover, I was pregnant, which added to our concerns. The solution seemed to be to build our own house. Dick bought a lot, drew up plans, and proceeded to build the house himself. It wasn't quite finished when we moved in, only a few days before our son Richard was born. Our only furniture was a used stove, a hand-me-down dinette set, a borrowed crib and chair, and an old camp bed that harked back to the family's Lee Vining days. But we managed and were happy.

It was in this little house of less than one thousand square feet that we raised three children and started the Kelty Pack business.

Dick did not return to his job at Lockheed. "I realized I was too much of an outdoorsman ever to be happy working inside again," he says. "Carpentry had always appealed to me. I had my own tools and enjoyed building our house." His timing was right, and he had no trouble getting a job working for a contractor, building houses for other returning veterans.

▪ Leader of the Pack

The early 1950s saw the tentative beginnings of what is today a thriving backpacking industry. At that time, there were few backpacking equipment companies. L.L. Bean was started in 1917, Eddie Bauer in 1920, and REI in 1938, but they were not the giants they are today, and their selection of merchandise was limited. Most hikers combed surplus stores for their needs. A few, like Dick, made their own.

"I made my first backpack when I was fourteen," he says. "For me, necessity was truly the mother of invention. I needed to haul my two blankets and food for the overnight hikes I took with my dad." Dick made a simple wooden frame using leftover flooring readily available from new houses being built near his home. The two side pieces were straight, and he boiled and bent the two horizontal pieces that joined them. A canvas panel was added to keep the wood from rubbing on his back. "I didn't know what to do about the bag," Dick recalls, "until I spotted my brother Phil's Boy Scout knapsack. Perfect! Before Phil could say no, I grabbed it, added some grommets, drilled some holes in the frame, and attached the bag to it. I had me a backpack."

Those happy days in the mountains with his dad came to an abrupt end when Clifford died in an industrial accident. At eighteen, Dick had suddenly lost all fatherly guidance and a good friend.

It was six years later, after World War II, before Dick resumed backpacking in earnest. After we had built our house and settled down, with a three-year-old son and a baby on the way, Dick's lifelong friend, Clay Seaman, suggested a trip to the Sierra. Dick was enthused at the thought of seeing the mountains again after so long, and so the two of them began to make plans.

Their biggest needs were backpacks. At a war surplus store, they found an army rucksack with a steel frame and a heavy canvas bag—for five dollars. Two down mummy bags and two pairs of combat boots completed their purchases, and they were off.

They drove up to Independence in northern California and parked at the trail's end in Onion Valley. The next morning they hiked over Kearsage Pass and down to Bullfrog Lake. The trip was a learning experience. Thrilled though they were to be back in the wilderness, their pleasure was tempered somewhat by blistered feet and sore shoulders and backs. When they returned, Dick began to reevaluate the backpack. Still thinking along traditional lines, he said to Clay, "We'll just have to make our own packs. What I'll do is make the side pieces longer so that we can lift the frame up once in a while to give our shoulders a rest when they get sore."

Like most innovations, the first Kelty Pack was a collaborative effort. Two classmates of Clay's from UCLA, Stan Ruttenberg and Marx Brook, both lovers of the mountains, were often in the Kelty garage sharing their views. They liked Dick's idea of the longer side members and volunteered to try the pack out. I still remember the excitement Marx exuded when he returned from that first trial hike: "Hey, Kelty! I stuck those long side pieces in the back pockets of my jeans, and voila! The weight shifted off my shoulders and onto my hips!"

Dick was thrilled that such a simple maneuver had transferred weight to the hips, which are better suited than shoulders to carry loads. "If only I could figure out a way to keep the pack in that position," he thought. And then it came to him that perhaps he could achieve the same result by attaching a waist strap to the bottom of the frame. He tried it and it worked. Today, the waist strap is standard on every commercial backpack on the market. It was the first of Dick's many innovative ideas that would improve the backpack.

A few years later, when Dick was selling the pack by mail order, he received a letter from a man named Herb Budlong, equipment chairman of the Potomac Appalachian Trail Club, who wrote, "I am pleased that someone has finally designed a pack with a waist strap. For years, I have been exhorting my fellow members to attach a waist strap to their army packboards."

After the waist strap success, Dick began to give more thought to other backpack improvements, such as making the pack frame lighter. Packs to that point were oppressively heavy. "Does the frame have to be made of wood?" he asked himself. "Why not use aluminum as the aircraft industry does to control weight?" He bought some aluminum tubing and ripstop nylon from a surplus store and began to experiment.

The first frame he made with this tubing still had straight sides, but they were slightly longer than before. The crosspieces were curved and riveted to the sides. Then he added shoulder straps stuffed with carpeting, a nylon band to help keep the bag off his back, and a waist strap made of one-inch cotton webbing. The ripstop nylon for the bag seemed flimsy, but it was used in parachutes and was actually quite strong. Unfortunately, it came in white only. Dick Rit-dyed it in the washing machine, causing the Kelty family's underwear to temporarily take on a green hue. It was a small price to pay. Using my domestic Singer sewing machine, Dick sewed a large, simple bag, attaching grommets to the sides. He then linked the bag to the frame by threading a stainless steel rod through clevis pins (surplus aircraft rivets in which he had drilled holes) that were pushed through both predrilled holes in the tubular aluminum sides and grommets in the bag. On those first few packs, the waist strap was sewn to the lower edge of the back band.

Dick couldn't wait to try out his new creation. At the first opportunity, he raced up to the Sierra for a long weekend. He returned, pleased but full of ideas on how to improve his design.

During the summer of 1951, our backpacking friends were excited over what was happening in the Kelty garage and kitchen (home of the sewing machine). And there was plenty happening. Not wanting to spend money on expensive tools, Dick often devised his own. He cut the aluminum with a "chop" saw, bent it to the shape he wanted over a hardwood form he made, and then took it to a welder. When he got the frames back, he gave them an acid bath to remove surplus flux, which if left on the metal would corrode it. Any remaining rough edges were sanded down.

Marx, Stan, and Clay offered to take Dick's latest prototype on a trip and give him feedback. Dick gratefully accepted their offer. In addition, he cajoled family members into tramping around the living room wearing packs loaded down with bags of chicken feed. He would bombard us with questions and instructions: "How does it feel? Is it pulling on your shoulders? Is that waist strap better? Hitch up your shoulders before you cinch in that strap!" One evening I heard a strange noise and called to Dick: "Hey, there's a funny noise coming from our weight bags!" After inspecting them, he laughed. "We've got weevils!" he exclaimed. From then on, we filled the bags with rock salt.

Quality and comfort were Dick's biggest concerns, but he also wanted to be sure his packs would stand up to the most rigorous conditions. To test durability and strength, Dick climbed up on the roof of the house and dropped off a fully loaded pack onto our cement driveway. We all rushed over to inspect the result. Incredibly, nothing had broken. The frame wasn't even bent. In another strength test, he had me put on a pack, and then he latched onto the two vertical side pieces of the frame with all his weight. The pack frame held up far better than my own 120-pound frame did.

Friends who had watched these developments urged Dick to put his pack on the market. "There's nothing like it!" they assured him. With a family to support, Dick was reluctant to give up his carpentry work with its assured income for the uncertain future of an entrepreneur. "Most people I talk to don't even know what a backpack is!" he said. "I don't know if I can make a living selling it." One encouraging sign, however, was that every backpacker who saw his creation wanted one.

After giving the matter a lot of thought, he said one day, "I think the Kelty Pack has a future, so I'll keep working on it. But it won't provide us with an income for some time. I'll have to keep doing carpentry work." He did this for four years, but we now had a greater vision—to make a success of the Kelty Pack.

Dick borrowed five hundred dollars against the house so that we could buy materials in quantity. His next step was to approach Vandegrifts, a sporting goods store in Los Angeles. The buyer there was quite interested, but wanted the packs for twelve dollars. She in turn would sell them for twenty dollars. There was no way we could make a profit selling the pack for twelve dollars. We used only top-quality materials, and the pack was practically handmade. Dick decided to eliminate the middleman and sell by mail order.

We then made our production a lot more efficient, turning our little dinette into a miniature sweatshop. We invested in two industrial sewing machines, so fast and powerful that they scared us to death at first. But we became quite proficient, and for hours on end Dick and I would sit side by side stitching away. We cut the nylon out on our Formica-topped table using a wood-burning knife. This both prevented unraveling and destroyed the tabletop.

Dick added a new feature—the "hold-open" frame. This was an aluminum frame threaded through the top seam of the bag and connected to the main frame. It held the bag open and allowed easy access to its contents. Improvements and innovations came quickly. The design was never static. Dick curved every component of the frame to follow the contours of the human back. He threaded two small rods through the crosspieces to prevent the bag from resting on the back, then added an extra back band to further prevent this from happening and to help keep the hiker's back cool. Two outside pockets were added. We found a better zipper. The aluminum zippers were light, but tended to break easily and corrode. Their replacements were made of a nickel alloy.

A suggestion from our friend Marx became a permanent feature of the Kelty Pack. It was a clever yet simple idea that enabled the back band tie cords to self-lock when tightened.

To spread the word about our product, we advertised in the *Sierra Club Schedule* for many years, our only means of advertising. Sierra Club members proved to be enthusiastic, loyal customers.

Even with such limited promotion, we had to hustle to keep up with the demand. Orders came in from all over the country and even overseas, thanks to customers who traveled widely spreading the word. The distinct design of the pack, different from anything else seen on the trail, proved to be a great conversation starter. This word-of-mouth advertising was so powerful that little else was needed.

When I became pregnant and could no longer put in sweatshop hours, we decided to hire our first employee. Liz Warme, a German lady Dick managed to lure away from a parachute factory, proved to be a tireless, faithful worker. Needing larger quarters, Dick rented a tiny building, a former barbershop on

Early Kelty Pack

Photo by Tom McMakin

San Fernando Road in Glendale. Meanwhile, he continued to do all the metalworking in our garage. Our neighbors were incredibly tolerant. The teeth-on-edge screech of aluminum being cut was almost unbearable, but they never complained.

Another of my five brothers, Richard, arrived from England and joined us in this family venture. The innovations continued. Heeding complaints from mostly female customers about sore shoulders and hipbones, Dick made two significant improvements. He replaced the carpeting in the shoulder straps and waist band with a new synthetic rubber and began to offer the pack in three sizes. Later he added the partitioned bag.

The partitioned bag was the result of Dick's determination to keep the weight of the pack high and close to the hiker's back. But when Dick sewed the first partitions, it took him a disappointing six hours. It was unacceptably slow. By employing factory methods of sewing, we eventually cut hours off that time.

Early instructions on how to use stuff bag

We received a visit from Jene Crenshaw and Helen Kilness, publisher and managing editor of *Summit* magazine. They wanted Dick to make them a nylon sack in which to stuff their down sleeping bags. When they gave Dick the measurements, he told them, "You'll never get sleeping bags in a sack that small!" "Oh, yes we will," they replied. "We've seen it done!" And that is how that neat little stuff sack came to be lashed to the bottom of backpack frames. Crenshaw recalls the time she and Kilness were on the trail and met some people from another country. "They looked at our Keltys and asked if we were carrying our bed frames!"

Some customers began to ask if the pack came in colors besides green. In the beginning, Dick felt he had no choice. The one-inch cotton webbing was available in olive drab only, and since he didn't want to mix colors, he ordered that color for the nylon fabric too. In addition, feeling strongly about the importance of making a minimal impact on the environment, he believed that green blended well with the terrain and that brightly colored packs would look out of place and make the trail seem crowded. In his view, the only advantage to having a brightly colored pack was for search and rescue. Consequently, you often heard that "Dick Kelty will give you any color you want just as long as it's green."

He did make one exception. In 1966 Nick Clinch, an old friend whose Kelty Pack was worn by Tom Hornbein on Everest in 1963, called him with a request: "I'm going to Antarctica, and I want a Kelty Pack. But I want a huge bag and I want it in red."

"Red?!"

"Yes. We're being sponsored by *National Geographic*, so it's important we get good pictures. We need some color."

"All right, Nick. I'll do it on one condition. You don't tell anyone where you got those red packs."

So he made some marvelous packs (Nick is still using his), with huge frames and carry bars overhead that allowed them to carry large loads.

Says Nick: "The trip was very successful. We had wonderful pictures to accompany our article in *National Geographic*. There was a Kelty Pack in every picture. I privately referred to those packs as 'Coolie Keltys' because we could put so much in them. Dick finally said, 'Okay, Nick, you can tell people those are Keltys.'

"I call Dick the Henry Ford of backpacking. I blame him for the overcrowding of the wilderness. By taking the weight off the hiker's shoulders and putting it on the hips, he took the misery out of the sport. He made it enjoyable for people to go backpacking. Until Dick came along with the Kelty Pack, backpacks made your shoulders hurt. It was just awful. We had to take shoulder breaks every so often. Dick's design was revolutionary."

Nick Clinch was not the only one who noticed the growing hordes of backpackers. We received a warning from the FBI that Dick was on Squeaky Fromm's hit list. One of Charles Manson's girls, she had targeted Dick because the Kelty Pack had enabled more people to go into the wilderness, potentially ruining it. Until she was incarcerated, Dick did a lot of looking over his shoulder.

The Kelty Pack business was not a get-rich-quick enterprise. Our first year, 1952, we sold 29 packs, taking in a gross of $678.85. Out

Hiking in 1956. Left to right: Dick Kelty, Nena Kelty, Janet Seaman, and
Clay Seaman

By the campfire:
Keltys and Seamans

Kelty family hiking in 1957: Nena, Anita, Richard, Dick

of that had to come sales tax, excise tax on the bag, and any shipping
incurred. In 1955 we sold 300, and in 1956, 497—still not enough
to provide us with a living, but encouraging enough for us to continue. It was an exciting time, watching interest grow and getting
great feedback from contented customers. But Dick still continued to
do carpentry work.

Backpacking enjoyed a growth spurt during the 1950s. Perhaps it
was an urge to return to nature after the killing and destruction of the
war. Whatever the reason, it was a time of much creative thinking by
people who loved the outdoors. Le Roy and Alice Holubar in Colorado
were noted for their quality construction of tents, sleeping bags, and

Carl Siechert hiking with Kelty's experimental flex frame

Photo courtesy of Carl Siechert

Richard and Angela
Kelty, 1962

First Kelty factory, 1961

jackets; Gerry Cunningham for many innovative ideas, including the Gerry Kiddie Carrier, a rucksack with a fiberglass frame, several tent designs, and packs for horses, dogs, canoes, and bikes; Jack Stephenson for his moisture barrier for sleeping bags and other designs.

Dick continued to experiment with his backpack design. He tried to think of a way to make the frame more flexible. "I finally gave up on the idea, deciding that it would not be that beneficial for the hiker," he says. "The North Face has a model called Back Magic, but otherwise nobody has come up with a flex frame that really changed the direction of backpack designs."

Dick recalls his friend Bob Silver's 1958 backpacking trip through the Middle East: "To give himself a rest, Bob put his Kelty on the back of a donkey. Unfortunately, the donkey decided to roll over on his back, breaking the two side members of the frame. Bob continued his trip, wearing what is probably the original flex frame."

The 1960s brought big changes to the industry and to Kelty Pack in particular. Manufacturing and retail were moved to a larger facility on Victory Boulevard in Glendale. A wholesale operation was established, and packs were sold to dealers. We began exporting to Canada and Japan, and were growing so fast that banks declined to lend us money for materials. "Grow slower!" they admonished. Finally, we had to move the manufacturing from the Glendale store to a factory in Sun Valley, California.

In the 1960s Kelty, simultaneously with other companies, started to manufacture internal-frame packs. A natural evolution from the soft day pack, internals were cheaper to make and required simpler tooling. With so much attention given to internal-frame packs, frame design suffered through a period of benign neglect. But in the late 1970s some manufacturers focused their creative energies on suspension, the hip belt, and even the frame itself. They used materials such as polypropylene, carbon-fiber, and plastic to achieve their goals. Many packs now have a hip-wrap, replacing the simple belt. (This idea is not new, having been patented in 1878 by Henry Merriman of Connecticut.)

After agonizing over what might happen to his employees, who were like family to him, Dick sold the company to CML in 1972. He stayed on for two years as a consultant. Kellwood later acquired it, and today Kelty Pack is a wholly owned subsidiary of Kellwood.

It is staggering to contemplate what has happened to the backpacking industry since those humble beginnings in 1952. At the 1997 Outdoor Retailer Winter Market Show in Salt Lake City, there were eighty-nine exhibitors of backpacks. Kelty alone sold over one hundred thousand in 1996 (including day packs).

Chapter Two

BEFORE YOU LEAVE HOME

City life: millions of people being lonesome together.

—Henry David Thoreau

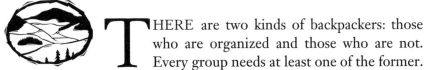 **T**HERE are two kinds of backpackers: those who are organized and those who are not. Every group needs at least one of the former. Even if you're not ordinarily a list maker, become one before a backpacking trip. In the backcountry, there are no Kmarts, and forgetting the silverware or the matches can be a major inconvenience, or worse.

The following checklist will help you make sure all tasks are done on time. You don't necessarily have to do everything yourself, but someone has to be responsible for making sure things are done correctly and on time.

Two Months Ahead

- Figure out who is going on the trip.
- Decide when and where you're going.
- Check permit regulations.
- Acquire maps and guidebooks.
- Begin breaking in new boots.

Get together with your backpacking cohorts and assess everyone's fitness and experience levels. Find out who has basic skills, such as loading a pack and planning meals, and who has advanced skills, like tromping through snow or wading across waist-deep streams. Encourage everyone to be honest; your harmonious backpacking trip depends on it.

Find out what each person wants out of the trip. If your group includes people with a wide range of skills and interests, consider hiking or driving to a base camp that allows the members of your group to choose from different hikes. For example, the campground at Tuolumne Meadows in Yosemite National Park is the trailhead for dozens of hikes of all lengths and grades.

Three Weeks Ahead

- Sketch out your main hiking route, emergency escape routes, and water sources.

- Determine the group gear with your mates.

- Make sure the gear works; replace or repair anything that doesn't.

- Plan a menu and start dehydrating, if necessary. (Dehydrate food; hydrate yourself.)

Once you've settled on the type of trip, it's time to pin down the location. Get out the map, decide how far you're willing to drive, and look for green splotches that indicate public lands. Veterans usually have a wish list, which may include thru-hiking the Appalachian Trail or descending into the Grand Canyon. Beginners would be wise to start on local and regional trails.

When you narrow your search to a small area, call a local outdoor store or trail club. Ask about the best guidebook for the area. Then call the government agency in charge for more information. Keep in mind that the person who answers the phone may not know the answers to your questions. You need to talk to a ranger, but they're out more than in. Find out when they come on duty, as the best time to call is usually early morning before they head out. Most ranger stations open between 7 A.M. and 9 A.M. Rather than leave a message, keep calling back.

Once you have the right person on the phone, make sure you ask all the probing questions, the ones you wrote down ahead of time. Don't be afraid to ask questions that appear to be answered in your guidebook. Conditions and regulations can change, and guidebooks can be inaccurate.

Consider asking the following questions:

> Not surprisingly, you can now use your computer to help plan your backpacking trip. SkillMaster Software's Adven-Sure program generates equipment lists based on individualized trip descriptions. Install the program, then specify group size, trip duration, planned activities, intended terrain, and desired travel style. The program spits out lists for both groups and individuals, plus a complete departure checklist. Contact SkillMaster at (303) 786-9559.

- How many miles of trails are there in the area? What kind of shape are they in? Are they well marked? Which ones do you recommend?

- Do you require permits? How far in advance must we apply for one? Do you run out of permits at certain times of the year? Is there a fee? Can I do it by mail or do I pick it up at the trailhead?

- Do you have designated campsites in the backcountry? How many? How quickly do they fill up? Are there fire restrictions?

- How many people do you typically see on the trails? What's the busiest time? The quietest?

- Is there an area that's less crowded? If so, why?

- How steep is the terrain?

- Is water widely available? If not, where?

- What wildlife will I see?

- Where can I order topographical maps of the area?

One Week Ahead

- Buy and repackage food.

- Verify departure plans with fellow hikers.

At some point, you have to figure out trailhead transportation. If you do a linear route, you may need a car at both ends. If you do a loop or an out-and-back route, you can manage with one car.

The Day Before

- Pack gear, checking each item off the list as it's put in the pack.

- Give a copy of your itinerary and return-time to a trusted friend or relative.

- Call a ranger, business owner, or management agency and check the weather and trail conditions at the trip site.

- Gas up the car. Check oil, air, and water levels.

Day of Trip

- Recheck the gear when you meet with your group. Revisit your checklist and probe for items that might be missing or that should be left behind.

- At the trailhead, put the car keys in a safe spot and tell everyone where that spot is.

- Have fun.

▪ Gear

Someone must take responsibility for ensuring that everyone has the necessary gear before departure. If you are backpacking with young

1974 Karakhouram Expedition—
Pakistani goat-herders wearing Kelty Packs

Photos by Chris Brown

children, inexperienced older children, or novice adults, you will have to help them make decisions as well. Let no one venture forth ill-equipped. Jim Hamilton of Geyserville, California, who has taken children backpacking for years, has no qualms about leaving someone home if he has inadequate equipment. As he says, "If the weather turns bad and someone in the group doesn't have rain gear, or his pack breaks, much more is at stake than just one person's discomfort."

The best way to minimize discomfort is to *take no more stuff than you need.* If you're fanatical, you'll lop off the end of your toothbrush and trim the borders of your maps, but everyone should watch their pack weight. Ounces add up to pounds and pounds add up to discomfort. Regard each item critically, asking, "Can I do without it? Will something lighter do the job? Something I'm already carrying?" For us, the portable shower is an easy call (it stays home), the fishing gear is more iffy, and the Swiss Army knife makes every cut.

First, lay out all your gear. Compare what you have to what you need. Use a complete checklist (see below). The main categories are food, equipment, and clothing.

Equipment purchases include both new and replacement gear. Does the stove work? Will your sleeping bags make it another year? Do they need cleaning? Are they sufficient for the temperatures you'll be facing? How's the tent? Still big enough? Do the seams need sealing? What other items do you need? Candles? Fuel? Fishing gear? Frisbee? Book?

Only you can decide what's essential and what's not. One rule is, if you're car camping and have space, take the borderline item; if backpacking, leave it behind.

Use the ESSENTIALS mnemonic to help you categorize gear:

Emergencies

Sustenance

Shelter

Extras

Navigation

Toiletries

Incidentals

Attitude

Light

Something to carry it all in

■ Checklist and Comments

Emergencies

☐ first-aid and snakebite kits

☐ waterproof matches in a case

- ☐ fire starter
- ☐ whistle
- ☐ signal mirror

Sustenance

- ☐ stove
- ☐ stove repair kit
- ☐ windscreen
- ☐ fuel
- ☐ fuel container
- ☐ lighter
- ☐ nestled pots and pans, with lids
- ☐ frying pan
- ☐ pot holder
- ☐ silverware
- ☐ food storage containers
- ☐ plastic bags
- ☐ large spoon
- ☐ spatula
- ☐ can opener
- ☐ cups
- ☐ plates
- ☐ bowls
- ☐ cooking grate
- ☐ garbage bags

- ☐ water containers
- ☐ water purification system (iodine, filter, or plenty of fuel)
- ☐ scrubbing pads
- ☐ dishwashing soap (biodegradable)
- ☐ paper towels
- ☐ dish towels
- ☐ tablecloth
- ☐ aluminum foil
- ☐ spices
- ☐ dry soups
- ☐ packaged dinners
- ☐ unleavened bread
- ☐ grains
- ☐ nuts
- ☐ dried fruit
- ☐ fruit juices
- ☐ candy/sports bars
- ☐ dry milk
- ☐ powdered drinks

Unless you're willing to live on cold food, you must carry a stove. Wood is scarce and fires are banned in many places, so you can no longer count on cooking over a campfire.

Select wide-mouth plastic water bottles. The wide opening makes it easier to fill, clean, and mix drinks.

An aluminum pie plate works as a lightweight pot lid; a Jiffy Pop popcorn container, with its built-in handle, is even better.

Endurance will be maximized by a diet rich in carbohydrates and low in fat.

Ordinarily, you would be wise to avoid fat-laden candy bars, but hiking or backpacking several hours a day isn't an ordinary expenditure of energy. One per day is all right.

For backpackers, freeze-dried foods are a wonderful development, but you can still satisfy most food needs, cheaply and easily, at the local supermarket.

Shelter

- ☐ tarp (with rope, stakes, poles)
- ☐ tube tent (with rope, stakes)
- ☐ tent (with fly, poles, stakes)
- ☐ bivouac sack
- ☐ ground cloth
- ☐ garbage bags
- ☐ mosquito netting
- ☐ sleeping bag
- ☐ stuff sack
- ☐ sleeping pad
- ☐ wick-dry socks
- ☐ wool socks
- ☐ nylon windbreaker with hood
- ☐ sweater
- ☐ bunting or pile jacket
- ☐ shorts
- ☐ long pants
- ☐ stocking cap
- ☐ baseball cap
- ☐ mittens or gloves
- ☐ rain suit

- ☐ emergency blanket
- ☐ hammock
- ☐ pillowcase
- ☐ underwear
- ☐ long underwear
- ☐ T-shirts
- ☐ bandanna
- ☐ insulated jacket
- ☐ gaiters
- ☐ hiking boots
- ☐ camp sneakers
- ☐ sandals
- ☐ thongs
- ☐ swimsuit
- ☐ sunglasses

Freshen sleeping bags and tents by hanging them on a line in the sun. Turn them frequently to prevent sun damage. At home, air them again. Avoid mildew by thoroughly drying tents and bags before stuffing them. Even if it didn't rain during your trip, they probably collected condensation. If you must stuff wet equipment, dry it at the first opportunity.

With care, a quality sleeping bag will last many years. Even if you have a good bag, remember the sleeping pad. If you go with an open-cell pad like Therm-a-Rest, keep your old closed-cell pad, which has the following uses:

- Under your stove—a tiny piece of pad insulates from cold and snow.

- In your boots—a little piece can be an innersole or a heel pad.

- Around a water bottle—a medium-sized piece offers insulation.

- Under you—a big piece can be a seat pad.

Car campers can take their favorite pillows. Backpackers should bring a pillowcase and fill it at night with clothes. Down vests and jackets make ideal pillow fill.

A coated-nylon tarp is versatile. It can provide extra shelter or ground cover. In torrential rains, rig a tarp as an umbrella over your tent.

A tube tent is fine as long as there are no mosquitoes and it doesn't rain more than a drizzle. Emergency blankets (metalized polyester) are handy. These are emergency blankets of metalized polyester, weighing about two ounces. They can be emergency shelters or reflectors and work as ground cloths. Consider putting one in everyone's day pack.

Large plastic garbage bags have myriad uses. Weighing almost nothing, one bag can protect your sleeping bag when you're crossing a stream, your pack in a storm, and your body in an emergency. Cut one open and use it as a dry emergency floor for your tent. Cut out neck- and armholes and fashion an emergency poncho. Use it as a liner inside your pack. Even use it for trash.

Extras

☐ extra food

☐ extra warm clothing

☐ extra water

☐ extra tent stakes

Water weighs more than two pounds a quart, so carry no more than you need. If you are hiking next to a river or are near lakes, carry only a little, keeping in mind that water shown on a map may have dried up, especially in the desert, and you don't always hike as far as you think you will.

Navigation

☐ maps

☐ compass

☐ pencil and a straight edge

Maps can be stored in a map case or resealable plastic bag. Fold a map to the section you will need that day on the trail. If you're hiking trails and have a topographic map, you probably won't need a compass. On the other hand, a compass is lightweight fun and a great learning tool.

Toiletries

- ☐ toothbrush
- ☐ toothpaste
- ☐ dental floss
- ☐ hairbrush
- ☐ comb
- ☐ sunblock
- ☐ lip balm, with sunblock
- ☐ soap (biodegradable)
- ☐ toilet paper
- ☐ moisturizing lotion
- ☐ deodorant
- ☐ insect repellent
- ☐ small towel
- ☐ towelettes
- ☐ tampons
- ☐ shaving kit
- ☐ baking soda
- ☐ trowel

Baking soda can be used as toothpaste, boot deodorizer, foot soak, and even a fire extinguisher. In the mountains, where dry skin can be a problem, moisturizing lotion may make the leap from luxury to necessity. If you get caught without sunglasses, you can fashion crude eye shields from food boxes, a paperback book cover, or a toilet paper tube. Cut slits just large enough to see through.

Incidentals

- ☐ rope
- ☐ Frisbee
- ☐ Hackey Sack
- ☐ Nerf ball
- ☐ crayons, felt-tip pens, pencils
- ☐ magnifying glass
- ☐ binoculars

- ☐ harmonica
- ☐ kazoo
- ☐ cards
- ☐ chess, checkers, backgammon sets
- ☐ books
- ☐ constellation guide
- ☐ coloring books
- ☐ plastic collection containers
- ☐ sketch pad
- ☐ field guides
- ☐ thermometer
- ☐ camera
- ☐ film
- ☐ fishing rod, reel, gear
- ☐ fishing license

Bring plenty of rope. It can be used for clothesline, hanging food, rescue, lashing down, and cattle rustling. Don't forget the fishing license. Revenue-hungry states are increasing the fines, such as a whopping $650 in California. If you play Frisbee in fragile back-country, take care not to scar meadows. Keep trampling to a minimum. Besides being a quiet toy, a Frisbee can serve as a plate, a platter, a cutting board, and a card table.

Attitude

- ☐ buoyant, upbeat personality
- ☐ willingness to adjust to nature and to others enjoying nature
- ☐ patience

Prepare to embrace the wilderness. The ability to appreciate nature is as important as any hardware. An upbeat attitude is the ultimate essential.

Light

☐ flashlight, with extra bulb and batteries

☐ candles

☐ candle lantern

Always bring a light with fresh batteries. To prevent your flashlight from accidentally being switched on in your pack and draining the batteries, use a rubber band or hair tie to hold the switch in the off position. Or simply reverse one of the batteries.

You can make your own candle lantern by softening the bottom of a candle and placing it in your cooking kit or an empty tuna can. With children or clumsy grownups in the tent, however, open flames are discouraged.

Something to Carry It All In

☐ internal- or external-frame backpack

☐ day pack

☐ fanny pack

☐ child carrier

☐ waterproof pack cover

☐ pack repair items (pins, rings)

Don't save weight by leaving behind your day pack. Whenever you want to drop your backpack and venture from camp, a day pack is invaluable for carrying small items.

Carrying repair items is a little like buying flight insurance. You hope you don't need them and most of the time you don't, but they provide peace of mind. If you have an external-frame pack, buy a package of spare clevis pins and attach one to each zipper pull on your pack, tent, and jacket. This allows you to grab a zipper in the dark or with gloves on. Plus, a broken pin won't ruin your next trip.

■ Packing the Pack

Once you know what you're taking, where do you put it all? Car campers can stash stuff in boxes and bags, but backpackers must be systematic. Try to pack your pack about the same way every time, a way that makes sense to you. You will grasp the need for systematic packing the first time you are caught in a storm and must madly rip through your pack in search of rain gear or a pesky tent stake.

Reserve space in the outside pockets of your pack for items needed most often on the trail: snacks, water, sunscreen, sunglasses, insect repellent, and map. Store toilet paper in a zipper-lock bag along with a plastic trowel (for digging catholes) in an outside pocket. Your first-aid kit should also be readily accessible. Tuck that warm sweater and rain gear under the top flap for easy access.

Place dense, heavy items, like the stove and tent, against your back as high as possible, putting the weight over your hips and feet. If you carry weight too low or too far back, you will tend to lean forward to compensate, stressing your lower back. Women, who naturally have a lower center of gravity, may want to experiment with packing the dense items more toward the midback. Ultimately, weight distribution is a personal matter. Some backpackers like to carry all their weight on their hips, while others prefer to balance it more between the shoulders and hips. Experiment with your pack's adjustment straps until weight distribution feels just right. With external-frame packs, the weight will naturally be higher up and more spread out across the width of your back.

Pack medium-weight gear farther down in the pack to lower your center of gravity and add stability. Your sleeping bag is a good item for the bottom of your pack. Lash long items like fishing rods and tent poles to the outside of the pack. Pad sharp objects to keep them from poking you, especially if you have an internal-frame pack.

Roll clothes into tight tubes and store in a bag. Store the fuel canister in two zipper-lock bags and keep it away from food and clothing. Put only leakproof water bottles inside your pack; don't use bicycle bottles.

The sleeping pad is usually strapped to the outside, unless it packs down really small. If you use a self-inflating pad, avoid a puncture by packing it in a heavy-duty stuff sack; don't strap it to the bottom of your pack, where it will take a beating every time

> Every increased possession loads us with a new weariness.
>
> —John Ruskin

you drop your pack. On the other hand, if you strap a rugged, closed-cell foam pad to the bottom, it will create a stable base that allows the pack to stand upright.

More Packing Tips

- When packing for a long trip, organize your food in stuff sacks of different colors. Breakfast might be in the blue sack, lunch in the red, and dinner in the green.

- Need a shower bag? Try a net bag, the kind sold in grocery and drugstores for washing lingerie. Thread a shoelace through the top as a drawstring, and you have a hanging bag for carrying toiletries. You can also use it to dry wet clothes on the outside of your pack.

- Nestle a plastic margarine tub in your cookware. Use it to store matches or scouring pads, or as an extra bowl.

- Use an empty Band-Aid box to hold a spartan first-aid kit. Add a needle and thread and tape two quarters (for an emergency phone call) to the inside of the box.

Now try on your loaded pack. Walk around with it; try going up and down hills. How does it feel? How does it sound? Annoying squeaks in a pack's hip belt or strap buckles can be silenced by applying lip balm or sunscreen to the noisy plastic. Just a dab or two will warm up and spread out to lubricate the obstreperous buckle without affecting performance.

■ Knowledge

It's always good to take some of this along. Below is a sample wilderness test. Try it on your group. Make it fun. People will learn more if you let them do their own research, rather than just telling them the answers. Make it an open-book test and urge them to take their time and seek creative answers. You may have to adapt some of the questions to suit the younger set.

The answers are below and scattered throughout the book. After you go through these questions, make up others, emphasizing the topics you believe are important. Then do the research.

 ## Sample Wilderness Test

1. True or false: Fast-moving water is always safe to drink.

2. True or false: Mosquitoes are attracted to dark colors.

3. Which clouds usually indicate rain?
   A. Cirrocumulus
   B. Altocumulus
   C. Cirrus
   D. Cumulonimbus

4. What's the major cause of death in national parks?
   A. Drowning
   B. Car accidents

    C. Bear attacks

    D. Falls

5. Choose the slowest runner:

    A. Grizzly bear

    B. Coyote

    C. Sprinter Michael Johnson

    D. Pronghorn antelope

6. Which piece of garbage takes the longest to decay?

    A. Candy wrapper

    B. Newspaper

    C. Tin can

    D. Glass bottle

7. What is DEET?

    A. Hiking organization

    B. Antihiking organization

    C. Poison found in certain mushrooms

    D. Chemical in insect repellent

8. What is *Giardia lamblia*?

    A. Water-borne parasite that makes you sick

    B. The fastest animal on earth

    C. Nerve tissue that is the first to be damaged
       by frostbite

    D. Italian soccer player

9. You're packing your pack. Which item weighs the
most?

    A. Gallon of water

    B. Five-pound tent

C. Large can of beans

D. Down sleeping bag

10. Which animal kills the most people each year?

A. Bees

B. Deer

C. Bear

D. Dog

Answers

1. False. With an estimated sixteen million Americans infected at any time with the intestinal parasite *Giardia lamblia*, you can bet a lot of people answer yes to this question. We now know that drinking from turbulent water is actually riskier than partaking from pools, where the giardia bug tends to settle to the bottom.

2. True. Mosquitoes also are attracted to heat, moisture, carbon dioxide, and whining—or so you can tell children.

3. D. Cumulonimbus clouds, the low-flying, dark, billowy ones, indicate rain is on the way. Find a weather book or the Boy Scout Handbook and study cloud formations.

4. A. According to 1991 figures reported in *Backpacker* magazine, sixty people drowned in national parks, thirty-four were killed in car accidents, twenty-five died in falls, and no one was killed by a bear.

5. C. Michael Johnson is pretty fast—for a human. He might hit twenty-five miles per hour. But a

grizzly has been clocked at thirty-two mph, coyotes at forty-three mph, and pronghorns at sixty mph.

6. D. *Backpacker* says the bottle will take up to 500,000 years to break down, the can 100 to 125 years, the candy wrapper 2 to 3 years, and the newspaper 1 to 2 years. That's why you carry out all trash.

7. D. DEET is the active ingredient in most mosquito repellents. It is certainly effective but it's best to stay with concentrates of less than thirty percent.

8. A. *Giardia lamblia* is a waterborne intestinal protozoan. Virtually unknown before 1979, giardia now exists in so many of the world's waterways that you get half-credit if you answered B—the world's fastest animal.

9. A. A gallon of water weighs 8.3 pounds, the tent 5 pounds, the sleeping bag 3 to 6 pounds, the can of beans 2 pounds. Carry no more water than you need to reach the next source.

10. B. About 130 people per year die through contact with deer, mostly by the animals darting in front of cars. Bees are a distant second with about 40 deaths; next come dogs with 14; bears are fifteenth on the list, with about 1 death every other year, lagging behind such acknowledged man killers as jellyfish and goats.

■ Home Projects

There are several projects you can do at home to make your backpacking trip more pleasant. Some suggestions:

Fire Starters

Here are four simple, effective fire starters that you can make at home.

- Line a tuna fish can with aluminum foil. Drape excess foil over the edge of the can. Cut several thin strips of cardboard and spread them in the can. Pour melted paraffin (old candles or crayons work) over the cardboard. Once the wax has dried, lift the foil out of the can and wrap the excess foil over the top of the fire starter, creating a small package. Unwrap it when you get to camp and set it on fire beneath a pile of tinder.

- Tightly roll four newspaper strips together and tie the bundle with string at two-inch intervals. Then cut the roll into segments, each one having a string tying it at the middle. Melt paraffin wax in a tin can set in a pot of shallow boiling water. Soak the newspaper segments in the wax, and then let them cool. They'll light quickly and last a good while.

- Roll cotton balls in petroleum jelly until completely covered, then pack them in a film canister (capacity thirty to forty balls). Pull a couple of cotton balls into a thin web, place it under a base of twigs, and light.

- Fill a plastic zipper-lock bag with the lint from your clothes dryer or belly button. Place beneath twigs.

Night-light

To make a "night-vision" flashlight, remove your flashlight bulb, wipe it clean with a dry cloth, and paint it with a waterproof red marking pen. Replace the bulb when the ink dries. The light will be enough to let you find your way around in the dark, but it will be less disruptive to your star-gazing campmates.

▪ Getting Out the Door

Preliminaries completed, pack packed, test taken, you are now ready to set out on your excellent adventure. Leave someone a detailed description of where you plan to go and when you plan to get there. Include alternate routes you are considering.

Chapter Three

EQUIPMENT: THE BIG-TICKET ITEMS

The least of things with a meaning is worth more in life than the greatest of things without it.

—Carl Jung

 **S**TEVE still remembers a blustery day in an Alaska campground years ago when he twisted his sputtering stove into pretzelized junk metal and heaved it into a garbage can. The moral is, always buy quality equipment from a reputable dealer—and don't lose your sense of humor. Quality gear will last longer and give you greater comfort than discount-store gear, especially when the going gets tough. Good gear is costly, but if you stay with camping and backpacking for the long haul, it will actually end up being cheaper.

Clerks in reputable outdoor stores can update you on the latest techno-logical innovations. In the meantime, here's a starter kit of information on the big-ticket items.

> "The biggest equipment error I ever made was buying a cheap backpack the first time I went to Europe. I still harbor a haunting vision of that fourteen-dollar Kmart special emerging onto the con-veyor belt in total disarray: The canvas pack is half off its frame; personal items are strewn everywhere. I am the laughing stock of Flight 379."
>
> —S.B.

Backpacks

Packs range from ten-dollar fanny packs to fifty-dollar day packs to five-hundred-dollar expedition models. Fanny packs are belts with a pouch. Day packs are small- to medium-size backpacks, some of which have padded shoulder straps and waist belts.

There are two types of large backpacks—internal and external frame. The external frame, the best choice for children, restricts movement but has a high center of gravity. The rigid frame can carry large, cumbersome loads comfortably. There are several points for securing gear to the outside of the pack. External frames sit away from your back and thus are cooler in hot weather.

> We recommend that children younger than about eight carry only a frameless day pack with padded hip belt and shoulder straps. Later, if your children will be hiking mostly on trails, they can move up to a junior external-frame pack. Many companies make aluminum-frame backpacks that adjust as your children grow.

Internal-frame backpacks have the frame sewn right into the fabric. They offer a lower center of gravity and greater freedom of movement (free-swinging arms, plenty of head room), but they do not handle large, unwieldy loads very well, especially if you must lash gear to the outside. They fit the contour of your back more closely, which makes them hotter but more stable.

Because internals are fatter and the weight rides lower, you have to bend forward at the hips to compensate. This can stress the back. The external frame, with its thinner profile and higher center of gravity, permits a more erect posture.

Backpacker magazine recently surveyed 140 thru-hikers midway through their 2,100-mile walk of the entire Appalachian Trail. Two-thirds were using external-frame packs, but internal-frame owners were happier with what they had. Ninety percent said they would buy the same brand again, primarily Lowe, Gregory, and The North Face. The most popular externals were Camp Trails, JanSport, and Kelty.

■ Pack Fit

Proper fit in a pack can determine how much you enjoy the trip. Here are some tips.

- Patronize a store that specializes in camping and backpacking equipment. It will have the greatest selection and the most informed people.

- Listen to advice, but take nobody's word for which pack is best. Run the tests yourself. Load weight into the model you are considering and walk around the store, feeling for any rubbing, especially at the shoulders or lower back. Make sure most of the weight rests on hips and buttocks, not on shoulders.

- Compare the pack's fit range with your torso and hip/waist measurements. To determine torso length, measure from the highest point of the shoulder (where it meets the neck) to the top of the hipbone. The frame is too small when you can't get the hip belt and/or shoulder straps far enough apart or you can't let out the shoulder straps enough. It's too big when the top flops around or you are unable to tighten the shoulder straps or hip belt.

- Ensure that the hip belt fits snugly—it should rest on your hipbones, not around the waist—then adjust the shoulder straps. The straps should be set wide enough apart so they don't pinch the neck, but narrow enough so they don't slide off the shoulders. Getting the shoulder straps and hip belt to work in harmony solves 90 percent of fit problems.

- Make sure the horizontal bar anchoring the top of the shoulder straps is the right height. When the pack is loaded, it should be even with the top of your shoulders.

- Some stores rent packs, allowing you to sample various models before you buy.

Pack Care

When you come off the trail, unzip all the pockets and shake out the dirt, sand, and crumbs. If the pack is dirty, sponge it off with mild soap and water. Air-dry out of the sun, for ultraviolet rays can damage the nylon.

Store packs in a cool, dry, airy place to discourage mildew.

Before the next trip, inspect packs for loose seams or damaged hardware at major stress points around the shoulder straps and hip belt. Repair zippers. Stitch any rips with a heavy-duty needle and upholstery thread. Use silicone spray on external-frame squeaks.

Innovations

- Mountainsmith, an innovative pack maker, has come up with a modular system called the Revolution. It has a padded frame to which you can attach pack bags in five different sizes (3,500 to 7,500 cubic inches) and configurations. The frame, featuring a "spinal chimney" to promote ventilation, has different components for men and women. Call (303) 279-5930.

- Kelty has created the LockDowns, a revolutionary new line of internal-frame packs that provide a custom fit. At the heart of the technology is a shoulder harness mounted on a stiffened panel that slides up and down twin aluminum stays. Once it's set for your exact torso length, it locks down into a solid unit with the pack bag. The result is perfect weight distribution and the most comfortable pack you'll ever carry.

Resources for Backpacks

The number of companies offering backpacks is growing every year. In its March 1997 issue, *Backpacker* magazine reviewed fifty-three of them, too many to list here. The following are some that offer a broad selection.

Camp Trails 1326 Willow Rd., Sturtevant, WI 53177; (888) 245-4985

Dana Design 333 Simmental Way, Bozeman, MT 59715; (406) 585-9279

Eastern Mountain Sports 327 Jaffrey Rd., Peterborough, NH 03458; (888) 463-6367

Ferrino 11315 Rancho Bernardo Rd., Suite 133, San Diego, CA 92127; (800) 566-0690

Gregory Mountain Products 100 Calle Cortez, Temecula, CA 92590; (800) 477-3420

JanSport P.O. Box 1817, Appleton, WI 54913; (800) 552-6776

Kelty 6235 Lookout Road, Boulder, CO 80301; (303) 530-7670, (800) 423-2320

Lafuma America 16745 Saticoy St., Unit 112, Van Nuys, CA 91406; (800) 514-4807

Lowe Alpine Systems P.O. Box 1449, Broomfield, CO 80038; (303) 465-0522

McHale Packs 29 Dravus St., Seattle, WA 98109; (206) 281-7861

Mountain Equipment, Inc. (MEI) 4776 E. Jensen St., Fresno, CA 93725; (209) 486-8211

Mountainsmith 18301 W. Colfax Ave., Golden, CO 80401; (800) 426-4075

Osprey Packs P.O. Box 539, 504 Central Ave., Dolores, CO 81323; (970) 882-2221

Outbound/Safesport 269 Columbia Ave., Chapin, SC 29036; (800) 433-6506

Recreational Equipment Inc. (REI) P.O. Box 1938, Sumner, WA 98390-0800; (800) 426-4840

Serratus 3103 Thunderbird Crescent, Burnaby, BC Canada V5M 2M9; (604) 444-3348

The North Face 2013 Farallon Dr., San Leandro, CA 94577; (800) 447-2333

VauDe Sports P.O. Box 3413, Mammoth Lakes, CA 93546; (800) 447-1539

Sleeping Bags

A sleeping bag is a shell, a nylon cocoon, filled with insulation. Your body provides the heat; a good bag merely retains it. How well a bag warms you depends primarily on its size, shape, type of insulation, and how it is contained in the bag.

Other variables you may find important include:

comfort rating	fill power	shell
fill weight	hood	zipper
loft price	stuffed size	weight

You must first decide on down or synthetic fill. Down is the fluff growing next to the skin of waterfowl. Only goose and duck down are used in sleeping bags, and goose down is considered superior.

Maybe, but it's by such a small margin that other factors can tip the scales the other way. In other words, a good duck can be better than a bad goose.

For equal warmth, down is light, compact, and pricey. Synthetic fills (like Polarguard, Hollofil, and Quallofil) are comparatively heavy, bulky, and inexpensive. On the other hand, they maintain loft and warmth when wet and provide better ground insulation than down.

Whichever fill you choose, synthetic bags are best for your children, especially if they're young and wet the bed. Synthetics are easy to wash and dry, and a damp bag still insulates well. Consider renting or borrowing bags before making a final decision.

Once you settle on type of fill, consider construction, size, and shape. Construction refers to the arrangement of baffles, the compartments inside the shell that hold the fill. Baffles distribute the fill evenly, keeping it from piling up at, say, your feet. Choices include slant tube, slant wall, slant box, and parallelogram baffles. Unless you are hiking from the equator to the top of Mount McKinley, don't fret about baffle construction. Loft and comfort rating are more important. You should, however, avoid a quilted bargain-basement bag that is stitched straight through the top and bottom layers; insulation along the stitching is near zero.

Sleeping bags come in three basic shapes: rectangular, semi-mummy, and mummy. Mummies are the lightest and warmest but are the most restrictive. Some are trimmer than others, but in most, if you turn over, your bag turns with you. This can induce claustrophobia in some people. Avoid this by crawling in the prospective sleeping bag for a snuggle test. Measure comfort by the sincerity of your ooohhs and aaahhs.

Most adult bags come in regular and long. Most manufacturers offer only one kids' size—"junior." Why not put a child or a tiny adult in a full-size bag? Because a bag that is too big for the occupant takes longer to heat up and loses heat faster. The excess space also adds needless weight to a load. On the other hand, a bag that is too small will be too cramped for a comfortable night's sleep.

Below are a host of other factors that might influence your choice of sleeping bag.

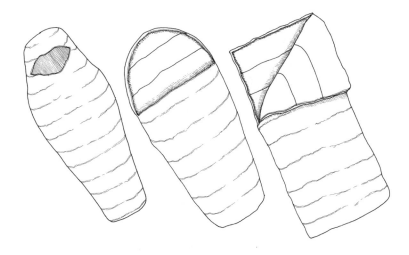

Comfort rating. Sleeping bags are given a temperature rating, usually plus forty degrees Fahrenheit to minus forty degrees F, which is supposed to be the lowest temperature at which the bag will keep you warm. The first problem is that individual differences can affect how warmly you sleep. The second is that comfort ratings are supplied by manufacturers, who tend to shade the numbers in their favor. Even if they don't help you compare bags from different makers, they will give you an idea where a bag fits in a particular manufacturer's line. Lower comfort ratings mean higher prices.

Fill power. This is the best measure of down quality. One ounce of down is placed in a tube and its volume is measured under a weight. The higher the result (the more cubic inches per ounce), the more efficient the down. A fill power of 550 is good; 650 excellent.

Fill weight. This is how much the insulation inside the sleeping bag weighs. Fill weight and comfort rating are related.

Hood. An enormous amount of heat is lost through the head and neck. A hood with a drawstring makes a sleeping bag versatile. In very cold weather, tighten down the hood so only your nose protrudes; on warmer nights, use the hood as a pillow.

Loft. Gently shake and fluff your sleeping bag and lay it flat. The thickness of the insulation after fluffing is loft. More loft (eight inches is excellent) means more warm air trapped between you and the elements. As a rough gauge of warmth, figure about four inches of loft keeps you warm down to forty degrees, six inches to twenty degrees, and eight inches to zero.

Price. Money is an object, of course. Bags are expensive, but they've inflated a lot less than hotel rooms. For quality down bags, expect to pay $150 to $300; for synthetic fill, you can do well for less than $200. You can find a kids' bag rated to fifteen degrees F for less than $100. You can find used bags at flea markets, thrift shops, and garage sales, or you can adapt one out of a used adult bag. This works especially well with bags having less than full zippers. Amputate the bottom two feet and resew it.

Shell. Cold air moving across the surface (shell) of a standard sleeping bag will draw warm air out of the insulation as you sleep. Laminating a nylon shell with ripstock Gore-Tex will substantially increase a bag's protection from moisture and heat loss without increasing weight.

Stuffed size. You should stuff quality sleeping bags, rather than roll them. Stuff sacks, usually of coated nylon, come in a range of sizes. How small a bag will stuff to is important for backpackers with limited space. Down is more compressible than synthetic fill, though the latter has narrowed the gap in the past few years. Compression stuff sacks with extra straps will make the package even smaller.

Weight. This is more important for backpackers than car campers. Most kids' bags weigh less than three pounds; most adult ones less than five pounds.

Zipper. Nylon coil zippers are better than tooth ones. Number seven zippers are stronger than number fives. A full zipper makes a bag versatile: unzip it partway and hang your leg outside; unzip it all the way and call it a blanket. But that full zipper also creates tiny holes that can leak warm air. Good bags have the zipper covered to prevent this.

Another issue is whether the zipper is on the right or left side. This is important if you want to zip one bag to another and share it with that special someone. If two bags have full zippers of the same size and type, with opposite configurations, they will zip together.

With care, a good sleeping bag will last for years. Store bags loose in a cool, dark, dry room. If you have space, hang them in a spare closet. Or use storage bags made of breathable cotton and roomy enough to avoid loft compression. Never store any sleeping bag, down or synthetic, compressed in a stuff sack or backpack.

> Right now, while you're strong, write on a piece of paper: "I will not let my child sleep with me in my sleeping bag." Now follow that rule, at least if you care about a good night's sleep.

You can sew two sheets together on three sides, insert your sleeping bag into the envelope, and use it on your bed as a quilt.

In camp, after pitching the tent, un-stuff, unzip, and fluff all bags to allow them to regain full loft. Next morning, air-dry bags on a warm rock or line. That will evaporate perspiration that has condensed on the insulation fibers.

Bags are best machine washed. Use a commercial front-loader, not a home top-loader. Use mild soap and the "delicate" setting. Remove it carefully; if you yank from one end, you can tear the baffles. Tumble dry thoroughly on a very low setting. Never drape a soaking wet bag over a line.

To keep your sleeping bag clean, double a sheet, then sew the bottom and partway up the side to create a liner that can be taken out and washed.

Resources for Sleeping Bags

Camp 7 3701 W. Carriage Dr., Santa Ana, CA 92704-6417; (714) 545-2204; (800) 224-2300

Caribou Mountaineering 400 Commerce Rd., Alice, TX 78332; (800) 824-4153

Feathered Friends 119 Yale Ave. N., Seattle, WA 98109; (206) 292-6292

Ferrino 11315 Rancho Bernardo Rd., Suite 133, San Diego, CA 92127; (800) 566-0690

Integral Designs 5516 Third St. S.E., Calgary, AB Canada T2H 1J9; (403) 640-1445

Kelty 6235 Lookout Rd., Boulder, CO 80301; (303) 530-7670, (800) 423-2320

L.L. Bean Casco St., Freeport, ME 04033; (800) 809-7057

Marmot Mountain 2321 Circadian Way, Santa Rosa, CA 95407; (707) 544-4590

Moonstone Mountaineering 5350 Ericson Way, Arcata, CA 95521; (707) 822-2985

Outbound/Safesport 269 Columbia Ave., Chapin, SC 29036; (800) 433-6506

Peak 1 P.O. Box 2931, Wichita, KS 67201; (800) 835-3278

Sierra Designs 1255 Powell St., Emeryville, CA 94608; (800) 736- 8551

Slumberjack P.O. Box 7048-A, St. Louis, MO 63177; (800) 233-6283

The North Face 2013 Farallon Dr., San Leandro, CA 94577; (800) 447-2333

Western Mountaineering 1025 S. Fifth St., San Jose, CA 95112; (408) 287-8944

Wiggy's P.O. Box 2124, Grand Junction, CO 81502; (800) 748-1827

■ Sleeping Pads

A pad may be the most underrated piece of gear in the battle against a sleepless night. It puts a layer of insulation between body and cold, hard ground, cushioning against roots, rocks, and old tent stakes. It also can be your life raft on a stormy night in a leaky tent.

Pads are of two basic types—closed-cell and open-cell. Common to both is foam.

Closed-Cell Pads

Closed-cell foam is a slab of tiny plastic bubbles, whole and unbroken (closed), so the pad won't absorb water. Lightweight, waterproof, and virtually indestructible, they offer decent insulation in three seasons and can be a supplemental pad in the winter. Because the rigid cell walls do not fully collapse under pressure, closed-cell pads are bulky to pack.

You can cut closed-cells to the exact length you want. If, for example, you're shorter than average, you may prefer a three-quarter-length pad. Simply trim the excess and use it as a water bottle insulator or seat pad.

Open-Cell Pads and Self-Inflators

Open-cell foam pads offer more comfort and insulation than closed-cell models, but their broken bubbles soak up water like a sponge. Encase a slab of open-cell foam in a heat-sealed nylon cover, however, and you get the warmest and cushiest of all backcountry beds—the self-inflator.

The self-inflating pad employs airtight construction and a simple plastic or metal valve to capture and hold air. When you unscrew the valve, the collapsed cells spring to shape, drawing air into the waterproof envelope. It is upon this pillow of air that you sleep, with minimal convective and conductive heat loss. A self-inflator weighs more and costs more, but many backpackers have decided it's worth it.

If you go with a self-inflating pad, be patient and let it inflate by itself. Unroll your pad and open the valve as soon as you get to camp.

By bedtime it should need only a couple of puffs to cap it off. Blow into your pad as little as possible, as your breath carries moisture that can break down the foam.

Children, who seem impervious to the rigors of lying on the ground, will usually sleep fine with the cheaper closed-cell foam. A half-length pad might be just right for them.

After each outing, give your pad a quick sponge bath. Allow ample time to dry, then store the pad in the usual cool, dry place. Leave it unrolled with the valve open; closing the valve may trap moisture inside and cause mildew.

Always pack a good repair kit. Use self-adhesive nylon tape for repairs. Fix pinholes with a dollop of seam sealer. Patch larger holes by cutting a rounded patch one-half-inch larger than the hole. Clean the area with stove gas or denatured alcohol. Use duct tape only as a last resort, as it leaves a gooey residue that hampers permanent repair.

To decide which pad is right, rank weight, warmth, bulk, comfort, durability, and cost in order of importance. Then factor in your own peculiarities. Do you sleep warm or cold? Are you big and tall or short and slight? Do you want to shave ounces? Regardless of the answers, don't lose sight of the ultimate goal: a good night's sleep for everyone, perhaps the most important element of a successful camping trip.

Resources for Sleeping Pads

American Camper 14760 Santa Fe Trail Dr., Lenexa, KS 66215; (913) 492-3200

Artiach/Appalachian Mountain Supply P.O. Box 8526, Atlanta, GA 30306-0526; (800) 569-4110

Basic Designs P.O. Box 1498, St. Cloud, MN 56303; (800) 328-3208

Cabela's 812 13th Ave., Sidney, NE 69160; (800) 237-8888

Cascade Designs 4000 First Ave. S. Seattle, WA 98134; (800) 531-9531

Crazy Creek Products P.O. Box 1050, Red Lodge, MT 59068; (800) 331-0304

Down to Earth 63189 Nels Anderson Rd., Bend, OR 97701; (541) 382-7285

Eastern Mountain Sports 327 Jaffrey Rd., Peterborough, NH 03458; (888) 463-6367

High Country Outdoor Products 19767 S.E. Sunnyside Rd., Damascus, OR 97009; (503) 658-4704

Hot Toddy P.O. Box 50986, Kalamazoo, MI 49005-0986; (616) 388-8664

Liberty Mountain Sports 9325 S.W. Barber St., Wilsonville, OR 97070; (503) 685-9600

Peak 1 P.O. Box 2931, Wichita, KS 67201; (800) 835-3278

Slumberjack P.O. Box 7048-A, St Louis, MO 63177; (800) 233-6283

Stephensons-Warmlite 22 Hook Rd., Gilford, NH 03246-6745; (603) 293-8526

Texsport P.O. Box 55326, Houston, TX 77043-4309; (713) 464-5551

Wenzel 1224 Fern Ridge Pkwy., St. Louis, MO 63141; (800) 325-4121

Wiggy's P.O. Box 2124, Grand Junction, CO 81502; (800) 748-1827

▪ Shelters

Your basic choices in backpacking shelters, from the primitive to the sophisticated, are: nothing, snow caves, tarps, tube tents, and three- and four-season tents.

Nothing

If conditions are right, nothing has a great deal to offer: lightweight, good packability, and the opportunity to see about forty billion stars. But let's say it's not a clear night. Let's say it's stormy or the bugs are swarming. Then, "nothing" doesn't cut it.

Snow Cave

This is strictly an emergency dwelling. Climbers caught on Mount McKinley might dig a snow cave, but most backpackers will not.

Tarp

You can buy a two-pound, waterproof tarp, with grommets, for a fraction of the cost of a tent. A well-rigged tarp offers shelter from rain and sun but little privacy or protection from wind and insects.

When rigging a tarp, as when opening a restaurant, location is everything. Seek good wind protection and stakeout points (scenic overlooks may provide neither). Look for firm staking soil and sturdy trees that will support your lines. Your living quarters should be on the lee side of the tarp, as sheltered from fluctuating winds as possible. If you're expecting much rain or snow, pitch the roof at a steep angle. As little as ten gallons of rainwater collecting on a flat roof can rip out spindly tie-outs. Whichever configuration you use, stretch the tarp surface tight; a strong wind will throttle any slack, tearing out grommets and ripping seams.

Practice in your backyard to learn a tarp's uses and limitations. Since most tarps are flat (some are shaped), you must use rope and/ or stakes and poles to hold it up and shape the material. With some creative rigging, many shapes are possible. With practice, you will be able to put up a tarp quickly even in bad weather.

Tube Tent

A tube tent isn't really a tent but an open-ended plastic or coated nylon sleeve. It's easily rigged by running a line through it and tying both ends to rocks or trees. It's cheap and light, but if the going gets tough, tube tenters invariably get wet.

Tent

There are two overriding reasons for carrying a tent: insects and weather. The cheapest tent, if it has a floor and no holes, will offer full protection against mosquitoes and even tinier no-see-ums. Most tents are adequate if the weather is mild and dry, but will they survive a weekend in the desert beneath an unrelenting sun? How about a snowstorm in the Rockies? Think of a tent as an insurance policy against the possible ravages of nature. You hope you don't need it, but you feel so much better if you have it.

Technology has made possible sturdy, lightweight tents that sleep up to six (eight if some are kids). Before you buy a tent, ask yourself the key questions: Will you be backpacking or car camping? In winter? At high altitude? What about price? Early on, you must decide between a three-season and a four-season tent. For most people who camp from late spring through early fall, three-season tents are adequate. Four-season tents have extra features, like an internal guy system, that allow you to survive a winter storm at high altitude.

Even in three-season tents, there are several options to consider.

Weight-to-volume ratio. Tents range from one-person models, weighing less than three pounds and suitable for one anorexic bicyclist, to cabin-style models weighing more than forty pounds and suitable for bowling tournaments. If you are backpacking, your tent will usually be the heaviest item in your pack. As with so many backpacking items, you have to balance the comfort of using a bigger model with the discomfort of carrying it. You should also figure how far you will be carrying it. If you are hiking the Pacific Crest Trail and have to lug every ounce of tent three thousand miles, you will place a disproportionate value on weight; if you are a casual weekend camper who carries the tent only a mile or two to the old fishing hole, weight is nothing compared to spaciousness.

Spaciousness. Sierra Designs has a two-person tent that weighs only three pounds, thirteen ounces. With a floor space of thirty-two square feet, it is fine for one adult or two kids. Two full-sized adults could make it, but they had better be married, or at least engaged, before trying to ride out a three-day squall in that shelter.

Most outdoor stores have pitched tents on display. When shopping for a tent, bring the whole family and crawl in. Assure yourselves that this mobile home you are buying is large enough to house you and your brood. If you are ordering from a catalog, determine the dimensions of the tent, then take a marker and an old sheet and draw the shape. Crawl onto the sheet and make sure it's big enough.

Packed size. This can be important even if you're not backpacking. Car trunks have gotten smaller, still another reason to eschew huge, bulky cabin tents for trim backpacking models. The packing size of good two-person tents ranges from about five by seventeen inches to seven by twenty-one inches. Even the largest of the quality six-person tents packs to about ten by thirty-one inches.

Ease of setup. You'll realize how important this feature is the first time you have to put up your tent in the rain. Things to look for: How many poles? Are they all the same length? Are they shockcorded (linked by an internal elastic cord)? For good tents, the answers are two to four, yes, and yes.

Some of today's tents are easy enough for, yes, a child to put up. In 1991, The North Face introduced the No-Hitch-Pitch system, with every pole preattached to one floor grommet and already threaded through the correct canopy rings. All the camper has to do is spread out the tent floor, push the poles into position, and snap the free ends into the remaining grommets.

Whatever tent you buy, always set it up at home before you head out into the wilderness. You don't want to be reading directions out there by flashlight. Besides, a single missing or broken pole can render your tent useless. Break a little nipple off one of your tent poles and, though it appears insignificant, it may be enough to disable the tent beyond use.

Shape. The A-frame is dead; long live the dome. Actually, a few A-frames endure, and many so-called domes aren't true domes. Nowadays any self-standing tent is commonly called a dome.

The greatest advantage of domes over flat-walled A-frames is usable space, especially headroom. Because the walls rise more or less vertically on all sides, domes have almost half again as much volume as an A-frame with the same floor area. You don't have to crawl on your belly or sit in the middle to avoid brushing against the sides of a dome. If you're tentbound for longer than a day, extra space can have a huge psychological impact.

Freestanding capabilities. Most good tents will stand on their own, using just the poles and no stakes. This means you can pick it up and move it after it has shape. You should still stake your tent, however, lest a sudden wind blow it into a nearby gorge.

Entrances. If there is only one door, it should be at the front or back, not on a side. The latter makes it inconvenient for the person farthest away.

Tautness. Quality tents are designed to be pitched tightly (although even the best tents need to be guyed in severe winds). Because cheap tents employ fewer poles and inferior fabric, they remain wrinkled even with the best pitch. That gives the wind something to bite into and whenever there is flapping nylon, seams start to separate, fabric starts to tear, and nerves start to fray. To test tautness, toss a quarter on the canopy. It should bounce right off.

Poles. If you choose a dome, the poles should be light, flexible, hollow, and shockcorded. Aluminum gets the nod over fiberglass, as it's easy to break a fiberglass pole tip.

No-see-um mesh. Quality tents have at least one "screen" door or window; many now have two or more. Nylon mesh should be fine enough to keep out the tiniest no-see-ums while allowing you to see outside. More and more of today's tents have mesh windows, on both the sides and the ceiling. Thus you retain that outdoor feeling while cowering inside your tent during the evening infestation of mosquitoes. If the weather is fine, you can remove the rain fly, improve air flow, and sleep under a canopy of stars.

Rain fly. The rain fly is vital to the moisture-control system. The most important thing a tent can do is control water movement. We tend to focus on keeping rainwater out, but the biggest problem is removing condensation inside. During sleep, respiration and perspiration cause water vapor buildup that can condense on cool tent walls.

Top manufacturers beat the problem by providing two walls: an inner breathable canopy and an outer waterproof rain fly. With double walls, the inner canopy stays warmer than the fly and internal moisture passes out through the canopy, condensing on the fly. It may drip back onto the tent canopy, but surface tension will prevent it from repenetrating and dripping onto you.

Insist on a full fly over your tent. Some inferior tents offer a tiny fly that sits atop the tent like a beanie. If the fly doesn't cover the entire tent, the nylon canopy must have a waterproof coating, which means interior moisture can't escape. This can make the inside of your tent feel like a cold steam bath.

Vestibule. Many tents include a separate covered area for cooking or stowing gear. This is handy in bad weather.

> If your tent doesn't have a vestibule, you can make one out of a yard or so of coated ripstop nylon. Cut it in a triangle, with one side to fit the front of the fly near the door. Sear the cut edges with a flame, holding the fabric taut. Then sew Velcro strips along the edge of the fly and on the matching edge of the fabric.

Internal gear holders. Look for loops, pockets, and attics. The latest—elevated mesh shelves—are all the rage in today's tents.

Seams. Stitching creates tiny needle holes that offer still another entrance for moisture. Defend against this with a commercial seam sealer. Most are applied like a roll-on deodorant. Sealing tent seams may be a good job for your children.

Color. This could be important. If bad weather forces you to spend days in your tent, your sanity could be at stake. Three days of staring up at bright orange walls could send you screaming into the woods. Quality tents generally come in muted, natural hues.

Extras. These might include a netted roof vent or separate storage sacks for stakes, poles, and fabric; or a ground cloth sized to fit perfectly under your tent and prevent water from collecting around uneven edges.

Price. Price depends on materials, workmanship, design, features, and options. Costs vary dramatically and, as with most things, you generally get what you pay for. The price range for quality two-person tents is two to four hundred dollars. Four-person tents top out at around eight hundred dollars. At the other end of the spectrum, you can find domes for less than one hundred dollars that seem like they might suffice. In fact, they might not last a weekend under a raging desert sun or a tropical deluge.

The most important consideration for most people is how well a tent protects in a driving rainstorm. That can be a tough call in a store. The worst tent in the world, assuming you can set it up properly, will be adequate when the weather is fine. Most tents will keep

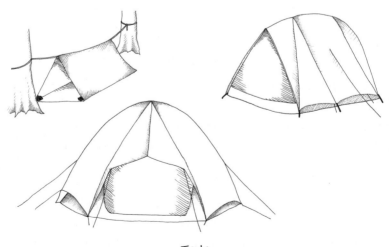

Tents
Illustrations by John Kelty

you dry in a sprinkle, a drizzle, and even a soft, steady rain. But a squall may reveal leaks you didn't know existed. At those times, quality takes on new importance.

Buying a Tent

- Find out if any local outdoor stores rent tents. If so, you can try one out before you buy.

- Ask friends, neighbors, and acquaintances about their successes and failures. You may even be able to borrow a tent for a test run.

- At the camping store, get in and out of demonstrator models several times. Now imagine yourself doing it in wind, rain, or snow. Check for good ventilation. See if closures are tight. Try the zippers to see if they work smoothly from outside as well as inside. Do they have storm flaps for protection against wind-driven rain?

Family in a tent
Photo by Rick Ridgeway

- No matter how much you like the demonstrator, inspect the tent you buy before you take it home. Make sure you have the stakes, poles, guy lines, and fly.

Tent Care

- Before pitching a tent, lay down a ground cloth to protect the coated floor. A Space blanket, weighing only a couple of ounces, works well.

- Before entering a tent, remove your shoes and leave them outside. Tracked-in debris rubs off the floor's protective coating.

- Before breaking down a tent, sweep it out, or, if it's a freestanding tent, pick it up and shake it out.

- Hand wash your tent. Set it up and sponge it with warm water and mild, nondetergent soap. Rinse thoroughly.

- Always clean and air-dry all components before storing. Never store a wet tent. If you must move on before your tent is dry, set it up again as soon as possible to let the seams dry.

- Never dry-clean, machine wash, or machine dry a tent.

- Store in a dry place, out of sunlight and away from rodents and heat sources.

- If you're storing a tent for a long time, let it hang or leave it loosely packed.

- You can roll or stuff a tent, but rolling usually makes a smaller package. When rolling, leave the doors and windows open to allow air to escape. Fold the collapsed tent into a rectangle equaling the length of the folded poles. Place the poles at one end of the rectangle and roll the tent tightly, pushing air out with the poles. When you reach the end, hold the roll tightly and insert it into its bag.

- Repair small tears and punctures with nylon tape.

- When you have a seam leak but no sealer, try lip balm, candle wax, or snow seal. They will seal for a while.

Innovations

Somewhere between a tent and a tarp lies the Altamate, which might be perfect when mosquitoes are not a problem. It is a shaped fabric lean-to supported at its peak by one stout pole (which doubles as a walking stick). The basic weight is 2.5 pounds, but extra options, including a ground cloth, can increase the weight to 6.5 pounds. The manufacturer claims the Altamate sleeps up to four and can withstand winds of fifty miles per hour.

Resources for Tents

Bibler Tents Dept. BG, 5441-D Western Ave., Boulder, CO 80301; (303) 449-7351

Diamond Brand P.O. Box 249, Naples, NC 28760; (800) 258-9811

Eastern Mountain Sports 327 Jaffrey Rd., Peterborough NH 03458; (888) 463-6367

Eureka 1326 Willow Rd., Sturtevant, WI 53177; (888) 245-4984

Ferrino 11315 Rancho Bernardo Rd., Suite 133, San Diego, CA 92127; (800) 566-0690

Garuda Mountaineering 333 Simmental Way, Bozeman, MT 59715; (406) 587-4153

Kelty 6235 Lookout Rd., Boulder, CO 80301; (303) 530-7670, (800) 423-2320

L.L. Bean Casco St., Freeport, ME 04033; (800) 809-7057

Marmot Mountain 2321 Circadian Way, Santa Rosa, CA 95407; (707) 544-4590

Moss Tents P.O. Box 577, Camden, ME 04843; (800) 859-5322

Mountain Hardware 950 Gilman St., Berkeley, CA 94710; (510) 559-6700; (800) 330-6800

Noall Tents 59530 Devils Ladder Rd. #26, Mountain Center, CA 92561; (909) 659-4219

Outbound/Safesport 269 Columbia Ave., Chapin, SC 29036; (800) 433-6506

Quest P.O. Box 5009, 2690 Lake Forest Rd., Tahoe City, CA 96145; (800) 875-6901

Recreational Equipment, Inc. (REI) P.O. Box 1938, Sumner, WA 98390-0800; (800) 426-4840

Sierra Designs 1255 Powell St., Emeryville, CA 94608; (800) 736-8551

The North Face 2013 Farallon Dr., San Leandro, CA 94577; (800) 447-2333

Walrus P.O. Box 3875, Seattle, WA 98124; (800) 550-8368

■ Stoves

Inanimate objects are classified scientifically into three major categories—those that don't work, those that break down, and those that get lost.
—Russell Baker

Backcountry overuse has lead to campfire restrictions in many areas, so a stove has been upgraded from luxury to necessity. When car camping, you can use a two- or three-burner stove with a separate fuel tank. When backpacking, choose a lighter one-burner model.

Selling points include:

Weight

Compactness

Ease of use

Fuel capacity

Burning time at maximum flame

Flame adjustability

Average boiling time

Stability

Effect of wind, cold, and altitude

Safety features

Ease of repair

Availability of fuel

Price

You will first have to decide between a stove that burns liquid fuel (gas or kerosene, sometimes both) or one that uses canisters of pressurized propane or butane.

Liquid-Fuel Stoves

When given a choice of fuels, most campers in the United States opt for white gas over kerosene or auto gas. It's readily available, burns cleaner, and is more efficient than the heavier fuels. Other advantages include moderate cost and easy evaporation of spilled fuel. On the downside, priming is required, the fuel is somewhat danger-ous, the stove must be insulated from cold and snow, and a separate fuel bottle is required.

The advantages of kerosene include easy availability and high heat output, and the facts that spilled fuel will not readily ignite and there is no need to insulate the stove from cold and snow. However, prim-ing is required and spilled kerosene is smelly and will not readily evaporate.

Roughly, one quart of liquid fuel should last one person a week. Double that if drinking water must be boiled or snow melted for water.

Multifuel Stoves

For versatility, it's hard to beat multifuel stoves, most of which burn white gas, kerosene, and auto gas. Although white gas, which burns hot, clean, and reliably in cold weather, would be most people's first choice, it's not always easy to find outside the United States. The first time you find yourself where the only fuel for miles around has an octane rating, you'll kiss your multifuel stove.

Many multifuel stoves have the added advantage of accepting fuel bottles of different sizes and brands. If you have such a stove, and you're heading out for just a weekend, you don't have to lug a huge bottle of fuel.

Cartridge Stoves

The advantages of butane or propane include no priming, immediate maximum heat output, a convenient no-spill fuel container, and easy lighting. However, butane and propane cartridges are heavy, and butane doesn't burn well below freezing.

Blended butane/propane cartridges recently hit the U.S. market after long being the standard in Europe. The new 80 percent butane/20 percent propane fuel was touted as more efficient in subfreezing conditions. *Backpacker* magazine confirmed that claim, but for the first two-thirds of the canister only. Because propane has a considerably lower boiling point and doesn't chemically bond with the butane, the propane burns off first, leaving behind plain old butane. Thus, cold-weather efficiency diminishes, making it necessary to warm up a near-empty blended-fuel canister. There are several ways to do that:

- Sleep with your fuel canister, then store it in your sleeping bag or under an insulated jacket. Keep it warm until mealtime.

- During cooking, periodically wrap your hands around the canister.

- Heat some water slightly and dip the canister for just a few seconds. Never immerse a fuel canister in boiling or near-boiling water.

- To incubate a canister that has already been warmed, make a wrap from a foam drink "coolie" or a closed-cell sleeping pad.

- Only as a last resort should you warm a fuel canister with a lighter. To avoid a possible explosion, never get a fuel canister any hotter than is comfortable to the touch.

To conserve fuel, carry freeze-dried foods, which require no cooking on the stove (just add boiling water). Soak dried foods before lighting the stove, cover pots while cooking, and shut off the stove ten minutes early and let dinner sit in a covered pot to finish cooking. Other fuel conservation tips:

- Apply flat black stove paint (available at hardware stores) to the outside of your cookware to increase heat absorption. After the paint dries, heat several quarts of water to burn off the initial odor of burning paint. The combination of a blackened pot and a tight lid can reduce boiling time by 20 to 30 percent.

- A wraparound windscreen reduces fuel consumption and boiling time by 20 to 50 percent, depending on wind conditions. A windscreen should fit snugly around the pot, with less than an inch between the two. With tank-under stoves, monitor the amount of heat that reflects down onto the fuel tank or cartridge because overheating can be dangerous. If the tank feels hot, open the windscreen a little. You can make your own inexpensive windscreen by cutting it out of a cookie sheet or aluminum pie tin.

> If you're planning to live on freeze-dried foods, it's easy to calculate your liquid fuel needs. First, total how many cups of boiling water you'll need to rehydrate the number of meals and hot drinks you're bringing. Second, determine how much fuel your stove uses to boil a cup of water. Now multiply the two numbers together. Add about 25 percent more fuel as a safety margin.

- Heat ordinarily lost to the ground can be reflected toward the pot with aluminum sheeting or foil.

Stove Safety Tips

- Read and follow instructions.

- Keep the stove clean and in good working order.

- Eliminate surprises by practicing with a new stove before beginning a trip.

- When carting the stove around, store the fuel separately.

- Fill your fuel tank using a filter funnel to keep debris out.

- Refuel stoves before each use so you don't run out in the middle of meal preparation.

- Never refuel a hot stove.

- Do not fill the fuel tank to the brim.

- Do not refuel a stove near flames.

- Do not pour fuel inside a tent.

- Replace the cap on the fuel bottle and on the stove before lighting.

- Place a pot on the stove to check stability before lighting.

- For pressurized canister stoves, light the match and hold it next to the burner before turning on the gas. When replacing a canister, make sure gaskets are clean. The screw threads should be easy to turn— don't cross-thread the fitting. Once the canister is attached, listen for a hissing noise that could mean a leak. Never throw an "empty" canister in the fire.

- Do not light gas stoves in enclosed areas, such as tents. A burning stove consumes oxygen and gives off carbon monoxide. If you must cook inside the tent because of bad weather, light the stove outside, then carefully move it inside the vestibule or near the door. Keep the stove stable and the tent well-ventilated.

- Do not light or operate a stove near spilled fuel.

- Mark fuel bottles clearly.

- For fuel storage, use only metal flasks or approved plastic containers (fuel dissolves some plastics).

- Do not closely surround a pressurized-gas cartridge with a windscreen; it could cause the cartridge to overheat and explode.

- Do not leave stoves unattended.

- If your stove has a removable key that adjusts the flame, remove it during operation so it doesn't get too hot.

- Carry spare parts, tools, and instructions for field repair. Clean holes and vents regularly.

In the end, the key to a safe, stress-free relationship with your stove is intimacy. Take it apart, clean it, and put it back together again until you can do it in a pelting rainstorm. You may have to someday. Get to know every orifice and gasket. Memorize how it sounds when it hums along efficiently, and develop an ear for any deviation from that sound.

Innovations

Tired of watching your food-laden stove tip and topple on uneven ground? Wilderness Concepts' new four-ounce stove stand (Mighty-Lite, $25) solves this instability problem for two of the most popular multifuel backpacking stoves, the MSR WhisperLite and the MSR XGK. Made of aluminum and Lexan, the Mighty-Lite supports both the stove and its detached fuel tank, providing a broad base to support group-size pots.

Resources for Stoves

American Camper 14760 Santa Fe Trail Dr., Lenexa, KS 66215; (913) 492-3200

Bibler Tents Dept. BG, 5441-D Western Ave., Boulder, CO 80301; (303) 449-7351

Camping Gaz/Suunto 2151 Las Palmas Dr., Suite G, Carlsbad, CA 92009; (800) 543-9124

Liberty Mountain Sports 9325 S.W. Barber St., Wilsonville, OR 97070; (503) 685-9600

Mountain Safety Research (MSR) P.O. Box 24547, Seattle, WA 98124; (800) 877-9677

Optimus/Suunto 2151 Las Palmas Dr., Suite G, Carlsbad, CA 92009; (800) 543-9124

Outbound/Safesport 269 Columbia Ave., Chapin, SC 29036; (800) 433-6506

Peak 1 P.O. Box 2931, Wichita, KS 67201; (800) 835-3278

Primus/Country Tool & Manufacturing Co. P.O. Box 188, Cherry Valley, IL 61016; (800) 435-4525

Pyromid Outdoor Cooking Systems 3292 S. Hwy. 97, Redmond, OR 97756; (800) 824-4288

VauDe Sports P.O. Box 3413, Mammoth Lakes, CA 93546; (800) 447-1539

ZZ Corp. 10806 Kaylor St., Los Alamitos, CA 90720; (800) 594-9046

■ Water Filters

Filters may seem expensive, but they last a long time, don't weigh much, and are probably the best solution to the water problem. (If you still doubt the need for a water filter, see "Giardia" on page 263.)

There are now many models, some smaller than your water bottle, almost none weighing more than two pounds.

Here are some other variables to consider when shopping for a water filter:

Ease of use. Is the filter comfortable to hold? Effortless to pump? Is the overall design appropriate for steep, slippery streambeds, or is it designed for laboratory use only? Are the hoses, prefilters, and accessories layman logical?

Rate of output. This figure reflects the manufacturer's stated output in pints per minute under "ideal" conditions. Manufacturers tend to be wildly optimistic about the performance of their filters. Glacially silted or murky water, a half-clogged filter, or kinked hoses can extend filtering time.

Pore size. This is the size of the openings in a filter element, which determines what size particles can be removed. Pore sizes are measured in microns. The period at the end of this sentence is about 600 microns in diameter.

Filter pores must be 4.0 microns or smaller to be effective against giardia, the most common backcountry bugaboo. To reject bacteria, pores should be 0.2 microns or less, but a filter this fine is subject to clogging and will need frequent cleaning in murky or silty water. (When treating cloudy or debris-littered water, let it silt out overnight and then strain it through cheesecloth or coffee filters.) Because viruses can be as small as 0.0004 microns, no field device that relies entirely on filtration will reliably remove them.

Filter type. Is it ceramic? Glass? Polyethylene? Does it combine physical filtration with chemical annihilation? (While the filter snags giardia, the chemical element kills bacteria and viruses.)

Prefilter. The prefilter fits on the end of the intake hose to strain out larger particles that would otherwise clog the main filter. Although a prefilter is usually an extra-cost option, it reduces cleaning and extends filter life.

Ease of field maintenance. Is cleaning the filter a simple matter? Can you easily diagnose and repair basic problems? Problem number one is clogging, so make sure yours can be easily cleaned or has a replaceable filter.

Durability. Does the filter hold up to the rigors of backcountry life? Do parts crack, break, or fall off? How long before cleaning is no longer effective and the filter must be replaced?

Packability. This is a function of both weight and bulk. Other considerations: Are there many loose parts to lose? Does it come with a storage sack? Does it leak all over your pack?

Cost. Katadyn offers an expedition filter for $725, but in a field test conducted by *Backpacker* magazine (December 1996) the overwhelming favorite was the PUR Hiker for a mere $50. The point is, there's quite a price range out there, and the most expensive water filter is not necessarily the best one for you. Shop around and make sure you're getting what you pay for.

Resources for Water Filters

American Camper 14760 Santa Fe Trail Dr., Lenexa, KS 66215; (913) 492-3200

Basic Designs P.O. Box 1498, St. Cloud, MN 56303; (800) 328-3208

General Ecology 151 Sheree Blvd., Exton, PA 19341; (800) 441-8166

Katadyn USA 3019 N. Scottsdale Rd., Scottsdale, AZ 85251; (800) 950-0808

Mountain Safety Research (MSR) P.O. Box 24547, Seattle, WA 98124; (800) 877-9677

Outbound/Safesport 269 Columbia Ave., Chapin, SC 29036; (800) 433-6506

PUR 2229 Edgewood Ave. S., Minneapolis, MN 55426; (800) 787-5463

Relags USA 1705 14th St., Suite 119, Boulder, CO 80302; (303) 440-8047

SweetWater 2505 Trade Centre Ave., Suite D, Longmont, CO 80503; (800) 557-9338

Timberline Filters P.O. Box 20356, Boulder, CO 80308; (800) 777-5996

WTC/Ecomaster Corp. 14405 21st Ave. N., Minneapolis, MN 55447; (612) 473-1625

When I lost my possessions, I found my creativity.
I felt I was being born for the first time.
—Yip Harburg

■ Backpacking Lite

I moved quickly and quietly because my pack was so light—16 pounds. A lean, clean pack makes for a clear clean mind. When you carry a light pack you recall what skipping is.
—Mark Jenkins

Since backpackers have to carry everything they think they might need or want in camp, tough decisions must be made. Do you carry that second paperback? The sweater Doris knitted for you? The Dutch oven?

There are some backpackers, Mark Jenkins among them, who are strong advocates of going light. Jenkins, the Rocky Mountain editor for *Backpacker* magazine, suggests we view our equipment as simply tools to help us explore the wilderness.

"Question the status quo," he says. "You don't need a sledgehammer to pound in a tack. You don't need a Bowie knife to part a bagel, and you don't need four T-shirts for one body. Less is more. Native Americans knew it. Thoreau knew it. John Muir knew it."

To pare your equipment effectively, rigorously evaluate the true function and need of every item you plan to take, and then toss anything that doesn't pass the test. Once you have selected an essential, find the lightest and most versatile version of it.

What follows is Jenkins's gear checklist for what he calls his Beartooth Lite Expedition, a four-day trek into the Beartooth Wilderness in southwestern Montana:

- *Backpack:* Kelty White Cloud (2 pounds, 12 ounces)

- *Sleeping bag:* Western Mountaineering Apache Super Gore-Tex (2 pounds, 10 ounces)

- *Sleeping pad:* Cascade Designs Ridge Rest (8.5 ounces)

- *Bivy sack (instead of a tent:* Western Mountaineering Fortress (1 pound, 8 ounces)

- *Rain jacket:* MontBell Versalite (7.5 ounces)

- *Fleece jacket:* L.L. Bean (14 ounces)

- *Rain pants:* MontBell Versalite (6 ounces)

- *Fleece hat:* Kmart (2 ounces)

- *Baseball cap:* Your choice (1 ounce)

- *Sunglasses:* Your choice (1 ounce)

- *Water bottle:* Nalgene (4 ounces, plus 5 ounces of water)

- *Iodine crystals:* (2 ounces)

- *Cook pot and lid:* Manufacturer unknown (8 ounces)

- *Stove:* MSR Whisperlight with 11-ounce fuel bottle and repair kit (3 pounds, 4 ounces)

- *Insulated mug:* (4 ounces)

- *Knife:* Swiss Army, small (2 ounces)

- *Compass:* Silva Polaris Type 7 (1 ounce)

- *Flashlight:* Tekna 2AA (4 ounces)

- *Miscellaneous:* Moleskin, toothbrush, plastic spoon, paper, pen, nylon cord, map, candle, toilet paper, lighter, sunscreen—smallest quantity and size of each (7 ounces total)

- *Food:* Purchased from Safeway (3 pounds, 8 ounces for four days)

If you decide to go ultralight, keep in mind the following tips:

- Especially if you're traveling in unfamiliar territory, carry well-stocked first-aid and survival kits.

- High-quality ultralight equipment tends to be more expensive.

Here are several useful items that weigh next to nothing that you shouldn't forget to take backpacking:

- Pillowcase. A jacket or sweater goes inside and—instant pillow!
- Waterproof sunblock lip balm (can be used on ears and nose, too)
- Footbag (Hacky Sack)
- Plastic garbage bags—for protection of packs and equipment and myriad other jobs
- Zipper-lock plastic bags
- Toilet paper—for various clean-up and hygiene purposes
- Magnifying glass—for studying specimens
- Star guide
- Space blanket
- Whistle—for distress signals
- Butane lighter
- Dental floss—for thread or shoelace
- Small binder clip—for attaching the ends of a stove windscreen or other clipping needs
- Shower curtain rings—for hanging items off your pack

- Water weighs 8.3 pounds per gallon. If you start drinking as soon as you get up in the morning and don't stop until you've downed two or three quarts, you'll be able to hike miles without needing a drink.

- Waxed dental floss, amazingly strong and almost weightless, is great for emergency repairs on packs, boots, and clothes. A small sewing needle can be stored inside the plastic floss container.

- If you travel with a partner, you can share the weight of the stove and pot, as Jenkins did to reach his final weight of sixteen pounds, thirteen ounces.

- Don't go ultralight in winter, except perhaps in Hawaii. Cold weather demands lots of warm clothes and plenty of food to stoke the internal fires.

Chapter Four

EQUIPMENT: THE INCIDENTALS

...[A] man's life consisteth not in the abundance of the things which he possesseth.

—Luke 12:15

Cookware

BACKPACKING cookware ranges from old coffee cans to state-of-the-art titanium pots and pans. Those at the front in the battle against weight will appreciate feather-light titanium cookware. Although it looks fragile, titanium is strong stuff. Ordinary aluminum cookware is not the best choice for backpackers because it dents easily and food sticks to its thin walls. On the other hand, nonstick, coated aluminum cookware is becoming more and more common in the camp kitchen. Although the nonstick coating will scratch off if you clean your pots with steel wool or your pocketknife, it's quite durable if you use it wisely.

Still quite common in outdoor stores are enamel and stainless steel mess kits. Enamel cookware, rustic looking with blue and white speckles, is actually made from lightweight stainless steel with a kiln-baked, fire-resistant finish. Enamel cookware is a bit heavier than aluminum and regular stainless, it's tougher to clean, and the coating eventually chips off, leaving rust spots behind.

Regular stainless steel is slightly heavier than aluminum, but it distributes heat well and is fairly easy to clean if the edges of the pots are rounded.

Regardless of which metal you choose, consider the following features:

- Tight-fitting lid.

- Nesting capability. Pots with built-in handles don't nest as well as those without.

- Blackened outer finish. This helps the pot absorb and distribute heat faster.

- Rounded edges. A slight curve from the bottom to the side of the pot makes clean-up easier. Rounded edges also encourage heat to creep up the walls of the pot for more even cooking.

- Lipped rims. A small curve on the rim adds strength and gives you something to hold on to with your gripper clamp.

- Gripper clamp. Look for handleless pots that work with a gripper clamp.

- Size. How big your pots are depends on your menu and the size of the group. Pasta, for example, demands a pot large enough to let the noodles breathe. In general, carry:
  - 1-liter when you're alone
  - 1.5-liter for two people
  - 2-liter for three people
  - 3-liter for four or more people

I don't even butter my bread. I consider that cooking.

—Katherine Cebrian

Cup

A cup takes on added importance in the backcountry. Many backpackers eat and drink out of one cup. Whether you're using your cup for macaroni and cheese, hot coffee, or cold water, you want it to insulate well. *Backpacker* magazine ran a test on six common camp cups. The insulation winner, by a long shot, was the lidded travel mug. Thirty minutes after boiling water was poured in, it was still a piping 160 degrees F.

In last place: the metal Sierra cup, the backpacker classic.

Insect Repellent

This can be a necessity for a backpacker, as mosquitoes seem to like the same places we do. Repellent won't keep them from buzzing you, but it will prevent them from biting you. A nonaerosol repellent weighs so little, there's no good reason not to take it (see "Mosquito Bites" on page 276).

Knife

Unless you plan to slit open a moose, a small blade should be sufficient. The Swiss Army knife is a handy gizmo, capable of performing several tasks, from whittling to opening wine. Such versatility is invaluable—look for it in other equipment. Since knives tend to be heavy, don't carry a knife with more features than you need.

The latest backpacking tool in the knife family is the pocket survival tool. Made of stainless steel, with interconnected parts to prevent loss, good ones have the following features: a variety of blades and screwdrivers, pliers, wire cutters, ruler, can and bottle opener, saw, awl, file, fish hook sharpener, scissors, nail file, and tweezers.

Light

Even if your trip is timed with a full moon, you will probably want to carry a lightweight flashlight. There are dozens of choices, but for backpacking consider only those that use lightweight AA and AAA batteries. A compact, lightweight headlamp with an over-the-head strap frees your hands for camp chores or shuffling cards. Fancier models have a spot-to-flood zoom lens that can be tilted from horizontal to vertical.

To add ambience, there's no better light source than a candle lantern. Most are tall, narrow, and unstable, but Olicamp's new Footprint Lantern is stubby, with little feet to keep it steady. The short votive candle sits in a holder that unscrews for easy lighting. The Footprint weighs 3.2 ounces. Contact: Liberty Mountain Sports, (503) 685-9600.

Map and Compass

If you're traveling through unfamiliar country, a topographical map and compass can be valuable. You can find both at most backpacking stores. Both items are lightweight, so if you're in doubt, you risk little by taking them along. When hiking on well-marked trails in familiar country, you might opt to take a map and not a compass. In places like the Cascades and the Rockies, where weather fronts can strike with little warning, sometimes creating a roiling whiteout, a compass can be a life saver. (See chapter 11, "Survival Skills," for tips on using map and compass.)

Silverware

Many backpackers reduce their utensil needs to a single tablespoon. As true silverware is heavy and can scratch your pots, consider Lexan, which is lightweight and durable. Cut off the handle so it fits in your cookware.

Sunglasses

If you hike and climb above tree line, surrounded by exposed rock and snow, sunglasses can be a necessity. Even on cloudy days, 60 to 80 percent of ultraviolet (UV) light can reach your unprotected eyes. The reflection off those light-colored surfaces can burn your cornea and cause temporary blindness. Look for reputable brands that have a certification sticker of the Sunglass Association of America.

If you plan to be in the high country for very long, take an extra pair of sunglasses. Because if you lose your only pair and become snow-blind, you are in deep trouble.

Manufacturers are not required to reveal how much UV protection sunglasses provide, but many do. Look for shades that block 97 to 100 percent of UVA and UVB rays and, unless you plan to cross a glacier, transmit 75 to 90 percent of visible light. Remember, there's no correlation between darkness of lens and level of protection from harmful UV rays.

Polycarbonate (plastic) lenses are lighter, cheaper, and shatter-proof. On the other hand, glass is more scratch-resistant, accepts antireflective coatings, and offers greater clarity. Consider photochromic lenses, which darken with increased visible light. If you're going to spend a lot of time on ice or snow, you might want sunglasses with side blinders.

Sunscreen

This is especially important at high altitudes, where the atmosphere is thinner and the reflection from rock and snow can be punishing. (See "Sun Injury" on page 291).

Watch

Some backpackers like to leave timepieces at home, all the better to keep their finger on the pulse of nature. Others prefer having the security of knowing exactly how long it is until sunset. Moreover, a watch with an alarm and a luminous dial can be valuable for that

The plastic wrapping used to cover a new mattress during shipping makes a great light-weight ground cloth. And it's free. Visit your local mattress store and offer to recycle one of their used wrappers. Trim it to fit your tent, or use it for other camp chores.

early-morning wakeup call when you want to climb a nearby peak. And if you know that thunderstorms roll in around two o'clock every afternoon, a watch will help you figure out when to turn back.

Avocet watches have the above features, plus an amazingly reliable altimeter and barometer. They are temperature-compensated and adjust nicely to atmospheric changes.

Water Bottle

Dehydration is a big problem in the mountains, where the air is dry and you tend to exercise more than usual. If you're going to carry only a quart or two of water, consider Nalgene wide-mouth, high-density polyethylene bottles. They are bombproof and lightweight. Another popular option: 1.7-liter Gatorade bottles. If you are camping or have limited access to water sources, you might prefer a collapsible gallon jug, which takes up less room when empty.

One company, CamelBak, has a hydration system that includes a collapsible bladder incorporated into a day pack. A no-hands drinking tube runs from the water supply to your mouth, allowing you to suck water anytime you want. It's the ultimate in convenience—as long as you don't already have a backpack to carry.

Chapter Five

FOOTWEAR

After twenty miles I make a bargain:
"God, if you lift the left foot,
I'll take care of the right."

—Kathrine Switzer

EVEN if you borrow your camping equipment and buy your clothes secondhand, you should spend some bucks on your boots. The right footwear can make the difference between a glorious day of hiking and a miserable day of wet feet, blisters, and even falls. Compared with tennis shoes, hiking boots offer better durability, cushioning, ankle support, and protection from the elements.

The first step in determining your footwear needs is to be realistic about your activity level. Consider what terrain you will be hiking. If it is sidewalks and cushy nature trails, tennis shoes will suffice. But if even once you will carry a backpack over rocky trails or cross-country, you need sturdy boots with lug soles.

Hiking boots, made of leather, nylon, or a combination, come in three basic styles. Low boots are lightweight, have flexible soles and soft uppers, and look almost like regular athletic shoes. They are cool, quick-drying, and don't need much breaking in, but they are not the best choice if you're carrying a backpack on rough terrain. High-top boots are heavier, have thicker soles, and offer more protection from impact and temperature extremes. High-top, off-trail boots are heavier still—sometimes more than five pounds each—with rugged midsoles and maximum ankle support. They will support a hiker over most any terrain, but their weight will slow down most children and trail hikers. Buy the lightest boot that will serve your needs. In terms of leg wear, one pound on your feet is equivalent to twenty pounds on your back.

Right Fit

Proper fit is critical, no matter what you hike in. Tight shoes limit the foot's natural elasticity during walking; loose shoes permit excessive foot movement inside the shoe, leading to blisters. Here are some tips for assuring the right fit:

> Back in my macho adolescent days, I decided to forgo boots and hike in tennis shoes. My boots were clunky old Raichles, and I figured I'd be lighter and quicker, and blah, blah, blah. On the last day, we did a gradual fifteen-mile descent on a fairly rocky trail. Had I worn hiking boots, I would have suffered nothing more than the usual aches and pains. Wearing tennis shoes, however, I was temporarily crippled. The bottoms of my feet were sore to the touch, and for an hour afterward all I could do was sit and moan. It was the last time I attempted a serious hike in anything but quality boots.
>
> —S.B.

- Shop for boots late in the day; feet tend to swell as the day goes on.

- To assure proper fit, take to the store the socks you will wear on the trail. A good sock should be thick enough to provide cushioning.

- Consider boots as large as possible for your growing children. One way to lengthen boot life is to fit them when your children are wearing, say, three pairs of socks. Next year, two sock layers may do it; after that, one thin sock and one thick sock may achieve optimum snugness.

- Ask questions of clerks to narrow down the number of boots you need to try on.

- Check workmanship. Do you see loose threads or faulty glue? Slip your hand into the boot and feel for rough edges, ridges, or seams.

- Check for flexibility. You should be able to bend the sole fairly easily across its widest point, where the ball of the foot rests. Conversely, the boot should have a stable heel and a rigid shank (the narrow part of the sole beneath the instep).

- Keep the boots unlaced and push first one foot, then the other, as far forward in the boot as possible. You should barely be able to fit your index finger between the heel and the back of the boot.

> Good boots cost money, and children, bless their ever-expanding little feet, will soon outgrow them. On the other hand, you want the best for your little darlings and real boots are safer. One father spoke of the time his four-year-old daughter was racing down a steep granite slope toward an abyss. He yelled for her to stop, which she did, slamming down hard into her boots. "Any other shoes would have hopelessly buckled and skidded," he said, "but her Vasque boots gripped like steel-belted radials an inch from the edge."

- Next, kick the heel against the floor. The back should feel snug but comfortable.

- Lace the boot snugly. Hold down the front of the boot. You should not be able to lift your heel within the shoe more than an eighth of an inch.

- Using your thumb and forefinger to exert pressure, check that the widest part of the foot rests in the widest part of the boot.

- Walk around the store for at least fifteen minutes. Try slopes or stairs. Your feet should not slide around, though you should be able to wiggle your toes. If boots don't fit in the store, they won't fit in the outdoors, though heavy leather boots will gain flexibility.

- Don't buy your hiking boots through a catalog unless the company has a good return policy. You must be able to return a bad fit.

- By using multiple socks to adjust the fit, you might find used boots at flea markets, thrift shops, or garage sales. Because children usually outgrow boots before they wear them out, outdoor stores sometimes carry used boots for kids. They may even give you a trade-in.

- Allow a week or two before a long hike to test your new boots and make sure they fit.

Boot Care

When you buy a pair of boots, find out the best waterproofing to use. As soon as you get them home, apply the first coat. Do it again before the first hike. Silicone spray works best on split-leather and fabric boots.

Clean your boots after a big hike. Resist the temptation to dry boots in an oven or over an open flame. Air-dry them thoroughly away from direct heat. Stuff newspapers, socks, paper towels, or rags into the boots to soak up moisture. Change the wadding if boots stay wet.

Spray the inside of boots with a fungicide to discourage the growth of molds. Store boots, unlaced and open, away from damp areas. Meticulous care prolongs boot life.

Foot comfort depends on boots, socks, and hygiene. Attack hot spots on your feet with moleskin, Spenco 2nd Skin, or duct tape before they become blisters. Wash your feet daily. Feet heat up and swell on long hikes and during the night. Aspirin and ibuprofen reduce swelling. Keep your feet dry with liberal sprinklings of baby powder, especially before long hikes. Feet sweat through about a quarter of a million pores.

Sport Sandals

The latest option in wilderness footwear is the sport sandal, which is lightweight, contoured, cushioned, and quick-drying. Its snug-fitting straps keep your foot securely in place, even on rocky trails, and high-traction outer soles can grip wet, slippery terrain.

Such high-tech features make the sport sandal a great second shoe on a backpacking trip. After imprisoning your feet in socks and boots for hours, airing them out in sandals is a slice of heaven.

Though sport sandals are touted as a hiking boot by some manufacturers, many podiatrists disagree, especially if you have flat feet or any type of foot abnormality. Sandals lack ankle support and greatly increase the risk of stubbed toes. The heel in many sandals is lower than the ball of the foot, which, according to Dr. Harry Hlavac of the California College of Podiatric Medicine, can strain the arch and Achilles tendon.

That said, a good pair of sport sandals will work for a backpacker in a pinch. Backpacking in the High Sierra recently, Jeff Doran of Troy, New York, developed quarter-size blisters on his heels, convincing him to try hiking in sandals. They gave him instant relief and caused no problems, even on rocky trails.

When buying sandals, test their fit by walking around the store for a few minutes. Make sure your feet are firmly centered and don't slide around. There should be about a quarter of an inch from your foot to the edges of the sandal.

To check for adequate support, grab the ends of a sandal and try to bend it. If it bends anywhere but at the toe area, support is inadequate.

Innovations

A Montana woman, tired of slipping on the ice, has invented the Taiga snow boot. It has a sole modeled after the traction of an animal paw. The thick sole is polyurethane and nonwoven felt, and the knee-high upper (resembling a mukluk) is made from Polartec 200 fleece. Call (800) 244-3675.

Resources for Footwear

Adidas 541 N.E. 20th Ave., Suite 207, Portland, OR 97232; (800) 423-4327

Alpina P.O. Box 23, Etna Rd., Hanover, NH 03755; (603) 448-3101

Asolo P.O. Box 800, Williston, VT 05495; (800) 892-2668

Danner 12722 N.E. Airport Way, Portland, OR 97230; (800) 345-0430

Fabiano 850 Summer St., South Boston, MA 02127-1575; (617) 268-5625

Garmont USA Adams Park, 75 Boyer Circle, Williston, VT 05495; (888) 343-5200

Hi-Tec 4801 Staddard Rd., Modesto, CA 95356; (800) 521-1698

Merrell Footwear P.O. Box 4249, Burlington, VT 05406; (800) 869-3348

Nike One Bowerman Dr., Beaverton, OR 97005; (503) 671-6453; (800) 344-6453

One Sport 1003 Sixth Ave. S., Seattle, WA 98134; (206) 621-9303

Raichle Geneva Rd., Brewster, NY 10509; (800) 431-2204

Reebok 100 Technology Center Dr., Stoughton, MA 02072; (800) 843-4444

Salomon 400 E. Main St., Georgetown, MA 01833; (800) 995-3556

Tecnica 19 Technology Dr., West Lebanon, NH 03784; (800) 258-3897

Timberland 200 Domain Dr., Stratham, NH 03885; (800) 445-5545

Vasque 314 Main St., Red Wing, MN 55066; (800) 224-4453

Yukon 555 S. Henderson Rd., King of Prussia, PA 19406; (800) 352-3331

Chapter Six

CLOTHING

Neckties strangle clear thinking.

—Lin Yutang

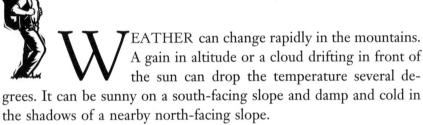 EATHER can change rapidly in the mountains. A gain in altitude or a cloud drifting in front of the sun can drop the temperature several degrees. It can be sunny on a south-facing slope and damp and cold in the shadows of a nearby north-facing slope.

To prepare for such a climatic mishmash, dress in layers. Because air is trapped and kept warm between each layer, two thin sweaters are more effective than one thick one. With several layers of warm clothes available, you can add or subtract to achieve the warmth needed. This provides maximum flexibility during weather fluctuations. Remember that having to take off clothes during a warm spell is a minor inconvenience; not having enough clothing when the temperature plummets can be disastrous.

The layer closest to your skin should wick away moisture. Cotton, a moisture absorber, is great in hot weather, not so great in cold weather. Wool retains its warmth when wet, but it can be unbearably scratchy. Synthetic fabrics like polypropylene or Thermal Dynamics are best for the inner sock and underwear layer. The middle, or insulative, layer can be a pile or fleece sweater. The outer layer might be a rainproof, windproof shell. Gore-Tex laminated onto nylon allows perspiration to escape but does not allow rain in. A hood keeps rain out and heat in.

As needed, add gloves, hat, extra socks, and other accoutrements that we'll talk about later. Not every clothing item must be purchased at an elite outdoor store. You already own most of what you need, even for cold-weather camping. To save money, look for hand-me-downs at flea markets, thrift shops, garage sales, and, with their permission, in your friends' closets.

Balaclavas

Though often confused with the flaky Greek dessert, a balaclava is actually a form-fitting hood that covers not only the head but the face and neck. Available in lightweight fleece, wool, and synthetic versions, it can be worn as a cap or pulled down over the ears to protect your face from wind and driving snow. Pull it all the way down into your turtleneck to eliminate air gaps.

Bandannas

Some backpackers carry only one swatch of cotton in their entire pack—a bandanna. Besides enhancing the cowboy look, a bandanna has many uses, including drying dishes, cleaning sunglasses, and damping down your fiery brow.

Caps

Even if you don't need a hat for warmth, take a broad-brimmed cap along to help reduce glare and protect your delicate face from UV exposure. Baseball-type caps will shield your eyes and nose. Caps in the manner of Lawrence of Arabia or the French Foreign Legion also protect vulnerable ears and neck.

Gaiters

Pebbles, burrs, thorns, mud, snow, ticks, and rainwater are a few of the hazards that can bedevil your feet and legs on a typical day—

and that's if you stay on the trail. You can defend yourself against these annoyances with a sturdy pair of ankle-high or, better yet, calf-high gaiters. These waterproof or water-repellent leg sheaths fasten by Velcro, snaps, or zipper; most use a cord or webbing instep strap to cinch tight around your boot. For serious bushwhacking, backcountry skiing, and deep-powder snowshoeing, gaiters are a must.

Gaiters keep moisture and cold out of boots and socks—preventing frostbite, blisters, and even hypothermia

Gloves/Mittens

In cold weather, it's important—possibly even life-saving—to keep your extremities warm. Fingers have to be nimble enough to pull a zipper, strike a match, prime a stove, and grab a handhold.

Whether you choose gloves or mittens is strictly up to you. Mittens make camp chores awkward, but they pack your fingers together for maximum heat retention. Gloves offer dexterity and adequate insulation for all but the coldest weather.

Either way, use a modular system for maximum adaptability. Start with a thin synthetic glove liner that will dry fast. Liners should be seamless around the fingers and fit snugly without cutting off circulation.

The middle layer should be an insulating layer of fleece or wool. On the outside: a waterproof, breathable shell to repel wind and water. If you plan to climb in your glove/mitten system, Gore manufactures a fabric called WindStopper, which is Gore laminated to fleece, the ideal combination of warmth and gripping power.

Extra features include palms and fingers reinforced with Cordura, Kevlar, or rubber; taped seams; wide cuffs for easy access; wrist leashes for a secure fit; and adjustable gauntlet closures to seal out spindrift.

Long Johns

The inner layer of clothing, closest to our skin, should offer insulation and wick moisture from the body. The greatest advance in textiles for outdoor adventurers in the past decade has been the development of lightweight, high-performance polyester underwear. Miracle fabrics like polypropylene, Thermax, and Capilene are perfect for long johns. They wick away moisture and are stretchy enough to permit extreme movements. They are machine-washable and, what's more, the moisture-moving quality won't wash out.

Rain Gear

Don't even consider rain gear that isn't waterproof (with taped seams) and fairly lightweight. Beyond that, assess the following variables:

Breathability. Does the fabric allow perspiration out as your body heat increases? Or does it seal you in tight, like a leftover in plastic wrap?

Ventilation. How well can you adjust the suit to changing weather with zippers and vents?

Freedom of movement. When you're clambering over rocks and under deadfalls, does the suit work with you or against you? Does it bind at the knees on high steps? Or ride up when you reach overhead?

Durability. What's its life expectancy? (Unfortunately, this may be difficult to determine until it's too late.)

Pockets. How many? Can you reach them while wearing your pack? Do they leak?

Hood. Does it protect your head and allow peripheral vision even when you're active?

Details. Are there wrist closures? Storm flaps?

Compressibility. Does the suit compress to softball-size (high score) or beach ball–size (low score)?

Aesthetics. Is the suit pleasing to the eye? Is the color compatible with nature?

Price. Can you afford it? This is no small concern with rain gear; the advantages of the new synthetic fibers do not come cheaply.

Socks

For hikers, feet are the first line of defense. As go the feet, so goes the hiker. Put thirty or forty extra pounds on your back, and the pressure on the feet increases.

Goal number one is to keep your feet warm and dry. Most people accomplish this by wearing at least two pairs of socks. On the inside is a thin, synthetic sock that wicks moisture away from the skin; on the outside, a heavier wool-nylon blend that provides cushioning and warmth. Avoid cotton, which absorbs moisture and causes blisters.

Shorts

Some hikers insist on wearing shorts on the trail, even in cold weather. Knowing that not much body heat is lost through the legs, they prefer the freedom of movement that shorts offer. Consider nylon in the summer and synthetics or cotton at other times of the year. An elastic waistband or drawstring avoids the problem of your belt getting hung up with your belly strap.

Trousers

For years, the basic choice on the trail was between jeans and shorts. Denim jeans, though very protective, take forever to dry and restrict your movement. Now there are high-performance trail pants made from synthetic fibers that are lightweight and durable. Consider these points when shopping:

Fabric. The ideal fabric is lightweight, durable, quick-drying, and comfortable against your skin. Avoid cotton and seek pants in one of the many nylon-based synthetic fibers that meet these requirements.

Cut. Trail pants are either roomy, allowing unrestricted movement, or snug and stretchy. Roomy cuts have ample ventilation to alleviate heat buildup but are still trim enough to fit under rain pants. Look for a gusseted crotch or a full gusset running from crotch to ankle, which allows freedom of movement. Snug cuts should stretch with you but be loose enough to allow some air flow. With either cut, the ankle should taper to avoid its snagging on bushes.

Length. Inseam lengths vary widely, so try before you buy. Ideally, the trouser bottoms drape just over the top of your boots to help keep out dirt and rocks.

Zippered legs. Zippers add versatility to your wilderness wardrobe, allowing you to adjust for temperature fluctuations. Beware of any rubbing by the zipper when you try them on.

Pockets. Look for pocket closures—snap, zipper, button, or Velcro—to assure that the contents don't spill out on the trail. Back pockets should be flat with no protruding flaps to catch on your belly strap.

Ankle closures. Snaps, buttons, or Velcro tabs at the ankles let you cinch the pants legs tight around your boots. Although this may be impractical while hiking, it can be valuable around camp to ward off cold air and biting insects.

Color. Dark colors hide the inevitable dirt better than light colors, but black may lead to overheating on sunny days. Khaki is the compromise choice of many.

T-shirts

The general rule for T-shirts is whatever draws moisture away from your skin is good. Cotton absorbs sweat like nothing else, but it traps it against your skin like a damp washcloth and chills you at first breeze. Because a damp torso is an invitation to hypothermia, leave your cotton T-shirts behind and carry a few synthetics. Look for loose-fitting, short-sleeved polypropylene tees.

Underwear

A lot of us grew up wearing cotton skivvies, which are truly wonderful in temperate climates but can't keep you dry on long, sweaty hikes. Cotton stays damp and cold, and may even cause a rash.

Quick-drying synthetics, on the other hand, wick water away from the skin. Look for snug-fitting polypropylene or polyester with flat, inconspicuous seams to minimize chafing. Men may prefer no fly because having one adds extra seams that can rub.

UV Clothing

Ordinary clothing does not completely block out UV rays. If you are fair-skinned, spend an inordinate amount of time in the sun, or have a family history of skin cancer, consider specially made sun-blocking fabrics that have tighter weaves and much higher SPFs. Finding UV clothing can be a challenge; try looking at products made by The North Face, Sun Precautions, and Ex Officio.

Vests

Sometimes a down, synthetic, or fleece vest is all you need to stop the shivering. The best ones are simple, compact, and lightweight. Down vests pack the smallest and are the warmest per ounce—when dry. Synthetic and fleece vests are slightly heavier and bulkier, but they dry fast. Look for extra features, such as deep cargo pockets with zippers or a windproof shell.

Windbreakers

In this day of expensive waterproof/breathable fabrics, the windbreaker is often ignored. For hard rains and wet blizzards, windbreakers are inadequate, but for most other conditions they will do just fine.

Two important elements of a windbreaker are fabric and design. The windproofness of a shell garment is determined by three factors—the density of the thread, the density of the weave, and whether or not the fabric is coated or laminated. All windbreakers cut the wind, so your choice will depend on your bank account and the ferocity of the wind where you hike.

Most windbreakers are made from either polyester or nylon. Although nylon is still the standard, polyester is lighter and almost ten times more hydrophobic than nylon, meaning it will dry much faster. Finishes, coatings, and membranes all adhere better to polyester. Both nylon and polyester fabrics can be woven into durable ripstop patterns.

The best windbreakers have (or don't have) the following features:

- A hood. Most of the time you won't need it, but when you do it's a real asset. If the jacket doesn't have a collar that the hood zips into, just tuck it down inside to keep it from flapping.

- No lining. Windbreakers are supposed to be light; hence, no lining.

- No taped seams. A windbreaker should be water-repelling, but not waterproof. Taped (waterproof) seams increase the cost of a windbreaker unnecessarily.

- Nonwaterproof fabric. Like taped seams, waterproof fabric is a feature best left to rainwear.

I base my fashion taste on what doesn't itch.
—Gilda Radner

Fabric Glossary

With the plethora of "performance" fabrics on the market, an abridged dictionary of clothing terms might help you sort through the choices.

> **acrylic:** generic name for soft, washable, colorfast synthetic fibers derived from polyacrylonitrile. Used in base-layer and insulating fabrics.

> **baffle:** a sewn chamber in an insulated garment or sleeping bag that prevents insulation from shifting.

> **ballistics cloth:** a thick nylon weave used in clothing, packs, and luggage for reinforcement. Named for its similar durability to bulletproof fabric.

> **boiled wool:** wool fabric that has been hot-washed and felted to give it a tighter, more weather-resistant, more shrink-resistant weave.

> **Capilene:** Patagonia's treated polyester base-layer fabric. The fiber surface is treated to make it hydrophilic. With the core hydrophobic, the combination lifts water away from the skin toward outer clothing layers without soaking the fiber. Commonly found in long underwear.

> **chemically treated fabrics:** base-layer fabrics whose outer surfaces have been treated with a hydrophilic chemical that wicks or draws sweat through to the outer surface. Examples: Capilene, Thermal Dynamics.

> **Cordura:** DuPont's abrasion-resistant, texturized nylon fabric usually used for making backpacks or, in

clothing, as reinforcements at high-wear areas, such as knees, shoulders, and arms.

down: the soft undercoating feathers of geese and ducks. Used in insulated garments and sleeping bags, it is naturally warm and lightweight when dry, but heavy and useless when wet.

fleece: commonly used, generic name for pile synthetic fabrics like Malden's Polartec, Draper's Eco-Pile, or Dyersburg's E.C.O. Fleece.

Gore-Tex: Gore's microporous membrane that, when laminated to an outer fabric, keeps rain out while allowing perspiration vapor to escape. "Three-layer" construction is a sandwich of Gore-Tex membrane laminated to one of a variety of tough outer fabrics and backed by a protective tricot inner face. "Two-layer" construction marries the Gore-Tex membrane to an outer fabric with a free-hanging liner.

Hollofil: single-hole polyester insulation used in sleeping bags and apparel, usually in cheaper brands. Hollofil II is a four-hole version that's slightly warmer than regular Hollofil, with improved stuffability.

hydrophilic: water loving; often used to describe the wicking characteristics of fabrics.

hydrophobic: water hating; used to describe the water-repellent quality of shell fabrics, and the moisture management or push-pull qualities of underwear fabric.

laminate: a composite fabric made by gluing layers together; often used to describe waterproof/breathable fabrics like Gore-Tex or Marmot's MemBrain.

loft: term used to describe thickness of insulation materials. High loft is thick and fluffy, low loft thinner and denser.

Lycra: DuPont's version of spandex.

microfiber: extremely fine, tightly woven fiber that combines natural breathability with wind and water resistance. Microfiber fabrics are used in performance outerwear, and are often laminated to waterproof/ breathable fabrics or treated with waterproof/breathable coatings.

MVT (Moisture Vapor Transfer): term used to quantify how much vapor a fabric can transfer from one side to the other.

nylon: generic term for fiber made from synthetic polyamides extracted from coal and oil. Coated nylon is coated with urethane on the inside to make it water resistant. Nylon will not be fully waterproof without sealed seams, but it's light, packable, durable, and inexpensive. It's used widely in outdoor clothing and gear.

pile: a generic name for synthetic fleece, often used to describe single-sided fleeces that are thicker and furrier than typical two-sided fabrics.

polyester: a synthetic fiber, frequently blended with cotton, rayon, or other synthetics, that features quick drying time, high strength, and abrasion and crease resistance.

polypropylene: a propylene/ethylene-based synthetic fiber that's hydrophobic, quick-drying, colorfast, and has good heat retention. It is subject to shrinkage and meltdown in hot dryers.

polyurethane coating: polymer-based waterproof coating applied to the inside of a fabric. In its heavy nonbreathable form, it's used in items like tents and packs; in its lighter, microporous breathable form, it's used in outerwear.

Quallofil: DuPont's seven-channel polyester, high-loft insulation with a soft, downlike feel. Used primarily in sleeping bags, but also in insulated outerwear and accessories.

rayon: generic term for fibers that are derived from trees, cotton, and woody plants and that have a shiny appearance and feel silky. Too absorbent for good moisture management, rayon is used mostly in base layers and trail clothes.

ripstop: fabric, usually nylon or polyester, woven with double thread at regular intervals to create tiny squares that prevent tears from spreading. Found in outerwear, sleeping bags, packs, and tents.

spandex: generic name for a synthetic fiber offering great stretch, good strength, abrasion resistance, and long-term resistance to body acids. It is always used in combination with another fiber, such as cotton, nylon, or polyester. DuPont's Lycra is the best-known brand of spandex.

storm flap: a piece of cloth that covers an opening—usually a zipper to keep out wind, rain, and snow.

Synchilla: Patagonia's name for its line of fleece.

taffeta: any fabric that is woven with a plain weave to give a fine, smooth look.

waterproof: term used to describe a fabric's ability to block out water completely. To be waterproof, clothing and tents must have taped seams and protected zippers.

waterproof/breathable (WP/B): term used to describe the degree to which an outerwear fabric prevents water entry while allowing sweat vapor to escape.

water/weather resistant: term used to describe materials that initially repel water but eventually get soaked. Most nylons, microfibers, and other shell fabrics are water resistant but not waterproof.

wicking: pulling moisture away from the skin and dispersing it throughout the material; a critical feature in high-quality base layers.

WindStopper Fleece: Gore's windproof pile fabric made of a windproof membrane laminated to fleece.

Zendura: a pile fabric from Borg made entirely from recycled plastic soda bottles.

Innovations

Hospitals use bacteria-fighting minerals called zeolites as purifying agents in linens and bandages. Now, an outdoor gear and garment maker, Mountain Hardware, incorporates zeolites in a new line of active odor-free underwear, dubbed ZeO2. Call (800) 330-6800.

Resources for Clothing

Adidas 541 N.E. 20th Ave., Suite 207, Portland, OR 97232; (800) 423-4327

Alpine Design 500 Coffman St., Suite 201, Longmont, CO 80501; (303) 776-8000

Altus Mountain Gear 75 W. Fifth Ave., Vancouver, BC, Canada V5Y 1H4; (604) 876-6044

Cabela's 812 13th Ave., Sidney, NE 69160; (800) 237-8888

Camp 7 3701 W. Carriage Dr., Santa Ana, CA 92704-6417; (714) 545-2204; (800) 224-2300

Campmor P.O. Box 700, Saddle River, NJ 07458; (800) 525-4784

Climb High 60 Northside Dr., Shelburne, VT 05482; (802) 985-5056

Columbia Sportswear 6600 N. Baltimore, Portland, OR 97203; (800) 622-6953

Critter Mountain Wear 108 W. Tomichi, P.O. Box 993, Gunnison, CO 81230; (800) 686-9327

Devold 14800 28th Ave. N., Suite 100, Plymouth, MN 55447; (800) 433-8653

Duofold Road #2, Route 309, Tamaqua, PA 18252; (800) 448-8240

Earthware P.O. Box 180, Francestown, NH 03043; (603) 525-4405

Eastern Mountain Sports 327 Jaffrey Rd., Peterborough, NH 03458; (888) 463-6367

Epic Adventure Wear 225 State St., Suite 113, Schenectady, NY 12305; (800) 975-3742

Ex Officio 1419 Elliott Ave. W., Seattle, WA 98119; (800) 644-7303

Feathered Friends 119 Yale Ave. N., Seattle, WA 98109; (206) 292-6292

Gerry Sportswear 1051 First St. S., Seattle, WA 98134; (206) 623-4194

Helly-Hansen 17275 N.E. 67th Ct., Redmond, WA 98052; (800) 235-4150

Hind P.O. Box 12609, San Luis Obispo, CA 93406; (800) 235-4150

Integral Designs 5516 Third St. S.E., Calgary, AB, Canada T2H 1J9; (403) 640-1445

Kokatat 5350 Ericson Way, Arcata, CA 95521; (800) 225-9749

L.L. Bean Casco St., Freeport, ME 04033; (800) 809-7057

Log House Designs Butterhill Rd., Chatham, NH 03813; (603) 694-3373

Longworth Industries/PolarMax P.O. Box 520, Candor, NC 27229; (800) 552-8585

Lowe Alpine Systems 620 Compton St., Broomfield, CO 80020; (303) 465-0522

Marmot Mountain 2321 Circadian Way, Santa Rosa, CA 95407; (707) 544-4590

MontBell America 940 41st Ave., Santa Cruz, CA 95062; (800) 683-2002

Moonstone Mountaineering 5350 Ericson Way, Arcata, CA 95521; (800) 822-2985

Mountain Hardware 950 Gilman St., Berkeley, CA 94710; (510) 559-6700; (800) 330-6800

Nike One Bowerman Dr., Beaverton, OR 97005; (503) 671-6453; (800) 344-6453

Not Just Johns 219 Grant St., Unit A, Newport Beach, CA 92663; (800) 642-6525

Outdoor Research 2203 First Ave. S., Seattle, WA 98134; (800) 421-2421

Patagonia P.O. Box 8900, Bozeman, MT 59715; (800) 638-6464

Recreational Equipment Inc. (REI) P.O. Box 1938, Sumner, WA 98390-0800; (800) 426-4840

Red Ledge 130 Commerce Rd., Carlstadt, NJ 07072-2502; (201) 939-2878

Royal Robbins 1314 Coldwell Ave., Modesto, CA 95350; (800) 587-9044

Sequel Outdoor Clothing P.O. Box 409, Durango, CO 81302; (970) 385-4660

Sierra Designs 1255 Powell St., Emeryville, CA 94608; (800) 736-8551

Solstice 2120 N.E. Oregon St., Portland, OR 97232; (503) 239-6991

Sun Precautions 2815 Wetmore Ave., Everett, WA 98201; (800) 882-7860

Terramar Sports Worldwide 10 Midland Ave., Port Chester, NY 10573; (800) 468-7455

The North Face 2013 Farallon Dr., San Leandro, CA 94577; (800) 447-2333

Wickers Sportswear 340 Veterans Memorial Hwy., Commack, NY 11725; (800) 648-7084

Wild Roses 130 Prim Rd., Suite 509, Colchester, VT 05446; (802) 862-3351

Woolrich 1 Mill St., Woolrich, PA 17779; (800) 995-1299

Wyoming Woolens P.O. Box 3127, Jackson Hole, WY 83001; (800) 732-2991

Chapter Seven

IN THE KITCHEN

Setting out well is a quarter of the journey.

—H. G. Bohn, *Handbook of Proverbs*

CAREFUL meal planning prior to a wilderness retreat is an absolute must. What you eat while carrying a heavy backpack over uneven territory at high altitude goes a long way toward determining how well you'll feel and perform. And in the backcountry, there's no corner grocery store to run to for that forgotten item.

Today's hikers benefit from studies by sports nutritionists. We now know that a diet rich in carbohydrates is the most practical way to deliver the energy that helps brain and muscles work best. But the body has a limited ability to store carbohydrates, so we must replenish the glycogen that carbohydrates produce by snacking every hour or so on something nutritious.

Washington's Center for Science in the Public Interest includes the following among nutritious backpacking snacks: granola and powdered milk, almonds, peanuts, cashews, and dried peaches. PowerBars, developed as an energy source for serious climbers and competitive athletes, are also a good food.

The exact number of calories you need depends on your body weight and metabolism, the weight of your pack, and how much work you do. A 154-pound male doing a strenuous hike may need four thousand calories per day. But all calories are not created equal. The recommendation is that 60 to 70 percent of your calories come from carbohydrates, 10 to 15 percent from proteins, and only 20 to 25 percent from fat, which is difficult to digest at high altitudes. On hiking days, try to get 40 percent of your calories from lunch and snacks.

The success of your wilderness menus depends in part on the quality of your shopping, repackaging, and packing. You have the option of buying freeze-dried or dehydrated meals at specialty stores, or you can comb the local grocery stores for dried or bulk food and adapt recipes from home. Freeze-dried meals are light and easy to prepare, but they are usually bulky, expensive, and sometimes skimpy for the ravenous hiker. For those who prefer to create their own meals, supermarkets, Oriental markets, and health food stores are great sources for dried foods, both packaged and in bulk. Wherever you shop, always read the labels to calculate the cooking time, bearing in mind that cooking will take longer at high altitudes. Also consider how much water you will have to boil. Both factors will directly affect the amount of precious fuel you'll consume.

Another alternative, especially if your trip is three days or less, is not to cook at all. Attempt this only in summer when hot food is a luxury, not a necessity. Going cookless allows you to lighten your pack by leaving behind your stove, fuel, pots, lids, handles, and soap. By eliminating cooking from your camp chores, you have more time to hike, read, or admire the sunset. Needing water only for drinking, you will have a freer choice of campsites.

If you decide to cook, here are your primary food options:

Freeze-Dried Food

The freeze-dry process sucks air and moisture out of the food, resulting in a remarkably compact, lightweight, and comparatively expensive product. If this is for you, and if you have no objection to meat, then Mountain House products (made by Oregon Freeze Dry) are a good choice. Pioneers of the freeze-dry process twenty years ago, Mountain House provides food for the military and space program, as well as for hikers, climbers, and backpackers. Responding to consumer trends, they have introduced some all-natural entrees. The beauty of their products is that most are instant—no cooking—and can be prepared right in their own pouch. Just add boiling water, stir, and let sit.

Another freeze-dry veteran is Richmoor, which offers all its regular entrees free of MSG. It too has an all-natural line—Natural High. If your group is large, look for meals that serve four.

To conclude your meal with a gourmet treat, try the astronauts' favorite—freeze-dried Neapolitan ice cream from Backpacker's Pantry.

Dehydrated Food

The dehydration process moves food through a drying chamber, where relatively low-heated air slowly removes the moisture, resulting in a heavier, heartier, less expensive product than freeze-dried. Dehydrated foods take longer to cook than freeze-dried. Whichever you choose, always make sure portions are adequate for your appetites. Cheap meals sometimes mean small meals.

■ The Trail Chef

Although it's more work, creating your own meals more or less from scratch has definite advantages. When you control the ingredients, you can cater to personal tastes and diet restrictions.

Unlike cooking at home, where you can browse through the refrigerator, pantry, or local supermarket, selecting whatever strikes your fancy, all meals for a backpacking trip must be preplanned. The planner should take into account nutritional value, calories, shelf life, cooking time, and weight. Any organizing or cooking you can do at home will make mealtime in the wilderness that much easier.

If you want to make your own fuel-saving meals, consider the following basic building blocks:

> Be clear about who in your party is supposed to take care of food purchases. If such assignments are left vague, you can count on hearing, "I thought you were bringing it!"

When considering wilderness cookbooks, look for ones that address the following important concerns:

- Recipes low in weight and bulk, but high in taste
- Recipes that rely on readily available foods
- Fuel needs
- Bear-bagging techniques
- Low-impact guidelines
- Winter cooking
- Meal planning for multiday trips
- Nutritional requirements for backpackers
- Dehydrating your own food

Some highly recommended cookbooks:

Cooking the One-Burner Way by Melissa Gray and Buck Tilton (ICS Books)

Hungry Hiker's Book of Good Cooking by Gretchen McHugh (Random House)

The NOLS Cookery by National Outdoor Leadership School (Stackpole Books)

The Well-Fed Backpacker by June Fleming (Random House; out of print, but worth tracking down)

- Bulgur. This is cracked, steamed, and dried wheat. It comes in three sizes, with the smallest best for quick cooking in camp.

- Couscous. Cracked, steamed, and dried wheat or millet, white or brown. Serve with something crunchy to give it more appeal.

- Roasted rice. Found in Chinese food stores. Slightly slower to rehydrate than ordinary rice, but tastier.

- Instant Oriental noodles. Precooked and dried, they are available in supermarkets and Oriental markets.

- Dried vegetables. A wide variety can usually be found in the produce section of good supermarkets. Peas and carrots take a long time to rehydrate.

- Instant soups. Combine one of the many flavors with bulgur, rice, couscous, or noodles.

- Dried fruit. Consider peaches, apricots, apples, and pineapple.

- Instant refried beans or black beans. Just add water.

- Instant grits and oatmeal. Great for breakfast.

- Concentrated tomato paste in a tube. Available in supermarkets, it is useful for pepping up pasta dishes or soups.

Whether you choose prepackaged meals or do-it-yourself, certain basic requirements, discussed next, are the same.

Breakfast

For that special someone who needs a caffeine fix before he stops growling like a bear, surprise him with MUD Gourmet Coffee bags. Packed with dark-roasted gourmet coffee (they come decaffeinated too), these individual filter bags deliver great taste without the fuss. A supermarket alternative is Folgers Coffee Singles. Other morning beverages include tea, Tang, lemonade, and instant breakfast drinks.

For the morning meal, consider granola (homemade or store-bought), instant cereals, longer-cooking cereals (soaked overnight to speed up cooking), fruit compotes, powdered eggs, and pancakes. For those quick trail starts, try a PowerBar or homemade energy bar.

Lunch on the Go

Many nutritionists suggest a steady diet of snacks between meals. In this way, you avoid that midday valley of fatigue. For years, the standard trail munchie has been gorp, short for "good ol' raisins and peanuts." There are dozens of variations on the market. Or buy the ingredients and mix them at home. This will give you what you want at a cheaper price. Other good snack items include fruit bars, dried fruit, fruit leather, chocolate bars, unleavened bread, crackers, peanut butter, cheese, and beef jerky. Prevent boredom by mixing in a variety of textures and tastes.

Packing Your Food

Repackage as much of your food as possible in heavy-duty plastic bags. Meals should be measured out and wrapped individually, with labels and directions clearly marked. Remember to save the cooking

You may want to dunk your dried fruit in boiling water, then store in the refrigerator to stave off lingering bacteria left during processing.

instructions. Push out as much air as possible from the bags. Use a bag with room enough to add water and stir the contents. Pack spices in pill bottles or film canisters. Place your last meal at the bottom of the pack, and your heaviest meal, which you will consume first, on top. Pack a couple of extra meals for emergencies.

Don't Leave Home Without It

As you gather the food for your trip, make a checklist of ingredients you think you'll need to prepare your meals, then go through each meal and check it against this list.

Here are some kitchen suggestions from seasoned backpackers:

☐ Seasonings. These are crucial for pepping up wilderness meals. Consider taking garlic, Tabasco sauce, mustard, curry powder, and your own personal favorites.

☐ Powdered coffee creamer. Add it to your powdered-milk mix to improve taste.

Hydrate your food while you hike. Pack your widemouth Nalgene bottle with food, and then add water before setting off in the morning. By the time you reach camp, your food will have soaked up the water. During cooking, remove the pan from the stove several minutes before food is ready to eat. Keep the lid on. Your food will continue to cook as it cools.

☐ Olive oil. Low in saturated fat, it has a longer shelf life than butter or margarine.

☐ Cabernet sauvignon. This is why they invented botas.

☐ Baking soda. It can be used for laundry soap, toothpaste, body deodorant, stomach settler, fire extinguisher, and, when dampened to a paste, itch inhibitor.

☐ Pita bread. It can double as a plate in a pinch.

☐ Honey, mustard, or peanut butter in reusable polyethylene tubes.

Innovations

While you bide your time waiting for your freeze-dried food to rehydrate, the food is gradually losing heat. The solution is the BackCountry Cozy from Wilderness Innovations. It's a metallic, heat-retaining nylon pouch weighing less than two ounces. For more information, call (800) 845-0941.

> You can make a backcountry oven with tin foil and two pots. Roll up four small balls of the foil and put them in the bottom of the larger pot. Set the smaller pot on the aluminum balls. Cover the large pot.

Who riseth from a feast
With that keen appetite that he sits down?
—William Shakespeare, The Merchant of Venice

■ Recipes from Friends

Easy Granola

4 c. rolled oats
⅓ c. vegetable oil
¼ c. honey
1 tsp. vanilla extract
⅓ c. brown sugar
¼ c. sesame seeds
½ c. coconut
1 c. slivered almonds

At Home
Spread oats on ungreased baking sheet. Bake at 350° F for 10 minutes. In large bowl, blend oil, honey, and vanilla. Add oats

and remaining ingredients. Mix thoroughly. Spread mixture on baking sheet and bake again at 350° for 10–15 minutes. When cool, break into chunks and store in refrigerator.

Muesli

3 c. quick-cooking oats

¼ c. sunflower seeds

¼ c. almonds or other nuts, chopped

½ c. raisins

½ c. dried apricots or other fruit, chopped

2 tsp. cinnamon

2 c. dried milk

½ tsp. salt

At Home
Mix ingredients and store in a zipper-lock bag.

In Camp
Add 5 cups water to dry mix. Let stand 30 minutes.

Glop

1½ c. quick-cooking brown rice

freshly ground pepper to taste

1 package onion cup-a-soup

2 Tbsp. dried celery leaves

1 Tbsp. thyme leaves

15 oz. can boned chicken

2–3 Tbsp. grated Parmesan cheese

At Home
Mix all dry ingredients but Parmesan cheese and place in plastic zipper-lock bag. Place cheese in smaller bag within the larger bag.

In Camp

Bring *3 cups water* to boil (use more or less depending on how soupy you like your glop). Dump in contents of large bag, reserving the cheese. Add chicken. Sprinkle individual servings with cheese. Serves two.

Mincemeat Whoppers

½ c. butter

2 oz. unsweetened chocolate

1 c. semisweet chocolate chips

2 eggs

1 c. sugar

¾ c. prepared mincemeat

1 tsp. vanilla extract

¾ c. flour

¼ tsp. salt

½ c. chopped walnuts

At Home

Preheat oven to 350° F. Lightly grease a 9" x 9" baking pan. Melt butter, unsweetened chocolate, and chocolate chips over very low heat in a heavy-bottomed saucepan. Stir frequently and remove from heat just before chocolate is melted. Continue stirring until chocolate and butter are smooth. Set aside to cool. Beat eggs and sugar until light. Add vanilla. Stir in flour, salt, walnuts, and mincemeat. Then add the chocolate-butter mixture. Pour into prepared pan and bake 20–25 minutes or until toothpick put in center comes out clean. Do not overbake. Cool and cut into bars. These bars freeze well.

Trail Logs

1 c. chopped walnuts
½ c. chopped cashews
½ c. dried apples
1 c. seedless raisins
¾ c. pitted and chopped dates
1 tsp. lemon juice
2 Tbsp. dark rum
powdered sugar

At Home
Combine nuts and fruit and run through finest blade of food chopper. Mix thoroughly. Blend in lemon juice and rum. Roll heaping spoonfuls of mixture into logs about 2" long by ¾" wide. Roll in powdered sugar and let dry uncovered for two or more days. Store in airtight container. Wrap tightly in foil when packing for the trail. Makes 24 to 30 rolls.

Boy Scout Chicken Luau
(A good first-day dinner; campfire required)

heavy-duty aluminum foil
2 chicken breasts
2 potatoes, sliced ½" thick
2 carrots, sliced
2 slices canned pineapple rings
16 oz. can stewed tomatoes
salt and pepper, to taste

At Home
Tear off large square of foil. Place chicken breasts in center. Cover with potato slices, carrots, pineapple slices, stewed tomatoes, and salt and pepper. Add more pineapple slices and juice if desired. Make a pouch with foil. Seal the edges well

by folding over a couple of times. Freeze well for a couple of days. If possible, place in ice chest on way to trailhead.

On the Trail
Place pouch in zipper-lock bag. Wrap well in towel and place in pack. This will keep well even in summer, but must be cooked on first day of trip.

In Camp
Build a fire. Place foil packet on red coals, and cook 45 minutes. Serves two, typically.

Trout Ceviche

On the Trail
Catch, gut, and clean fish. Cut meat from bone into bite-size pieces. Place in small sealable container with juice of 2 lemons, 1 lime, chopped cilantro, scallion, dill, and salt and pepper. Let sit for 3–4 hours, turning occasionally, or put into your pack to marinate while you hike. You may want to place the container in a stream to chill the ceviche before eating.

One-Pot Pasta

8 sun-dried tomatoes
1 smoked sausage
garlic
6 oz. angel hair pasta
1 carrot, thinly sliced
handful of green beans, cut in half
splash of olive oil
salt and pepper, to taste
Parmesan cheese, to taste

In Camp

Soak tomatoes in *4 cups water* for 15 minutes. Slice and sauté sausage with garlic. Set aside. Remove tomatoes from water and set them aside. Boil tomato water and add pasta. Add sliced carrot and beans, and cook until pasta is al dente (about 4 minutes). Strain water. Add tomatoes, a splash of olive oil, salt and pepper, and sausage and garlic. Serve with Parmesan cheese and Chianti to two very happy campers. (If you prefer your vegetables less crunchy, drop them into the water before the pasta.)

Spiced Fruit Rice Pudding

¾ c. instant brown rice, uncooked

½ c. dried milk powder

½ tsp. nutmeg

2 Tbsp. lemon juice or lemon flavoring

¼ c. honey

½ tsp. cinnamon

¼ tsp. dried ginger

1 c. dried fruit, chopped

At Home

Mix all ingredients and place in zipper-lock bag.

In Camp

Add ingredients to *2½ cups water*. Bring to boil, then simmer 5–10 minutes or until rice is cooked and fruit is tender. Stir to prevent pudding from burning. Serves two.

Resources for Food

Mountain House Oregon Freeze Dry, P.O. Box 1048, Albany, OR 97321; (916) 241-9280

Richmoor P.O. Box 8092, Van Nuys, CA 91409; (818) 787-2510

Trail Wise Box 15421, North Hollywood, CA 91615-5421; (818) 766-4065

Adventure Foods Rte. 2, Box 276, Whittier, NC 28789; (704) 497-4113

Alpine-Aire The Outdoor Kitchen, P.O. Box 1600, Nevada City, CA 95959; (800) 322-MEAL

Bakepacker Strike 2 Industries, E. 508 Augusta Ave., Spokane, WA 99207; (509) 484-3701

Dri-Lite Backpacker's Pantry, 1540 Charles Dr., Redding, CA 96003; (916) 241-9280

Harvest Foodworks 40 Hillcrest Dr., Toronto, ON, Canada M6G 2E3; (416) 533-7479

Perma-Pak 40 E. Robert Ave., Salt Lake City, UT 84115; (801) 486-4159

Stow-A-Way P.O. Box 957, East Greenwich, RI 02818; (401) 885-6899

Wee Pak P.O. Box 1450, Ketchum, ID 83340; (800) 722-2710

Chapter Eight

ON THE TRAIL

I walk every day, save in blizzards and cloudbursts, between
two and three miles across open wheat fields and through
cool, tall woods. I pursue the same path, year after year,
and neither I nor the dogs ever tire of it. I watch the deer,
and the fox, and the rabbits, and the squirrels, and the
skunks, and especially the birds, and I have never seen
the same scene twice.

—James Michener

Preparation

Success comes before work only in the dictionary.
—Anonymous

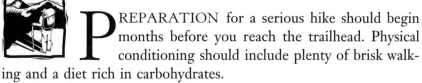 PREPARATION for a serious hike should begin
months before you reach the trailhead. Physical
conditioning should include plenty of brisk walking and a diet rich in carbohydrates.

Include as many people from the group as possible at the planning
session. Everyone appreciates the chance to offer an opinion—even
if no one pays attention to it. Consider the condition of everyone in
the group, particularly the weakest hiker. By looking at topographic
maps, get a fix on total miles, hiking days, and difficulty of terrain.
Then ask the tough question: Can each person in the party do it?

Before leaving home, test your equipment for comfort and con-

dition. Lace on your hiking boots, load up and strap on your pack, and go out walking on uneven terrain. Adjust the pack straps and bootlaces; find a comfortable fit and eliminate "hot spots" before you hit the trail.

Adults and older children should carry no more than one-quarter of their body weight, younger children less than that, and the youngest only a token amount, say a day pack with a teddy bear in it. You want them to feel part of the action, but if you saddle small people with too much weight, you risk turning the hike into a death march.

At the trailhead, look for walking sticks for everyone. You can buy fancy varnished staffs at outdoor stores, but why not use what nature provides? Besides amusement and image enhancement, a custom-fitted staff can help you balance on rocky terrain or while crossing streams; it can be a snake prober when stepping over logs and rocks or be used to push aside brush encroaching on the trail. You can even drive your stick into the ground and rest your pack against it.

If you are breaking in a rookie hiker, it helps to know your route and destination. Then your voice will carry the proper authority when you inevitably say, "Not much farther to go." Encourage everyone to complain silently—maybe the impossible dream. One person's open negativity can sap the strength of the whole group.

Photo by Carl Siechert

Children and adults new to exercise tend to be unprepared for "working through pain," but perhaps you can persuade them to demonstrate a little self-discipline. Remind them that the longer you fool around on the trail, the later you'll arrive in camp.

There are two schools of thought about limbering up before a hike. Tradition suggests you stretch your hamstrings, calves, feet, shoulders, and back; revisionists hold that just hiking slowly eliminates the need for elaborate warm-up. Children, being both undisciplined stretchers and youthfully limber, can usually begin walking with impunity.

Photo by Carl Siechert

Seek a natural stride, swinging your legs from the hips rather than kicking out with the knees. By pivoting at the waist and leaning forward slightly, the stride will automatically lengthen. If the terrain is level, your feet should strike the ground heel first and roll forward, with a final push-off being delivered by the last bone of the big toe.

Strive to keep your feet beneath your torso, planting them firmly on the ground and stepping around rather than on obstacles that might teeter. Arms should dangle, swinging freely, but not in an exaggerated way. Keep the head up and the shoulders relaxed, dropped back rather than hunched up. Avoid shuffling, which raises dust and wastes energy. Avoid slumping—it's easier to carry a load when walking fairly erect. If anyone walks bent over like Groucho Marx, find him a longer walking stick, which will help keep him erect.

Can't decide whether you want your hat on or off? Attach a small carabiner to the top of your pack and clip your hat to it when your head gets too warm. You won't have to stop, and your hat is handy when you need it.

Establish hiking rules early. Young children should stay in sight, older ones within earshot. As their voices get stronger, they can go farther ahead. When Steve grew to be a better hiker than his parents, he used to soar ahead to the next trail junction, then hike back to them, soar ahead, and hike back. Although he was, for a time, out of earshot, he never made a route decision without consulting his parents.

If you have agreed to break into smaller groups, arrange check-in points (often trail junctions) where everyone meets at certain intervals. Each group should have its own map.

Help members of your group see the big picture—the entire hike. It does no good to sprint the first half-mile in record time if the effort is so exhausting that you can't finish a three-mile trek. Better to expend energy evenly.

Uphill

> One climbs, one sees. One descends, one sees no longer, but one has seen.
> —Che Guevara

> Hills make all men brothers.
> —Dr. George Sheehan

Try to find and hold a steady pace on uphills. It will be slower than the pace you maintained on level ground, but it will require greater effort. Gunning it on hills burns a lot of energy. For example, ascending a fourteen-degree slope (rising fourteen feet in elevation for every hundred feet in horizontal distance) requires nearly four times the effort of walking on level ground. Add a backpack and the effort rises even more.

Photo by Rick Ridgeway

Don't lift your feet higher than necessary. Shorten the stride and lean forward slightly to keep the pack weight over the feet. Breathe deeply and rhythmically. On exceptionally difficult slopes, it is better to take six-inch steps and keep moving, no matter how slowly, than to take the frequent rest stops a faster pace would require. Starting and stopping consume extra energy.

On steep grades, you may have to walk on your toes. Toe stepping adds power and balance but soon fatigues calf muscles. Try alternating heel and toe steps to spread the load over different muscles.

When the climb is very steep or the load very heavy, try the "rest step" or "limp step" to flush away the acids of fatigue from the joints. There are two ways for the body to rest without actually stopping: You can allow the lead leg to go limp just after that foot is placed for a new step and just before the weight is shifted to it; or you can relax the trailing leg just after you transfer weight to the lead leg. Most people prefer to let the trailing leg go limp, and that is the easiest method to learn.

Downhill

I like long walks, especially when they are taken by people who annoy me.
—Fred Allen

When you leave established trails and go cross-country, you increase the risk of getting lost, or at least misplaced. When that happens, stop, take a few deep breaths, and consult your topo map. A common mistake is to look at the map first and then look up and try to make sense of the surroundings. Instead, scan the topography first; note macro features such as mountains, rivers, and canyons, and then find them on the map. Determine your position relative to those features, and then refine your estimate using nearby micro features.

At first blush, downhill would seem easier than uphill. But descending, though easier on the lungs, is actually twice as hard on hip, knee, and ankle joints. Putting on the brakes taxes the quadriceps, the big muscles in the front of the thigh. Downhill walking forces the foot to travel farther through the air with each step, so it's easier to slip and sprain an ankle on tippy rocks. Pounding downhill on your heels can jar your spine and make your whole body sore. On the other hand, if you put your weight forward, you may develop blisters on your toes. Cushion the shock of each downward step by rolling your hip forward and planting your foot with the knee slightly bent. As you transfer weight, allow the knee to flex so that it acts as a shock absorber.

Cross-Country

If you pick 'em up, O Lord, I'll put 'em down.
—The Prayer of the Tired Walker

When you leave the security of a trail, you are traveling "cross-country." Instead of relying on an established course, you must find your own way, often confronting swamps, deadfalls, and rocky ridges. With weight on your back, little inconveniences like scrambling over

Photo by Carl Siechert

Photo by Rick Ridgeway

Photo by Carl Siechert

deadfalls or slipping between rock and river become hazards. Going cross-country requires greater balance, strength, competence, and caution than walking on trails. Stick to the trails until you are ready for more.

Fording Streams

> Action absorbs anxiety.
> —standard medical axiom

Hiking in the spring may force you to cross water without a bridge. Look for rocks or fallen logs that might form a natural bridge or for narrows you can bridge with a standing broad jump. Failing that, you may have to get wet.

Before you do, assess the situation. How deep is the water? How about the footing? Do you leave your boots on or go barefoot? If you leave them on, you protect your feet but get your boots wet—do you have spare socks and shoes? Barefoot—maybe in calm water over a sandy bottom. It might be best to wear sneakers for the crossing and change back to boots on the other side. If so, make sure your boots are secured in or on your pack, so they can't get lost if you fall in.

When wearing a pack on a dangerous crossing, loosen the shoulder straps and unbuckle the belly strap so that you can jettison the load and keep from drowning. Use your walking stick as a third leg for balance and for probing loose, slippery rocks.

If the water is swift and dangerous, send the strongest swimmer across first, roped but carrying no pack. Then tie off both ends of the rope. A taut line between trees on both sides will provide security and peace of mind. Choose a wide, shallow ford over a narrow, swift one. Start on the upstream side and angle downstream to minimize your battle against the current. Avoid crossing above a falls or other hazard.

Wet Weather

Today I have grown taller from walking with the trees.

—Karle Wilson

When the weather turns foul, don your rain gear as soon as it starts to rain, not an hour later when you're soaked to the bone. Gaiters will keep rain from running down your legs and into your boots. Fold your map to the section you'll need and seal it in a zipper-lock bag. Keep your frequently used items handy. Put your map, toilet paper, snacks, and water in a fanny pack or a side pocket of your pack for easy access. Store anything that rain might harm, like a camera, in plastic bags.

Line your sleeping bag stuff sack with a garbage bag to make it more waterproof, especially if you carry your bag outside your pack. Carry a watch on overcast days when you can't gauge the time by the sun. Darkness can descend quickly, especially in the mountains.

Carry blister first aid, even if your boots are broken in. Prolonged rain softens even the most calloused skin, making it more vulnerable to blisters. If it's raining a lot, wring out your socks periodically during the day. Don't forget to towel dry your feet and powder them. One way to prevent blisters is with duct tape. Carry it by wrapping several turns around the handle of your flashlight. When you apply it to your feet, smooth out all the wrinkles.

If you wear glasses, a baseball hat will shield them from the rain. Don't reduce your eating and drinking just because it's cold and rainy. Chilly, wet weather demands that you take in even more fuel and fluids to ward off hypothermia. Hike in shorts, even in wet weather; bare skin is preferable to clingy wet fabric.

Photo by Rick Ridgeway

Pace

> He travels fastest who travels alone.
> —Rudyard Kipling

At the trailhead, explain to all that you have a destination. En route you're going to explore, enjoy the beauty, and have fun, but you also have a goal—say, Lake Woebegone by dark—and that means you have to keep moving. Also, remind the fast starters to maintain a steady pace to the finish.

Most backpackers travel one-and-a-half to two-and-a-half miles per hour, but there are plenty of exceptions. Two fit twenty-year-olds hiking fairly level ground on good terrain may hit four miles an hour in spurts; a family with toddlers may not make four miles in a day.

Photo by Rick Ridgeway

Be prepared to amend (or abandon) your timetable, whatever it may be. Urge slowpokes along, but don't insist they reach a destination by a certain time. Be flexible, especially with neophytes who you hope will return to the wilderness. Be prepared to accept defeat—bad weather, injury, illness, mosquitoes, or someone wimping out can alter your plans. Plan a bailout route, just in case.

Hiking compatibility may be difficult to achieve because of the differences in capabilities of the members of your group. Every hiker, research suggests, has an ideal pace, an optimum speed that requires minimal energy per step. It's a challenge to coordinate the movements of several hikers with different ideal paces. To get everybody from A to B, consider pacing, rest stops, maintaining energy, and foot care.

If you plan to stay together, the slowest walker should begin in front, setting the pace. Later, you may want to rotate the lead, as many people are front-runners who get an energy boost when they lead. The responsibility makes them more open to learning about blazes, ducks, and other trail signs. One way to rein in faster hikers is to keep adding gear to their packs until they slow down.

If the troops begin losing their will to walk, it may be time for a serious break. Drop packs, relax, and explore. Go swimming, fishing, or bug hunting. Side trips refresh some hikers, making the final haul easier.

When hiking with kids, have an adult bring up the rear to assure that no one wanders off the trail or calls a sit-down strike. From the caboose, you can help those who fall behind by readjusting their packs, pulling up their socks, and maybe showing them better ways to go over or around obstacles.

Rest Stops

> Our minds are lazier than our bodies.
> —La Rochefoucauld

Rest stops are important, particularly for young children, but prolonged stops can suck the momentum out of a hike. Whoever coined the phrase "take five" had it about right, for breaks longer than five minutes are often counterproductive. Even on sunny days, long rest stops cause the body to cool, muscles to stiffen, momentum to shred. Even a slight breeze can knife through sweat-damp clothing and start a child shivering. Carry a light windbreaker for such moments.

Make the most of stops. Take a breather, of course, but also do your chores. Peruse the map, find food or water in your pack, urinate, put on shorts, take off jacket, check feet, pull up socks, and adjust boots. Some people prefer not to stop for a full-blown lunch; instead, they eat a good breakfast, hit the trail soon after sunrise, fill everyone's pockets with nuts and dried fruit, keep a slower pace (if necessary), and limit rest stops to five minutes every half-hour or so.

One of the hardest lessons for newcomers to learn is to maintain a slow, steady pace, minimizing the need for frequent rest stops. Children especially are sprinters. Without killing their enthusiasm, grown-ups need to moderate the pace and stretch out their performance. On the other hand, you can't be too authoritarian about it. You will have to adjust the stops and pace to your weakest hiker. If the hike is being interrupted by more stops than you would like, compromise. Persuade members of your group to rest with their packs on, lightening their load by leaning against a rock or a tree.

This eliminates rehoisting the pack and getting used to the weight all over again.

Rest stops also offer opportunities to savor the country. Try to stop beside a stream or lake, at the top of a slope, in the first shade after a shadeless stretch, where a tree or rock offers a seat, or anywhere the view is spectacular. If it's an extended rest stop, make it fun. Go exploring; try to find something new; identify a snow plant, a bird's nest, or those animals wriggling in the water.

It's always nice to take a rest when you feel you've earned it. Promise your group a rest stop after, say, a hundred more steps. For variety and distraction, count backward. After a rest stop, you will once again have to rein in the fast starters, lest they burn out. We have seen youngsters go from sitting to sprinting to walking to trudging to stopping, all in less than a minute.

Motivation

> I never knew a man to go for an honest day's walk
> for whatever distance, great or small...and not
> have his reward in the repossession of the soul.
> —George Trevelyan

Motivating reluctant hikers may demand ingenuity, patience, and more tricks than a circus sideshow. Which tricks you employ depends on the ages and dispositions of those hikers. In the case of your children, start walking with them early in their lives. When they are old enough to sit up, start carrying them on your back in a kid pack. Your baby will enjoy the stimulation of seeing new places, feeling the wind, and hearing the ambient sounds; you'll benefit from the exercise.

There are kid carriers rated up to 60 pounds, but you probably don't want to schlep your second-grader around on your back. Your children will likely be pedestrians by age three or four. At that point, you can move on to short walks and backyard overnighters. Don't advance to car camping until you're sure your children are ready.

After car camping, if interest is high, try a short backpacking trip, say two days and one night. A short trip reduces the weight you have to carry and keeps you close to the trailhead in case problems arise. One hiking couple refers to ages two to five as "the lost years." Indeed, motivating a four-year-old to walk two miles can be like pulling teeth with tweezers. You can reward them with praise and food, but with their sprinter's approach and short attention span, nothing works every time or for very long. Try counting steps, playing games, singing, looking for wildlife, and identifying pretty leaves, rocks, wildflowers, and birds.

Some families find it effective just to talk. Increasing the chatter can distract kids and boost morale. Be a cheerleader, if necessary: "We're more than halfway . . . water just ahead . . . see that bird? . . . you're doing great, a real mountain pace." Try to include water in your destination. Most children will be motivated to finish a hike if they know they can swim or throw rocks in the water at trail's end.

I recently hiked to the top of Yosemite's Half Dome with two dads, each of whom carried his daughter (ages two and three) on his back. It was an eighteen-mile, eleven-hour hike with huge altitude gains and losses, but the kids reacted as though it were a stroll in the park. Neither ever complained. The reason: They live in Yosemite and have been on trails since they were infants.

—S.B.

Daydreaming has a bad rap, but it can move us along. When you round a bend and see someone crumble at the sight of a steep, switchbacking trail leading to some distant pass that might as well be on Mars, tell them to start daydreaming. Recommend that they think of something pleasant and absorbing and embellish it until it takes over their thoughts. If all goes well, the hike will proceed on a kind of automatic pilot.

Try teaching your reluctant hikers visualization, the first cousin of daydreaming. It's part imagination (a strong suit for children) and part concentration (not always a strong suit). This technique can be powerful. Steve has interviewed dozens of world-class adventure athletes—climbers, mountaineers, hang-glider pilots—and most cite visualization as a key to their success.

Here are some visualization possibilities for hikers: Imagine you're a gazelle, cheetah, or some other fleet animal; you're tough, strong, graceful, and can go forever. Imagine crowds of people lining the course, cheering you on to greatness (we tend to do better when others are watching). Moving uphill, picture yourself suspended from helium balloons. Moving downhill, picture yourself as a liquid, flowing over rocks or roots. Moving on level ground, picture a giant's gentle hand at your back. Moving into the wind, imagine you are a bullet or knife slicing through the heavy air. Above all, see yourself relaxing.

When your hikers tire of looking for birds' nests, squirrel burrows, and trees that resemble Aunt Ellen, introduce trail games (see below). When you run out of trail games, try bribery. Offer treats for so many steps, say a lemon drop or an M&M or stocks and bonds, when they make it to the rock that looks like Uncle Ferg and another when they get to the next trail junction. If you're like most parents who monitor their children's candy consumption, you might try using nuts or dried fruit as rewards. But don't be surprised if they lack candy's motivational power.

If all else fails, accept the stops and the slower pace. Get into your kids' adventure, their microworld; let them drop their packs and explore something they've spotted off the trail. Pull out the binoculars or magnifying glass and check out that colorful bird or bug. Remember your overriding goal is more ambitious than merely reaching Lake Muckamucka by lunchtime; it is to make the experience so much fun that everyone will want to do it again.

There is an intense but simple thrill in setting off in the morning on a mountain trail, knowing that everything you need is on your back. It is a confidence in having left the inessentials behind and of entering a world of natural beauty that has not been violated, where money has no value, and possessions are a dead weight. The person with the fewest possessions is the freest. Thoreau was right.
—Paul Theroux, The Happy Isles of Oceania

Trail Games

It's a rare beginning hiker who is able to provide his or her own entertainment on the trail. Young children have both a short attention span and a low boredom threshold. Those traits, combined with the common perception that hiking is drudgery, can result in a veritable whinefest if the entertainment slackens. Try to capitalize on youngsters' imagination. Although your idea of fun may not be shuffling along the trail making choo-choo sounds, that may be just the ticket to keep reluctant hikers moving.

Aesthetic appreciation may not be fully developed in some hikers. Instead, they may become obsessed with their physical condition. Be prepared to hear, "My feet hurt," "This pack is too heavy," "I'm thirsty," "My mosquito bites itch," "Are we almost there?" To yank them out of themselves, consider playing some of the following games while hiking:

> Some parents play a game called Treasure Map when their young hikers are nearing the end of their rope. With exaggerated solemnity, Tim Hallahan, for example, of Oakland, California, will pull from his pocket a folded Kleenex, peer at it, and announce, "I found this treasure map. If you follow the directions, you'll find a great treasure. First, touch five tree trunks." Off goes his son, Brett, miraculously rejuvenated. "Next, walk around a trail sign two times." Now Brett is skipping. "Then walk one hundred steps with your left hand on top of your head...."

Categories

One person picks a category (like cartoon characters, video games, marine mammals) and starts by naming an example (Tweety, Doom, humpback whale). The others follow in turn until someone repeats an item or draws a blank.

Who Am I? (Twenty Questions)

One person thinks of a character, either alive or dead, real or fictional. The others ask twenty yes-or-no questions, trying to determine who the character is. Encourage logic; discourage wild guesses, such as "Are you Gandhi?" on the third question.

Where Am I?

This is structured like Who Am I? One player begins by asking, "Where am I?" Other players try to find out by asking yes-or-no questions. The answer may be a very small place, such as atop the dashboard or in a trouser cuff, so players are encouraged to use their imaginations.

Sames and Differences

Have everyone look at an object of their choice—leaf, rock, tree, cloud—then encourage them to discover another object that is similar in some way. Ask, "In what ways is it the same? In what ways is it different?" Urge them to be specific and use all five senses. If they need more guidance, give them an example, like a branch of a tree and a branch of a river. What's the same about those two things? Shape? Name? What's different? Texture? Size? Movement?

Ghost

This word game works best for two people, though more can play. Alternate the start, with the first person stating a letter and the second person following with another letter, continuing in turn, with each player having a particular word in mind. You lose if you inadvertently complete a word of three letters or more or if you are challenged and cannot state a legitimate word that you are spelling. Each loss earns a dreaded letter: G-H-O-S-T. First one to T loses.

I Went to the Store

This game may seem like nothing more than mind candy, but it's actually a good memory exercise.

Any number can play. Someone begins by announcing "I went to the store and bought _____," filling in the blank with just about any A word imaginable, say, *artichoke hearts*. The second player repeats the A word, adding a B word of his own creation, as in "I went to the store and bought artichoke hearts and black-eyed peas." And so on, through the alphabet. A player who cannot repeat the litany of purchases is out, and the others continue until only one player remains. Hearing the items repeated will facilitate recall, allowing the game to go on for a surprisingly long time.

Trail Songs

Trail songs should be upbeat, energizing, and exploratory (almost anything with a banjo will do). Avoid funeral dirges. Possibilities include "She'll Be Comin' 'Round the Mountain," "This Land Is Your Land," "Zippity Do Dah," "Heigh Ho," and "Little Miss Mack." Avoid songs like "One Hundred Bottles of Beer on the Wall," which will threaten your sanity.

In the end, your choice of songs will be dictated by the answers to these questions: Can you sing a lick? Do you know the words to any songs? What works with your group?

Whatever strategies you employ to motivate reluctant hikers—and you may employ them all—keep 'em hiking. We're planting seeds here and, if nurtured properly, they will someday blossom into a full-blown appreciation of hiking through nature. As long as we don't allow our own goals to detract from newcomers' hiking experience, they should be back for more.

> So be conscious of your feet and perhaps they will
> lead you on the Wayless Way.
> —Chloe Scott

Innovations

An organization called Hike America offers more than a hundred medallions depicting famous trails and national parks that can be collected and affixed to a hiking staff. There are shields for such venerable trails as the Pacific Crest, John Muir, and Mount Rainier's Wonderland Trail, as well as fourteen versions of the Appalachian Trail (one for each state it passes through). Medallions cost $2.95

each; a chestnut staff is $19.95. For more information, contact Hike America, P.O. Box 5684, Redwood City, CA 94063; (800) 880-4453.

Trail Glossary

access trail: a trail connecting the main trail to a town, road, or another trail; critical for long-distance hikers who must resupply.

A.T.: the Appalachian Trail.

blaze: trail marking. A blaze can be a painted symbol on a tree, a sign, or a cairn. The Appalachian Trail is marked with two-by-six-inch white blazes placed at eye level.

bleeder: an angled depression built into the trail to drain water off the path.

BLM: Bureau of Land Management.

blowdown: large uprooted or broken tree that has fallen across the trail.

box canyon: a canyon surrounded on all sides by walls.

break-in: the time period your body, mind, or boots take to get used to the rigors of backpacking.

buffer zone: protective land on both sides of the trail that insulates the hiker from activities such as development, mining, or logging.

cache: supplies, especially food, hidden near the trail for future use.

cairn: a small mound of stones that marks where a trail passes.

causeway: a section of trail that passes through swampy terrain and has been built up with rock or dirt to create a permanently dry path.

chaparral: a dense thicket of shrubs and small trees, common in the Southwest and Mexico, that can survive low rainfall.

clearcut: an area in which all trees have been cut.

col: a gap in a ridge or a pass between two peaks.

cranking: hiking at a fast pace.

cross-country: hiking across open country rather than on a trail.

double blaze: two painted blazes that denote a change in direction or a trail junction.

end-to-ender: someone who hikes from one end of a long-distance trail to the other.

ephemeral creek: one that flows for only a brief period of time.

fastpacker: someone hiking too fast to smell the roses. Fastpackers travel light, get a great workout, and cover more ground than a conventional backpacker in the same amount of time.

grade: a trail's degree of inclination.

half-gallon club: A.T. thru-hikers who can consume half a gallon of ice cream in one sitting.

knob: a prominent rounded hill or mountain.

layover day: a day off from steady hiking.

pass: a narrow gap between mountain peaks.

power hiker: someone who covers long distances day after day.

saddle: a ridge between two peaks.

scree slope: a rock-covered slope with an angle of about thirty degrees that contains small gravel.

side trail: a path, usually dead-end, off the main trail. Side trails often lead to an interesting feature, such as a waterfall or a scenic overlook, that the main trail skirts.

skirt: to go around a mountain, often at an even grade, rather than climbing over it.

snowbound: describes a section of trail that is buried under so much snow as to be impassable.

snow bridge: a span of snow, often over a creek, that is hollow underneath. The weight of a hiker may sometimes be enough to collapse such a bridge.

switchback: a zigzagging trail up the side of a steep hill or mountain.

talus slope: a rock-covered slope with an angle of forty-five degrees or more. The rocks are larger and have sharper edges than those on scree slopes, making a talus slope more dangerous and difficult to climb.

tarn: a small mountain lake.

thru-hiker: someone who attempts to cover a long trail, such as the A.T., in one continuous trek.

toxic socks: a thru-hiker's socks after a few weeks on the trail.

trail corridor: all the lands that make up the trail environment as seen by the hiker.

trail name: the nickname a hiker adopts, often based on his or her personality, lifestyle, or hiking style.

trailhead: the start of a trail, often at a road.

traverse: lateral, oblique, or zigzagging movement, as opposed to straight-line movement up or down a slope.

treadway: the trail bed in which you walk.

undulating trail: a trail that follows a wavelike course, often going in and out of gullies.

wash: the erosion of soil by moving water.

waterbar: a rock or log barrier that diverts water off the path.

white-out: a visibility condition caused by thick clouds scudding over a snow-covered landscape. Because the light coming down from above is equal to the light reflected off the snow, there are no shadows and no visible horizon.

yellow-blazing: a long-distance hiker taking to the roads instead of walking the trail.

Yogi-ing: a thru-hiker behaving in such a way that strangers picnicking nearby offer their food.

yo-yoing: the act of a thru-hiker completing a trek, then turning around and going back in the opposite direction, then turning around again.

Chapter Nine

IN CAMP

When you're safe at home you wish you were having an
adventure; when you're having an adventure you
wish you were safe at home.

—Thornton Wilder

■ Selecting a Campsite in the Wilderness

 YOUR campsite is your home away from home, so it's okay to be particular. After a hard day on the trail, settling into camp is refreshing for body and spirit. The ideal site—discovered, not created—has level spots for tents, water nearby, available deadwood, a beautiful view, seclusion, and protection from weather and falling rocks.

Your chances of finding the perfect spot are better if you think ahead. Plan your daily mileage based on possible campsites. If you can't preselect your site, start looking for good spots well before dusk. Know how long it takes you to set up camp and make dinner, and leave enough time before dark.

Upon arriving at your destination, drop your pack at the first campsite that looks good, then scout out other possible sites. If you keep your pack on, you'll tend to pick the first site just be-

Sprinkle vegetable oil on any standing puddles around camp. The thin film suffocates mosquito larvae. Don't worry—there will be trillions left for the bats and birds.

cause you're tired. You'll also be tempted to camp right on the shore of that stream or lake. Don't do it. You should camp at least two hundred feet from water; in many places, it's the law.

If insects are a problem, seek higher ground where breezes will keep them away. Look for animal signs—tracks, scat, bedding sites—and avoid their homes and commuting routes. Stay away from "widowmakers," trees that have fallen and are leaning against another tree.

The most important quality in a campsite is a relatively flat sleeping area. Kids like to help with the selection. After choosing what seems like the best spot for your tent, spread out your ground cloth and lie down. If there is an incline, lie with your head uphill. Close your eyes and imagine what it will feel like at four in the morning. Is it comfortable? Consider the terrain for nighttime potty duties. Is it safe? If not, search elsewhere.

■ Pitching a Tent

Try your tent out in the backyard first. Learn how to pitch it there before you try to do it in the wilderness. When selecting a site, look for a relatively level area that will drain rainwater. Avoid low spots, grassy areas, and direct sun when possible. Extended solar exposure causes nylon to fade and break down, though the fly will help protect fragile netting and uncoated nylon. The ground should be durable enough to resist impact but soft enough to allow you to pound in stakes. Granite, for example, fails this test.

Tie strips of nonadhesive orange reflective tape to tent stakes or ropes to make them more visible at night. Use sticky reflective tape on camp items you might have to find quickly in the dark—your flashlight, for example. The tape is available in hardware stores and bicycle shops.

If the ground is soft, push the stakes in with the heel of your hand or the sole of your boot. If it's fairly hard, try gently pounding the stakes in with a rock or hammer; be careful not to bend them. If the ground is impenetrable, you can use extra nylon cord and tie the guy lines to rocks or trees or place a big rock on a tied stake lying on the ground. If the stakes pull out of soft ground or sand, you can tie the guy lines to a "deadman"—a stake, stick, or stuff sack filled with soil—and bury it perpendicular to the main pull.

Stake your tent out tightly. Quality tents are designed to be pulled out taut. If you leave wrinkles, the wind will do a flap-dance on your tent. All other things being equal, point your tent door toward the east or southeast to capture the morning sun.

Cooking

Until just a few years ago, wilderness campers who wanted hot food had to cook over a fire. That was back when backpackers were scarce, wood was plentiful, and stoves, if they existed at all, were heavy and primitive. Today, with wood often scarce, a portable stove is considered essential equipment by most backpackers.

Even if firewood is ample, you should usually cook on a stove. Besides conserving wood, it will provide a dependable, controlled flame without the need to build a fireplace, hunt for wood, nurse a fire, fight smoke and falling ashes, or deal with sooty pots or wildly varying heat output. The major drawback of a backpacking stove is that it provides only one small single burner, which means only one dish at a time can be cooked.

> He who believes that where there's smoke there's fire hasn't tried cooking on a camping trip.
>
> —Changing Times

Never cook in your zipped-up tent. Besides being a fire hazard, it coats the inside of your tent with condensation and produces carbon monoxide, an invisible, odorless gas that, when inhaled, reduces the blood's ability to transport oxygen. If you are battened down in your tent, a burning stove may consume all the oxygen, producing symptoms that include headache, nausea, and breathing difficulties. Those symptoms you assume to be altitude sickness may be, at least in part, carbon monoxide poisoning. When cooking, use the tent's vestibule, or put the stove right outside the tent while you remain inside.

The number-one enemy of stove efficiency is wind. If the wind is so disruptive that even a part of the stove's burner will not stay lit, efficiency is being seriously compromised. If it's not corrected, fuel will be wasted, cooking time prolonged, and food may never completely cook. Most windscreens that come with stoves are ineffective, and so you may have to build a protective wall. Position your stove in a hollow and build a windbreak on the windward side out of rocks, pieces of wood, deadfalls, sleeping bags, or whatever is available. Maximize efficiency by using lids that fit snugly on every pot and by reducing the distance between pot and burner to about one-quarter inch.

If you must cook over a fire, be prepared to build or remodel the fireplace. An efficient design for cooking is what's called the half-dugout. After choosing a location that is convenient and safe (avoid trails, stream and lake shores, rocks, dry grass, brush, overhead branches, and mossy ground), clear a circle about four feet across. In the center of that circle, use a sharp rock or trowel to dig out a rectangular area about one foot wide, two or three feet long, and four inches deep. Find two rocks about the size and shape of bricks (concave tops are better than convex), and place them on either side of the pit, about a foot apart, parallel to each other and to the path of the prevailing wind. On the downwind end, place a larger rock or rocks to form a chimney. The resulting structure is U-shaped.

Now you can place your lightweight backpacking grill over the pit. Support it on the two bricks, as close as possible to the chimney and about two inches above ground level—that is, six inches above the pit bottom. On windy days, you may have to dig deeper. If there are no rocks and the grill sits directly on the ground, the pit must be deeper still. Regardless of the size and depth of the pit, be sure the grill is secure and will not slide or wobble.

Cook your food with the smallest fire possible. Inexperienced fireplace builders tend to excavate too large a firebox and to set the grill too high. Increasing grill height from six to ten inches may triple the amount of wood needed to cook dinner.

Once you have the fire started (see "Making Fire" on page 225), everyone in your party should wear shoes when in the area. Stray embers can burn for quite a while, causing a serious foot injury. Stray embers can also damage nylon clothes, tents, and sleeping bags, so keep your gear well away from the fire. Polypropylene can melt with very low heat, causing your gloves or underwear to melt and stick to your skin like napalm.

When adding ingredients, always remove pots from the fire, lest you burn yourself or spill. Use gloves, pot grabbers, or pot holders to protect delicate hands.

> When compelled to cook, I produce a meal that would make a sword swallower gag.
> —Russell Baker

■ Washing

> One hand washes the other, but both wash the face.
> —Zen saying

Washing—both dishes and body—is covered in chapter 16, "Wilderness Ethics"; suffice it to say here that you should simplify cleanup as much as possible. Even if you favor lounging about sipping brandy after dinner, soak your pots and pans immediately after completing your meal to avoid hardening of foodstuffs. Leaving dirty pots and pans out overnight increases your chances of attracting animals to camp.

To clean your body, there are now no-rinse shampoos and body baths available at outdoor stores. Slather on, wipe off, and you're clean. Biodegradable and pH-balanced, they were developed for nursing homes and hospitals and used by U.S. troops during the Gulf War and on NASA flights. To avoid an unpleasant residue, use plenty of the product and make sure your towel is dry and absorbent.

> Miss your warm shower? You don't have to. Carry a one-liter plastic soda bottle as a water container. Bring an extra cap in which you've poked ten to twenty tiny holes (after removing the inner plastic seal). When you're ready to shower, fill the soda bottle with warm water and screw on the modified cap. Tie string or rope around the neck and hang it, or have someone hold it and sprinkle away.

Odds 'n' Ends

Soon after you get to camp, take off your boots and put on running shoes or sandals. Your feet will go "aahhh" and you won't trample the camp area.

To fasten a rope to a tent or tarp lacking a grommet or loop, place a smooth pebble, an inch or so wide, on the underside of the fabric where the grommet should be. Gather the fabric into a hood around the pebble, holding it at the neck. Tie the rope around the neck to secure it.

To rig up a no-peg clothesline, double your nylon cord and twist it repeatedly. Slide laundry in between twists and it will hold even in the strongest wind. When hanging clotheslines or mirrors, don't drive a nail into a tree.

If there is no rain threatening and you're not tentbound, unzip your sleeping bag and hang it on the line. Turn it frequently to prevent sun damage. That will freshen your bag after a long night of perspiring.

Heavy-duty garbage bags have multiple uses around camp. Reshaped with a knife and some duct tape, they work as a pack cover, makeshift poncho, or ground cloth for your tent.

Car campers can hang a sixteen-pocket shoe organizer for odds and ends. You can stash water bottles, candle lanterns, flashlights, socks, gloves, pens, notepaper, and even shoes.

If you want to read in the tent, make a lantern by standing a flashlight on end and placing a wide-mouth quart water bottle over it.

As we've long suspected, smoke does follow us around the campfire. It's attracted to the vacuum formed by a large object like your body. If you build a small stone wall near the fire ring, the smoke will be drawn that way, leaving you in the clear. When drying clothes and gear by the fire, place nothing closer to the flames than the distance at which you can comfortably hold your hand.

■ Cold Weather Camping

Fluff your sleeping bag before you crawl inside. Air trapped within the fibers will help retain body heat.

Plastic produce bags are remarkable foot warmers. Wear the bags between your liner socks and thick outer socks. They also make good mittens.

If you expect freezing temperatures, turn your water bottles upside down. Because water freezes from top to bottom, the mouths of the bottles will remain unclogged, unless it's cold enough to freeze the entire contents. Even colder? Sleep with your boots in your sleeping bag to keep them from freezing.

If you wake up cold, do muscular-tension exercises (isometrics) in your sleeping bag. Push your palms together, hold for a few seconds, then repeat. The exertion will make you warmer.

■ Games and Activities

When you eliminate the trappings of civilization, such as TV, telephone, and automobile, it's amazing how many more hours a day seems to hold. Unless you are moving camp every day, chores will consume only a tiny percentage of your camp time, leaving you plenty of time for games and activities. Although you and your campmates may be capable of entertaining yourselves, here

While camping in Yosemite Valley in the 1950s, my family's evening entertainment often included a visit to what was then an open dump near Camp Curry. On warm summer evenings, we would loiter in the parking lot, next to other like-minded tourists, and wait for the bears to come scavenge for dinner. As dusk deepened, about a dozen burly black bears would amble out to begin their nightly ritual.

This desultory prowl over mounds of garbage was an undignified affair, as I now see, but I didn't think so then. The dump afforded me the chance to study bears in a way that would be impossible during a panicky retreat. But one day the government concluded that the dependent relationship fostered by an open dump ran counter to the national park philosophy. Today, it has been replaced by bear-proof Dumpsters.

—S.B.

are some ideas you might want to explore *before* you hear that plaintive cry, "There's nothing to do."

Conundrums

The following problems will enlighten as well as entertain. They can be posed and solved on the trail, but they will probably play better in camp, where it's easier to concentrate. If only two or three people are working on a problem, it will take a while to solve it. Counsel patience.

State each situation, being careful not to say too much, and then ask for yes-or-no questions that ferret out "what's really going on."

1. A man walks into a bar and asks for a drink of water. The bartender looks at him, reaches under the bar, pulls out a gun, and points it at him. The man thanks him and walks out of the bar.

What happened? The man had the hiccups. The bartender, seeing this, decided to scare the hiccups out of him. When it worked, the man thanked the bartender and left.

2. A man is lying facedown beside a puddle of water in an otherwise empty room.

What happened? He stabbed himself with an icicle.

3. A man is trying to go home; another man, wearing a mask, is waiting there for him.

What is happening? The man is a baseball player trying to score; the other man is a catcher.

Headwork

These are thought-provoking questions that don't really have one right answer. Here are some examples, but you can probably think of others.

- What noise might a dog make if it were in trouble?

- Why are the holes in a salt shaker bigger than the holes in a pepper shaker?

- If beings from another planet landed on Earth and wanted to see the most beautiful thing on our planet, what would you show them?

- Why are some beaches rockier than others?

- If you could eat only one food for the rest of your life, what would it be? Do you think you'd get tired of it?

- Name some things that can't be bought with money that are just as valuable as things that can.

- Why aren't human teeth as sharp as sharks' teeth?

- When is it helpful for people to yell at each other? When is it hurtful?

- Try to make up a story that begins, "I am the smallest person in the world."

Kim's Game

Rudyard Kipling's *Kim* is a story about a boy who developed great powers of observation through practice. Kim's Game has its origins in that book.

Any number can play. Place twenty or more common objects—knife, compass, spoon, etc.—on a table, allow the players to study them for one minute, then cover them with a cloth. Each player then lists as many objects as he or she can recall. Remove the cloth. Score one point for each item correctly remembered and subtract two points for each item listed that's not on the table.

In one variation, everyone studies the objects for one minute as before, then they turn their backs while you move six or eight objects around on the table. The players have thirty seconds more to study the table, then list the objects moved.

In another variation, you remove six or eight objects. The players then look for thirty seconds and list the objects that were removed.

The Senses

Blindfold the other members of your party and have them sit quietly for a while. At the end of the time limit—maybe two or three minutes—have them write down what they heard, smelled, and felt.

Now let them try it again, this time with the knowledge that they should be observant. Point out the differences in the senses recorded when they knew they were supposed to be tuned in. After all, weren't the same things there the first time?

Aniverbs

Human behavior can sometimes be described vividly by using a verb derived from the animal kingdom. Have the members of your group list as many as they can. Below are eleven that come to mind.

> 1. Ape—to mimic (The small child will sometimes *ape* his parents' worst mannerisms.)
>
> 2. Badger—to pester (The mother *badgered* her daughter to clean her room by putting her dirty clothes in her bed.)
>
> 3. Dog—to trail persistently (Whenever he appears in public, Michael Jordan is *dogged* by fans.)
>
> 4. Fox—to deceive by ingenuity (For years the fugitive out*foxed* the police.)
>
> 5. Horse—to engage in rowdy play (The kids *horsed* around until they were tired enough for bed.)
>
> 6. Monkey—to play or tamper with something (The boys *monkeyed* with their bicycle lock until it came loose.)
>
> 7. Snake—to move or crawl like a snake (The soldier escaped by *snaking* through the bushes.)

8. Weasel—to evade (The student *weaseled* out of explaining why he was late to school.)

9. Whale—to thrash (She *whaled* on her brother for using her toys without permission.)

10. Wolf—to eat voraciously (The boy *wolfed* down lunch so he could get back to the baseball game.)

11. Bull—to crash into or through (The fullback *bulled* over left tackle for a first down.)

Rock, Scissors, Paper

This classic can provide a diversion for two or more people, as well as help decide who is going to do the dishes or filter the water.

Each player holds the left hand out, palm up; the right hand is clenched into a fist, and with a rhythmic count of "one, two," each player hits his fist into his palm. Synchronized with "three," the fists become rock (keep the fist), paper (flat hand), or scissors (two fingers extended). The scoring is simple: paper covers rock, rock breaks scissors, scissors cut paper. Play the best of seven . . . or ninety-seven.

Make a Square

Ideal for two players, this game requires only a sheet of paper and a pencil. It takes time to set up, so if it's a favorite with your group, you might want to photocopy several "game boards." They look like this:

```
.   .   .   .   .   .
.   .   .   .   .   .
.   .   .   .   .   .
.   .   .   .   .   .
```

Just about any number of dots will work, but you might try ten rows and ten columns to start, giving you one hundred possible squares that can be filled in.

The object is to complete as many squares as possible. The first player connects any two horizontal or vertical (not diagonal) dots.

The second player connects two more dots. They can be completely separate from the first or join the line the first player made. The first player then connects another pair of dots, being careful not to form the third side of a developing square. If player A does just that, player B can complete the square in his turn. When you complete a square, you get to put your initials inside and draw another line. Thus you can complete multiple squares during a turn. The winner is the player with the most squares.

Cross Out

We're not sure what this game is called, so we call it Cross Out. A game for two players, it can be played with pencil and paper or with twigs in the dirt.

Place the twigs (or draw the lines) in a pattern like this:

or like this:

Players take turns removing (or crossing out) one or more twigs (lines) in any single row. The object is to leave the last twig for the other player.

Dual Triangles

Since you already have twigs (make sure they're at least a couple of inches long), ask the children to form two triangles with five of them. (Clue: The two triangles share a common base.)

Quintuple Triangles

Same game, except this time participants are asked to form five triangles with six sticks of varying length. (Answer: One triangle is inside the other, upside down, its vertex touching the midpoint of the outer triangle's base.)

Trick Sticks

Don't throw those sticks away. The problem this time is to make three and a half dozen, using only six sticks.

As the name suggests, there is a trick to this one. In order to get it, participants must know their Roman numerals.

I   I   I   V   I

You may have to provide hints, but this exercise certainly rewards creative thinking.

Tic-tac-toe

You know this one. It's for two players, one using X, the other O. The board is created by the two horizontal and two vertical lines shown below, creating nine boxes. Players take turns placing their symbol in a box. Three X's or three O's in a row—up, down, or diagonally—wins.

Tongue Twisters

These are phrases that are hard to repeat without making a mistake, usually one that causes you to trip over your tongue and others to dissolve into gales of laughter.

Each person tries to repeat the twister quickly or, in the case of long ones, say it just once. You can keep score or not.

Some examples:

- *Toy boat, toy boat, toy boat*

- *Rubber baby buggy bumpers*

- *She sells sea shells by the seashore*

- *Peter Piper picked a peck of pickled peppers*
  A peck of pickled peppers Peter Piper picked
  If Peter Piper picked a peck of pickled peppers
  Where's the peck of pickled peppers Peter Piper picked?

- *How much wood would a woodchuck chuck*
  If a woodchuck could chuck wood?

- *A cup of coffee in a copper coffee cup*

- *Ten thin tin things*

Hot or Cold

This game should be played in either a noisy campground or in complete solitude; otherwise, the tumult might drive your neighbors crazy.

One player is "it"; we'll call her Doris. Doris leaves the group. During her absence, the group chooses one object for her to touch.

Doris is called back, and as she approaches, the group begins rhythmic clapping to indicate how close she is to the object. The louder the applause, the closer she is; the softer the applause, the farther away. When the object is touched, pick a new person to be "it."

Charades

Again, play this game only when noise won't disturb others around you.

In the simplest form, each willing person stands before the group and acts out a book, movie, or famous character, using body language and hand gestures but no words, while members of the group shout out their guesses. The actor can attempt to convey the big picture (example: acting out a man crossing a desert for *Lawrence of Arabia*) or do it word by word (as you might for *Little Big Man*). It is not in the spirit of the game to try to spell the title by shaping letters with your fingers.

In an uninhibited group, Charades can produce riotous laughter, directed at both the actor and some of the off-the-wall outbursts from the audience.

If only a few are playing, you can take volunteers to be onstage. If you have a lot of people, you may prefer to form teams and compete against the clock. If sensitive or insecure kids are playing, reassure them that you are laughing *with* them and not *at* them.

Crazy, Mixed-Up Kids

With everyone seated, players slap their knees twice, clap their hands twice, and then grab their right ear with their left hand and their nose with their right hand. On signal, they slap and clap again, but reverse positions—right hand to left ear and left hand to nose. Repeat the routine, getting faster and faster until everyone is laughing and completely mixed up.

Huckle, Buckle, Beanstock

Place a common object in a visible but not obvious place. The players, who know what's been stashed, walk around looking for it. The first one to spot it sits down, looks away from the object, and says—you guessed it—"Huckle, buckle, beanstock," then waits for the others to find it.

Gossip (Telephone)

You need several people to play this game. Start by whispering a message in the ear of someone, who then attempts to whisper it to the next person, and so on. Typically, by the time the message comes around to the first player, it bears little resemblance to the original, which makes everybody laugh like lovable idiots.

Cards

Even if you're backpacking, a deck of cards is worth its weight. Young children love games like Fish, Old Maid, Crazy Eights, and

War. Older kids and adults can play Rummy, Gin Rummy, Casino, Canasta, Hearts, Solitaire, or Poker, using twigs or moose droppings for chips.

Chess and Checkers

You can find tiny chess and checker sets that fold up and weigh next to nothing. Checkers can also be played by drawing a board in the dirt with a stick and using black and white rocks for checkers.

Gee Whiz Water Quiz

If the members of your group have a working knowledge of math, especially percentages, give them the Gee Whiz Water Quiz. They won't get many answers exactly right, but it should increase their understanding of where water goes and of the need for conservation.

1. How much of Earth's water is fresh?

2. How much of Earth's total freshwater is available for human use?

3. Where is the greatest amount of freshwater on Earth?

4. How much water does the average American use a day?

5. What percentage of a living tree is water?

6. What percentage of your brain is water?

7. What percentage of an adult body is water?

8. How much water is needed to produce a Sunday newspaper?

9. How much water is needed to produce an American car, including tires?

10. How much water is used to produce a fast-food meal, including hamburger, fries, and soft drink?

Answers

1. 3 percent; 2. 1 percent; 3. The polar icecaps, which contain six million square miles of water—enough to feed all the world's rivers for 100 years; 4. 200 gallons; 5. 75 percent; 6. 75 percent; 7. 65–70 percent; 8. 150 gallons; 9. 39,000 gallons; 10. 1,400 gallons

■ Activities and Hobbies

The wilderness is a regular learning laboratory. Being in nature lends relevance to the study of astronomy, botany, biology, medicine, mineralogy, geology, meteorology, ornithology, entomology, ichthyology, zoology, map reading, navigation, and a host of survival skills.

Although it's inevitable that some subjects will interest you and yours more than others, all of them will be more compelling in the wilderness than in the classroom.

Ornithology (Birds)

Birds seem to have a special hold on children. (Steve's daughter's third word, after "mama" and "dadda," was "doot," which was infant-talk for "bird.") What is it about birds that attracts us? They are active and attractive; they are diverse and ubiquitous; they sing songs, build nests, and come to feeders; and best of all, they fly. Boy, do they fly! Arctic terns may rack up twenty-two thousand frequent-flyer miles a year; some swifts reach speeds of up to two hundred miles per hour;

short-tailed shearwaters migrate in flocks up to four hundred thousand strong; homing pigeons can find their way home from one thousand miles away.

Although their numbers vary from place to place and season to season, birds are just about everywhere. More than 650 species are regular breeders or frequent visitors north of the Mexican border. Birds nest on sandy beaches and rocky cliffs, in marshes and deserts, along city streets and country roads, and in garages and barns.

If you're going to be a bird-watcher, learn to be quiet. Walk slowly and steadily, or not at all. Don't wear bright clothes. Get an early start, especially if you're looking for land birds in spring. They are noisiest and most active from dawn to midmorning.

Birding can be done alone or in a group. Many birders enjoy the solitude of an early morning walk or a restful hour near a pond or stream. On the other hand, a group provides companionship, extra pairs of eyes, and, if there is at least one experienced observer along, a steeper learning curve. Many areas of the country have bird clubs (often a local chapter of the Audubon Society) where you can meet other birders. Try calling the biology department of the local high school or college or the nearest natural history museum to find out about such clubs.

> The conservation movement is a breeding ground of Communists and other subversives. We intend to clean them out, even if it means rounding up every bird-watcher in the country.
> —John N. Mitchell

To identify birds, you need to develop an eye for detail. Learn to concentrate on certain features:

Posture and movement. The way a bird perches or moves often reveals its identity. Wrens cock their tails; woodpeckers and goldfinches have an undulating pattern of flight. Field guide illustrations don't always convey this type of information; that's why it's valuable to have along an experienced birder.

Size and proportions. When you see a bird you don't recognize, compare its size with a bird you do know—say, a robin or a crow. Note whether the bird is slender or robust, and whether its legs or bill are unusually long.

Songs and calls. Birds have two sets of vocal cords, and some have been re-corded singing two songs at once (don't try that at home). Recognizing a bird by sound is often easier than iden-tifying it by sight, especially with small birds in deep foliage. Of course, you have to learn the sounds. You can listen to recordings, but for beginners, it's better to apprentice with someone who has a good ear for bird calls.

Singing is usually most persistent in the morning, although some species don't seem to care what time it is. One researcher recorded a male red-eyed vireo repeating his refrain 22,197 times between dawn and dark.

According to a report by the U.S. Fish and Wildlife Service, Americans spend almost as much money annually watch-ing and feeding birds as they do supporting their favorite sports teams. Bird-watchers shell out at least $5.2 billion for travel, binoculars, bird-seed, and other accoutre-ments, while sports fans spend about $5.9 billion on football, baseball, and other sporting events. The point is that as popular songbird species con-tinue to decline, as they have for the past fifteen years, it's bound to have a significant effect on an im-portant segment of the U.S. economy.

Color and markings. These attributes most strikingly reveal a bird's identity, although some species change colors depending on season, sex, or age. With experience, you will be able to absorb more and more information in a quick glance and will learn the special characteristics that separate closely related species—say, the bill color of a tern or the wing bars of a vireo.

Nest and eggs. With a little practice, you will be able to identify the nest and the eggs of many species. Field guides describe the variations in both. Do not disturb nests or steal eggs.

Whether you are compiling a life list (of species seen and iden-tified) or you just like watching birds, you will want a decent pair of binoculars (as well as a pocket-size field guide, pen, and notebook). If you are backpacking and counting ounces, you may opt for pocket-size binoculars. (For example, Nikon's new Sprint 10x21 binoculars weigh only 8.8 ounces.) Petite binocs are fine when the sun is high, but full-size models deliver a brighter image, which is important in low light.

The key to evaluating binoculars is the numbers marked on every pair: typically 8x24 or 10x25 on compacts, 7x42 or 7x50 on full-size glasses. The second number is the diameter, in millimeters, of the binocular's objective lenses. Doubling the diameter, say from 25 to 50, *quadruples* its light-gathering capacity. Cheap binoculars are available for less than $50. At the other end of the spectrum, the Leica 7x42 BA, compact and waterproof, weighing thirty-two ounces, costs $1,650.

Entomology (Insects)

When you go camping, you'll likely share your accommodations with a variety of insects. About three-quarters of the animal species on Earth, about seven hundred thousand, are insects. There are more than one hundred thousand insect species in North America. Although delicate walkingsticks and bright butterflies get rave reviews, the vast majority of people say they don't like insects. Actually, insects have much to recommend them. They fill vital ecological niches, supply humans with medicine, keep other insects in check, and play an important role in the reproduction of flowering plants.

They also expand our awe of the miracle of life. Consider the many ways insects defend themselves. The walkingstick uses camouflage; bees sting; some caterpillars have stinging nettlelike hairs. Take note of insects' deceptive complexity. The eye of a dragonfly has a thousand parts; an ant society is amazingly sophisticated.

Most children are innately fascinated by creepy-crawlies. If your child shares this interest, make available an insect field guide and a lightweight magnifying glass. Hunt bugs together. Most nature stores have a meshed, cylindrical bug house, a fairly benign way to study insects before they crawl or fly away.

We can tell others to refrain from killing insects and even to put them back where they found them, but this runs counter to the instincts of many young people. The hope is that with knowledge comes respect.

Fishing

> Time is but a stream I go a-fishing in.
> —Henry David Thoreau

Fishing is a good activity for people of all ages—if they're interested. It's active, involves one in nature (albeit in an adversarial way), teaches new skills, and reinforces important qualities, such as the patience to wait, oh, two days for a nibble.

You can't just pass out rods and reels and expect beginners to perform flawlessly. To become proficient anglers, they will need careful, patient instruction and lots of practice. This is especially true if they are learning to fly-fish. Before they've paid their dues, they may break rods, cast lures into treetops, snag old boots, separate their reel from their rod, snarl their line into something more complex than Rubik's Cube, and come up empty in dozens of lakes and streams. Ah, but the eventual rewards: Mountain trout is maybe the best eating on the planet.

If you fish in high-impact areas, you should scatter fish guts and leftovers far and wide, at least two hundred feet from water and campsite. In alpine backcountry areas, don't throw the remains back into lakes or streams; chilly mountain waters act like a refrigerator, preventing rapid decomposition. And seeing fish guts in an otherwise pristine lake is a slap in the face of the wilderness backpacker.

Day Hiking

There is nothing quite like replacing backpack with day pack and setting off over hill and dale, by trail or cross country, many pounds lighter in spirit and load. Hiking is marvelous exercise and great for the soul, but caution is needed.

The most basic caveat is never hike alone. People of all ages should have a partner every time they leave camp. (Obviously, that rule has been broken by many otherwise responsible people, including John Muir and Henry David Thoreau.) If anyone in your group leaves camp alone, insist upon an itinerary. Look at a map and discuss details.

Night Hiking

At night, we lose much of our feelings of dominance over nature. Our eyes, through which we gather most of our information, become all but useless, forcing us to rely on other senses. We tend to think of nighttime as cold and empty ("the dead of night"), but actually the night is filled not only with stars but with the pulse and hum of life itself.

Writer W. H. Hudson liked to prove this to dinner guests. He would lead them into the dark forest that adjoined his estate and ask them to stand quietly. When all was still, he would fire a revolver he'd hidden beneath his coat, and suddenly the air would be filled with a mad chorus of howls and shrieks, with animals crashing through brush to flee the noise. "The wild outcry," he called it. "The extraordinary hullabaloo."

Such a hullabaloo is possible because an estimated 85 percent of the world's mammals are active at night, or at least around dawn and dusk. Sixty percent of carnivores hunt at night. Only humans, apes, monkeys, some birds, and a few other species prefer daytime.

Night creatures have complex eyes with a mirrorlike membrane that reflects light to the retina twice, giving the brain two chances to make it out. It's that reflection that we see in our headlights—white for coyote, yellow for raccoon, red for woodcock.

Take a friend or family member to visit a place at night that you saw earlier in the daylight. If it's cold, dress warmly and take sleeping pads. Carry a flashlight if necessary, but then turn it off and sit quietly. Hug a tree, stroke a flower, sniff, listen. If you must talk, whisper. Later, ask questions: How did it feel? What's different now that it's night? Did the other senses come into play? Hearing? Touch? Smell? Why do you think so many animals are more active during the night?

Mineralogy

Rocks have a life story. They are "born," they move around, and they change size. Some have beautiful colors and others have interesting shapes. Although most adults take rocks for granted, children seem to have a special intimacy with them.

Geologists divide rocks into three types based on their origin:

Sedimentary rock is the easiest to understand. The mud and decaying plant and animal material that sifts to the bottom of a lake is sediment. The layers of gunk at the bottom are pressed tightly together by the weight of ensuing layers (don't try this at home: it may take millions of years) until they become hard as rock. Then perhaps the lake disappears, the land is tilted by earthquake, and the sedimentary rock is exposed. Sandstone, which is reddish and sometimes embedded with fossils, is a common sedimentary rock. Compared to other rocks, sandstone is soft and easy to break up.

Igneous rock is born deep in the Earth, where everything is hot and liquid. As molten igneous material slowly slides toward the cooler surface of the Earth, it solidifies into rock. Igneous rock is also formed when a volcano erupts. Molten lava spews onto the surface, eventually cooling and solidifying. This type of rock is usually extra hard. Granite and obsidian are igneous.

Here are two exercises for you and your rock-loving kids. Begin by asking, "What is dirt?" After listening to a litany of wild answers, urge them to find out for themselves. Have them pick up a handful and examine it. What do they see? Rather than just one thing, dirt is really made up of myriad plant bits, seeds, dead insects, and tiny rocks.

Next, put together a row of rocks of descending size. Begin with one about the width of a thumbnail, lining up smaller and smaller pebbles until they are too small to pick up. When you reach that point, add a pinch of sand to the end of the row. Ask questions like, "How are rocks and sand alike?" (Hint: hard mineral matter.) "Why are they round or close to it?" (Hint: erosion of corners.) "How did sand become so small?" (Hint: water erosion.) If your audience is mature enough, build up to the big question: "How did rocks get here?"

Metamorphic rock is any rock—sedimentary, igneous, or previously metamorphosed—that has had its form altered. For example, proper conditions and intense pressure will change shale (a soft, flaky, sedimentary rock made up of compressed mud) into slate (a hard, dark, metamorphic rock used in blackboards).

Photography

Great photography is a complex mix that includes composition, subject matter, lighting, and other variables.

Having said that, it's getting easier all the time to learn how to take good pictures that are fun to look at back home. Photography is a recreational skill almost anyone can learn, especially with today's point-and-shoot cameras. Remember the following basic points:

- Remove the lens cap.

- Hold the camera steady.

- Don't shoot into the sun.

- Keep fingers away from the lens opening.

- Take a deep breath and hold.

- Slowly squeeze the shutter button.

- Clean the lens often.

Also, avoid these temptations whenever possible:

- Trying to fit everything in. Simplify pictures by taking separate shots instead of grouping them all together.

- Dead-centering your subject. Compose photos according to the Rule of Thirds: Mentally divide the tableau into three horizontal sections and three vertical sections. Place your subject, or main elements, where the lines intersect.

- Shooting in the middle of the day, when the light is boring. Shoot early or late in the day to enhance texture and colors.

- Expecting too much from your flash. Most small flashes will illuminate nothing beyond fifteen or twenty feet.

- Expecting too much from your lens. Snap a picture with a compact camera of an animal in the distance, and the animal will appear tiny in the final picture. Those great close-ups we see in books and magazines are made possible by big, expensive lenses.

- Combining ultralight and ultradark areas in the same frame. Your eyes can handle the contrast in a sun-dappled forest, but film can't. Shoot forest scenes on overcast days.

- Using boring, repetitive camera angles. Instead of standing all the time, kneel down, climb higher, look for other shooting positions. Turn the camera.

- Ignoring rogue details. Be alert for the merging shadows or the branch sticking out of your subject's head.

- Including too much overcast sky. Yes, you can take good pictures on cloudy days, but don't show large sections of cloudy skies, since film renders it poorly.

Pictures of people should:

- Have a center of interest.

- Have contrast.

- Show action, though not too fast.

Pictures of scenery should:

- Lead the viewer's eye to the center of interest.

- Have good background.

- Be framed, perhaps by two trees.

Remind novices that photography requires delayed gratification. The real enjoyment comes days or weeks later when you pick up the developed pictures and you feel the accomplishment of being able to say, "I took that!"

Scatology

This is the study and collection of mammal droppings. While it's not for everybody (nor is it the stuff of polite dinner conversation), scat does offer excellent clues about the animals in the area. Serious scatologists can determine the range of an animal, seasonal changes in diet, and population density. Back in the lab, samples can be scrutinized for parasites and indications of disease.

> One wildlife researcher, Olaus Murie, has a collection of 1,200 scat specimens, dried, varnished, labeled, and wrapped in plastic bags. Murie's collection is in constant demand for classes and seminars. Imagine how proud his mother must be.

Scat is indeed a valuable learning tool. In Great Smoky Mountains National Park, black bear researchers from the University of Tennessee have injected bears with a harmless isotope that shows up in their scat for up to three years. This allows them to identify individual animals and gather information without recapturing or even seeing the bear.

But you don't have to be a scientist to appreciate good scat. Young children delight in pointing out trail poop. By examining droppings for the basic characteristics of size, shape, and content, even laypeople can identify the responsible animal. Deer drop little pellets thirteen to twenty-two times a day that are easily distinguished from a moose's but might be confused with a rabbit's. Bobcats and mountain lions, like house cats, try to bury their scat, so look for scratches in the soil. In fact, scat is often only one of many clues. Look for tracks or fur caught on branches. Flies are a sure sign of fresh scat.

Star Gazing

There are one hundred billion stars in our galaxy, but only about six thousand are visible to the naked eye under ideal conditions (the most powerful telescopes can pick out, oh, about a billion). For thousands of years, people have grouped the stars into figures called constellations. Legends and myths have been passed down about them. It's fun to learn the myths and pass them on to others while pointing out the star clusters in the sky. Visit your library for a book about legends of the constellations.

A good starting point is the Big Dipper, probably the most visible constellation in the northern sky. Four stars make up the cup and three bright ones seem to complete the handle. Actually, the handle's midpoint is composed of two stars. Can you see them? Indians, who called these two stars the squaw and the papoose, used them to test the eyesight of young braves.

The two stars that form the side of the bowl farthest from the handle are called the pointers; if you follow their line upward, they take you to the North Star, which, because it is almost in a direct line with the axis of the Earth, doesn't seem to move as the Earth turns. All other stars seem to rotate around the North Star.

The North Star is also the first star in the handle of the Little Dipper, which is fainter than the Big Dipper. If you follow a line from the middle star of the handle of the Big Dipper through the North Star, you'll come to a big W, which is Cassiopeia, the Lady in the Chair.

Acquire a star chart and continue to "connect the dots" and identify constellations.

Storytelling

If not a lost art, storytelling is certainly an endangered one. But when sitting around a campfire or lying in a sleeping bag, storytelling is a natural entertainment. All you need is patience and a modest gift of gab.

Well, maybe a bit more. Here are a few tips for the beginning storyteller.

- Don't try to make up stories from scratch at first. Read adventure, mystery, or history stories in books and magazines, and retell them in your own words.

- Avoid unsuitable stories, overly sentimental ones, talking down to your audience, stories in dialect, and mumbling. For younger children, avoid off-color, sarcastic, and very scary stories.

- Look and feel relaxed; if not, your audience will sense your discomfort and uncertainty.

- Be enthusiastic, conveying emotion through changes in volume and tone. Children can detect indifference like a Geiger counter detects uranium.

- Have the framework of the story established before you start. Don't forget that a good story has a definite beginning, middle, and end.

- Start strong; try to catch your listeners' attention from the first words.

- Make the details clear, especially of the events, characters, and setting.

- Include vivid action. Emphasize verbs over adjectives and adverbs.

- Make the narration "visible" to the audience. Include sensory experiences besides sight. In other words, don't tell them, show them: hear the wind howl through the trees or smell the pine needles on a crisp, fall morning.

- Sprinkle in humor, but don't overdo it unless your kids are so young they can't recognize corn. Mix with dramatic inflection and pauses.

- Remember that "brevity is the soul of wit." If you are telling a long story, condense it into five to fifteen minutes. If it is a sure winner, you can tell it in installments, keeping your audience hanging until the next chapter.

Joseph Pulitzer, writer and newspaper owner, used to advise his reporters to write their stories

briefly, so people will read it;

clearly, so they will understand it;

forcibly, so they will appreciate it;

picturesquely, so they will remember it; and above all,

accurately, so they will be guided by its light.

Change "read" to "listen to" in the first line, and it's good advice for the storyteller.

Here's a traditional campfire story to get you started.

"One time I had a real scary encounter with a grizzly bear" (adding quickly, "Of course, there are no grizzlies around here"). "I managed to climb a nearby tree just ahead of the bear's snapping jaws. Seated on a branch, I watched in terror as the enraged bear clawed and chewed at the trunk of the tree. Then he shook it in an attempt to knock me from my perch. But the tree was too big and soon the bear gave up and disappeared into the woods.

"I started climbing down the tree, but before I got very far, the bear returned, this time with another bear. Together they chewed and clawed and shoved at the tree, but the tree was too strong. They too disappeared for a time, but were soon back, this time with a third bear. It was no use—the tree was too big for the three bears, and when they finally disappeared into the forest, a wave of relief washed over me.

"I again started down the tree. But to my horror, the three bears came back! And this time, each of them was carrying a beaver."

Bear stories are usually well received, as long as they're not too scary. This one really happened:

A woman who had just bought a new camera, complete with telephoto lens, was determined to get a good bear picture on her visit to Great Smoky Mountains National Park. When a black bear scrounging for handouts wandered into her campsite, the woman moved closer to the animal and raised the camera. The suddenly magnified image of the bear scared her out of her wits. Turning to run, she collided with a tree and knocked herself unconscious. The curious bear ambled over for a look.

When the woman regained consciousness, the bear was gone. A fellow camper, trying to be friendly, handed her a Polaroid he'd taken of the bear standing over her, licking her face while she was out. Seeing that, she fainted.

Here's another true story—if the storyteller can be believed—that should lead to some interesting discussion. Know your audience, as this one might frighten younger children.

It was 1924, and Albert Ostman, a Scandinavian lumberjack, was camped on the Powell River in western Canada. From the Indian guide who had taken him in to that wild area, he had heard about Sasquatch, a name that means "wild men of the woods." These creatures, though large and hairy, were reputed to be quite humanlike.

After finding a good place to camp the first night, Ostman dismissed the Indian. He made a bed of branches and hung his food on a pole, high above the ground. But in the morning, he found some of his supplies missing. At first he suspected a porcupine. When the same thing happened the second night, however, he knew it wasn't a porcupine. The salt was untouched, and porcupines always go for salt.

On the third evening, resolving not to sleep, he took off only his boots, putting them at the bottom of his sleeping bag. In the middle of the night, he was half asleep when suddenly he was picked up and carried, still in his sleeping bag. For maybe thirty minutes, he was jounced about in that confining sack, before being thrown to the ground. It was still dark. He heard voices but could make out no words.

When at last he poked his head out of his sleeping bag, he looked up to see four giant two-legged creatures. It was a Sasquatch family—mother, father, son, and daughter. The father was a huge, hairy, barrel-chested fellow, between seven and eight feet tall, and Albert assumed he had been the one to carry him through the woods. He was talking and gesticulating to Mrs. Sasquatch, who seemed to be objecting to something.

"What do you chaps want with me?" Ostman asked, but no one answered.

> If you feel ill-equipped to tell a story, consider reading one. The possibilities are unlimited, but here are a few favorites:
>
> • The Jungle Book by Rudyard Kipling
> • Alice's Adventures in Wonderland by Lewis Carroll (though some kids will incorrectly think they are too old for this one)
> • The Wind in the Willows by Kenneth Grahame
> • The Hobbit by J. R. R. Tolkien
> • The Merry Adventures of Robin Hood by Howard Pyle
> • Twenty Thousand Leagues Under the Sea by Jules Verne
> • Treasure Island by Robert Lewis Stevenson

At daybreak, he discovered he was trapped. They were camped in a natural bowl high in the mountains with only one way out. For seven days the lumberjack was held prisoner. The young male offered him grass and sweet roots to eat. In turn, Ostman offered the males some of his snuff. The "old man," as Ostman called him, took all that was left and ate it. His eyes began to roll, and he dashed off to a nearby spring for water. Seizing the opportunity, Ostman fled to freedom.

He told no one about the Sasquatch adventure for many years, fearing, understandably, that few people would believe him. When he finally did go public, he provided detailed descriptions of the creatures. They were herbivores, he said, eating evergreen tips, grasses, roots, and ferns. The female, over seven feet tall, had a wide pelvis and drooping breasts. The male had long forearms, short fingers, a hairy body, and a two-inch penis.

* * *

Do Sasquatch really exist? True believers point to the dozens of sightings since 1920, the photographs of footprints, and the three films that have been produced. The footprints, they claim, are exactly the type a huge humanoid would make.

People who do not believe in Sasquatch ask some vexing questions: Why hasn't one been captured? Why haven't pilots in fire-prevention helicopters spotted them? How can they find enough vegetation in the mountains to sustain such big bodies?

If the Sasquatch do exist, what exactly are they? Some anthropologists believe they are a lost tribe of Indians living a primitive existence in the Northwest. Others call them aliens. Some even suggest they are a new species of orangutan.

Swimming

Most people love water play. The focal point of most vacations is an ocean, lake, river, or swimming pool. But every year in the United States more than a thousand children fourteen and younger drown, the second most common cause of accidental death in children (after car accidents). Teach your kids to swim and watch them well. Beyond that, enforce the following safety rules:

- Adapt slowly to extremely cold water.

- Don't go in the water when you're overheated, overtired, or after eating a meal.

Although they get a lot of bad press, sharks kill an average of only one swimmer per year in the United States. The overwhelming percentage of open-water rescues are caused by rip currents and hypothermia. Because water is an extremely efficient conductor, immersing your 98.6° body in a 60° bay is an invitation to hypothermia. If your core temperature drops just a few degrees, your brain and other vital organs become affected. Uncontrollable shivering sets in, your speech starts to slur, and coordination and judgment begin to erode.

How long can we stand cold water? There are plenty of variables, including body fat percentage, but an old saw, called the 50-50-50 formula, asserts that in 50° water, 50 percent of the people will die in 50 minutes.

Mom had that one right.

■ Beware of unfamiliar swimming holes. Verify that a place is safe.

■ Don't swim above waterfalls.

■ Investigate the depth of any pool before you dive in.

■ Don't be macho in the water by overestimating your ability to stay underwater or swim long distances.

■ Be sensitive to the safety of others.

■ As a parent, don't rely blindly on waterwings or flotation devices to save your children.

Tree Identification

> Bamboos are straight and pine trees are gnarled.
> —Zen Saying

North America has the world's tallest, oldest, and most massive trees. It is home to nearly sixty oak species, thirty-five pine, and more than a dozen maple. About 750 species of trees grow wild north of Mexico.

Some trees have leaves, others have needles (really just long, narrow leaves). All contain chlorophyll, the green pigment required for photosynthesis. Some species, like giant sequoias and weeping willows, are immediately familiar; others must be identified through a process of elimination. With a field guide, consider the following variables when trying to identify a tree:

Leaves. Pinpoint the general type of leaf—needlelike, scalelike, or broad

Have you seen a big tree? A record for that species perhaps? Contact American Forests, keeper of the National Register of Big Trees, and nominate it for champion status. Backpackers stand a better than average chance of discovering prime specimens. For more information about nominating a tree or locating current champs, contact: Bill Cannon, American Forests, P.O. Box 2000, Washington, DC 20013.

and flat—then look at the size, shape, texture, color, and arrangement. Most broad leaves alternate on the twig (maples, with their paired leaves, are a notable exception).

Flowers. Blossom size, shape, and color can help you determine to which group a tree belongs.

Fruits. Closely related trees bear similar fruits. Acorns are oak fruit, and cones are conifer fruit.

Bark. In winter, when deciduous trees lose their leaves, bark may offer the best chance of identifying a species. Consider color, pattern, and texture.

Shape. This involves height, crown width, arrangement of branches, and other variables. Shape varies with location. A forest tree will be taller and its crown narrower than the same species growing in the open.

Wildflower Identification

More than fifteen thousand flowering plants grow north of the Mexican border, and identifying a few can be fun. Consider bringing along a flower field guide. Children may enjoy wildflower coloring books.

The vast array of flower colors, shapes, textures, and scents serves only one function: to produce the seed for a new generation. Every flower contains egg-producing female organs (pistils), pollen-producing male organs (stamens), or both.

Since flowers seldom pollinate themselves, most species need the help of an outside agent to transfer pollen from the stamen of one flower to the pistil of another. Many grasses and plants rely on the wind; others depend on insects or birds, attracting them with color or smell. In exchange for distributing its seed, the flower may supply nectar to its animal allies.

Flowers have long provided food and medicine to those with the knowledge to use them, but some are poisonous. Do not randomly eat flowers.

Pranks

Although we don't officially encourage practical jokes, some of the following suggestions submitted to *Backpacker* magazine are amusing—at least to contemplate. Before you engage in such juvenile behavior, however, make sure the recipients are as fun-loving as you.

- Pile some Milk Duds or chocolate-covered raisins not far from camp. After bragging to your mates of your ability to identify animals from their signs, wander out of camp until you come upon the chocolate "droppings." Pick up one of the top ones and pop it in your mouth. Savor it, rolling it around in your mouth as though trying to discern the species, all the while enjoying the shocked looks on the faces around you. It works best on a young, gullible audience.

- Separate the two halves of a few Oreo cookies and replace the cream filling with toothpaste. Hand them out around the campfire.

- Run a length of rope under someone's tent. Tie a knot in one end and, as your friend is nodding off, slowly retrieve the rope from the other end.

- When your tentmate falls asleep, fill his hand with toothpaste or shaving cream, and tickle his nose.

- Tell youngsters the story of the "Giant Campground Earthworm" while a coconspirator sneaks behind a tent, zips himself into a mummy bag, and starts crawling toward the others. This is a favorite with the under-ten crowd.

- Before campmates awake, make bear tracks by pressing your fist into the dirt and opening it while keeping your fingers slightly curved. Dot the top of each knuckle to imitate claws. Encircle the tent with tracks, and then yell "Bear!"

Bedtime

Before it gets dark, gather and arrange the items you might need during the night and first thing in the morning. Place them strategically in the tent or near your bed so that you can find them in the dark. You might include diapers, toilet paper, tissues, flashlight, books, water bottle, or rain gear.

If you have young children who go to bed before you, do your tent time—reading books, telling stories, singing songs—then kiss them good night and leave. Chances are, your kids will get less sleep than they do at home. In the evenings, they tend to be energized by their new surroundings; in the mornings, there is no shortage of sleep disturbers, from the sounds of nature to dawn's early light.

The last adult to crawl in should batten down the hatches. Make sure that:

- All food and garbage is safe from animals.

- The fire is safely contained.

- Pack pockets are open (so exploring rodents won't chew through to get inside) and packs are secure from the weather, if necessary.

- The path from tent to toilet is clear.

Leaving Camp

Before final departure, police your campsite. Check for trash and forgotten articles. Pick up other people's mistakes. Check not only the ground but the trees. Did you get your clothesline? Food-hanging rope? Tent stakes and guy lines?

Douse all fires until they are dead, then douse them again. Do some landscaping, smoothing out heavily trodden areas and filling in any holes or trenches your party dug. Set a good example for your children and other members of your party by leaving the campsite in better shape than it was when you arrived. Be guided by the adage, "Take only photos; leave only footprints."

Chapter Ten

WINTER BACKPACKING

A lot of people like snow. I find it to be an unnecessary
freezing of water.

—Carl Reiner

BACKPACKING in snow demands special equipment and skills. If you doubt that, consider that slipping on snow is the number-one cause of backcountry accidents in Grand Teton National Park. Just a seemingly ordinary fall on a patch of snow can result in a sprained wrist, twisted knee, or broken leg—and possibly require a rescue.

To avoid such a calamity, take a snow course. There are numerous guide services throughout North America that can teach you how to walk on different angles and types of snow with and without ice axe and crampons. You will learn about kicking steps, self-arrest, and many other valuable techniques.

If the snow is patchy and shallow, you may be able to hike in your boots. But in winter, especially in the mountains, you will almost certainly have to ski or snowshoe to your campsite.

Winter weather can be totally unforgiving of the mistakes you make, so you have to know what you're doing before you go snow camping. It can be relaxing fun if you do it correctly; if not, it can

People often come to the Jenny Lake ranger station and ask whether they need an ice axe to travel some trail they've heard is covered with snow. If they come in with their own beat-up axe, chances are they won't even need it because they already know how to travel on snow. If they come in without one, and are planning to rent one in town, chances are it won't do them any good anyway, and they should simply stay off the trail.

—Ranger Jim Springer

be fatal. If you are older than forty-five or out of shape, check with your doctor before you begin something as strenuous as backpacking on skis or snowshoes. Work up to cold-weather overnighters by taking ski lessons, talking to experienced people, reading books, and acquiring your own short-term experience.

Unless you are a highly experienced winter camper, don't try to take your children on a cross-country ski camping trip. Even if you're the reincarnation of John Muir, start with slow, short day hikes. Test equipment—and resolve— in your backyard (if snow-covered), or within shouting distance of your parked car. Once everyone in your group has become a strong skier and an able summer camper, consider an overnight excursion. Even then, keep trips short, avoid bad weather, and take enough gear and clothing to assure a cozy camp. Consider going in the spring, with its longer days and warmer weather.

For beginners, the choice of terrain is very important. Flat terrain is easier, but hills are more interesting and challenging. Until you learn to control your speed, avoid long, steep downhills. Also avoid deep snow, steep open slopes, snowy ravines and riverbanks, snow-laden trees and ledges, and ice overhangs. Learn to spot drifts from far off. If you fall in snow, brush it off immediately, before it can melt and soak clothing. Avoid chilling; it could lead to hypothermia.

Respect the power of winter, and scale down from your summer mileage. Start later in the day, to let the sun cut through the chill, and quit earlier. Tolerably chilly weather can become intolerable once the sun dips behind the hills, which in winter elevations can be unexpectedly early.

■ Cross-Country Skiing

Cross-country skiing is a fun way to share sport and wilderness with friends and family. It has lagged behind downhill skiing in popularity in the United States, but for all-around aerobic benefits, it's the front-runner. By using muscles in the shoulders, back, chest, abdomen, buttocks, and legs, cross-country skiers can burn as many as six hundred to nine hundred calories per hour. Olympic-level cross-country skiers expend upward of one thousand calories per hour and have set records for the highest level of oxygen consumption (VO_2 max), indicating excellent aerobic fitness. The kick-and-glide technique, combined with two-arm poling, offers a more complete workout than running or cycling.

Cross-country skiing has other advantages over downhill, including cheaper equipment and a lower risk of injury. Cross-country skiers don't have to make reservations at high-priced ski resorts, nor do they have to fight lift-line crowds. Once you're gliding along the ski trails, the sport is an exhilarating mix of exercise and meditation.

> In January 1990, Leo Hennessy was putting up signs on a cross-country ski trail in a remote area north of Boise, Idaho. A few old ponderosa pines poked about six feet above the snow. Just before dusk, without warning, one of those two-hundred-year-old pines burst into flames and crowned out in five minutes. Hennessy's first thought was biblical—God's own burning bush. He later learned the more secular truth from the Forest Service: The area had recently been control-burned and the fire had no doubt been smoldering in the tree's roots for days.

Depending on where you live, you may be able to ski in a nearby park or even in your own backyard. Most people don't need a lesson before starting out, but a good teacher can do wonders.

Equipment

Cross-country skis, are narrower, lighter, and longer than downhill skis. They're available as either waxable or waxless. The bottoms of waxless skis are molded into patterns that allow for gliding uphill as well as downhill. Most novices find it easier to start out with waxless skis because they're less hassle and provide more downhill control. Once they become more proficient, they usually opt for the speed and superior performance of waxable skis.

> A good way to make sure you get the right length skis is to stand and reach your arm straight up; your ski should measure from your wrist to the ground. Beginners, however, may find slightly shorter skis more maneuverable.

Until recently, all cross-country touring skis were made of wood and thus had to be waxed. Many still are today. When the proper wax is applied, the skier can glide uphill without slipping backward. The type of wax used depends on temperature and snow conditions. Although waxing for cold, dry snow is easy, it can be maddening in wet or changeable snow. For temperatures below freezing, hard waxes are best; for spring skiing, klisters, which have a softer consistency, are squeezed from a tube onto the skis. Waxing is a fine art, and experience will improve your technique.

The cross-country ski boot resembles a hiking boot. The binding attaches only to the front of the boot, leaving the heel of the rear leg free to lift off the ski. Although this provides less control on turns, it lessens the chances of blowing out a knee or ankle.

Most cross-country skiers will want their poles about armpit high, though adjustable poles are a great benefit on, say, a long, sidehill traverse. Touring poles should have a metal tip, a strap large enough to accommodate your heavily mittened hand, and a sturdy shaft made of fiberglass or cane. The pole basket is light, breakable plastic, so carry spare baskets in your repair kit.

If you are new to skiing and live in a snowless area, practice inside on a rug (with unwaxed skis). Clear out a room and get used to your boots and skis (save the poles for later). Become accustomed to those weird appendages attached to your feet. If you live where snow covers the ground, begin by trying to circumnavigate your house; or ski to the end of the block and back. Get used to carrying a loaded fanny pack or day pack. Learn how to move without crossing your skis, how to get up from a fall by yourself, and how to buckle and unbuckle your bindings.

Tips

When learning to cross-country ski, start by just walking, first on the flats, and then on increasingly steep up- and downhills. Graduate eventually to bending your knees and gliding along with your body at a forty-five to sixty-degree angle to the ground. The upper and lower body should work together in a rhythm of kicks, long glides, and poling strokes.

Cross-country ski machines, available in many gyms and health clubs, mimic the sport's motions and give you a good workout, but they won't help improve your technique on the snow.

■ Snowshoeing

When the going gets tough, the tough often turn to snowshoes. Even accomplished cross-country skiers will occasionally confront winter conditions that cry out for an alternative means of transportation. When the trail peters out and you're face-to-face with three feet of soft powder and a dense forest, you'll be glad you brought those snowshoes.

One huge advantage of snowshoeing is that it requires almost no experience. It resembles hiking, in that you travel one step at a time. You may have to adjust your backpacking gait slightly and you'll probably want to start out using ski poles for balance, but it won't be long before you're striding easily through the snowy woods. Although walking on snowshoes burns more energy than skiing, capable snowshoers tout the sport as quiet, relaxing, and contemplative.

Before spending two or three hundred dollars on a pair of snowshoes, attend a snowshoe demo or festival and sample some of the available models.

Snowshoe Anatomy

Decking. The decking is the material of the snowshoe's surface area. In the old days, the decking was catgut webbing strung across a wooden frame. Although this type of shoe is still available and quite functional, the new breed of snowshoes relies on solid sheets of rugged, lightweight materials like Hypalon (a rubbery, resilient nylon), vinyl, or polyurethane-coated nylon, all of which offer better flotation with a smaller surface area. (The smaller the surface area, the more natural your stride.)

Shape. Made of either traditional wood or lightweight aluminum tubing, most frames fall in one of three categories. Oval shoes offer the best flotation; shoes with tapered tails track best because the tail acts as a rudder; asymmetrical shoes allow the most natural gait.

Bindings. This is where the most radical design changes have occurred in recent years. Today, you have three basic choices of bindings: lace-up, buckle, and ratchet.

- Lace-up bindings are simple, secure, and widely adjustable; they work with light or heavy hiking boots, as well as insulated pack boots.

- Buckle bindings use nylon webbing and molded plastic buckles, just like the ones on your backpack. Although buckle bindings are lightweight and inexpensive, they sometimes jam with snow and can loosen as you walk.

- Ratchet bindings, borrowed from snowboarding, are the newest development in snowshoes. They buckle across the toe and behind the heel for quick, easy, and secure adjustments. But they are heavier and costlier than the other bindings, and testers for *Backpacker* magazine found it difficult to adjust them properly. You tend to want to tighten them down, "but then the hard plastic bands bind into your foot. Loosen them too much and your foot slides around," said one tester.

Weight. Some snowshoes weigh less than two and a half pounds; others more than five pounds. All other things being equal, or even slightly inferior, a lightweight snowshoe is tough to pass up.

Size. Backcountry snowshoes generally come in three sizes: eight by twenty-five inches, nine by thirty inches, and ten by thirty-five inches, although there may be slight variations by brand. The size that's right for you depends on two things: your weight with loaded pack and snow conditions.

Total weight	deep, dry, powdery snow	dense, wet, compact snow
under 150 lbs.	8 x 25 in.	8 x 25 in.
150 to 175 lbs.	9 x 30 in.	8 x 25 in.
175 to 200 lbs.	10 x 35 in.	9 x 30 in.
over 200 lbs.	10 x 35 in.	10 x 35 in.

▪ Winter Wear

The layering techniques you learned while summer camping are even more critical in winter. Both skiing and snowshoeing burn loads of calories, which means you generate a lot of heat even on the coldest days. Wear enough for warmth but not too much. Even a slow-moving skier should become warm enough to shed a layer or two. Try to peel off outer garments before sweat dampens inner layers. Parents must be alert to the layering needs of young children, who may be slow to speak up.

When choosing winter clothes, look for wool and synthetic fills, which retain heat better than cotton or down when wet. Snow-camping instructors like to say "cotton kills."

On both the upper and lower body, you should have on a breathable inner layer of long underwear made of lightweight, high-performance polyester, such as Capilene or polypropylene, to provide valuable insulation and wick perspiration away from your body. The next layers can be a fleece or pile shirt or sweater covered by a nylon windbreaker or rain jacket. In dry-snow areas, you can substitute a wind shirt or wind jacket. If you are traveling in cold weather with stop-and-go children, you may need a fiberfill-insulated jacket on top of other clothing layers.

As a third layer, consider fiberfill-insulated overpants with a nylon outer shell. Such pants should have two-way, top-to-bottom leg zippers. With rising temperature or increased activity, you can open the leg zippers as far as necessary. When you stop skiing or playing in the snow, you can rezip the pants. If it gets warm enough, the leg zippers will allow you to remove the overpants without removing your boots.

In between your long-john bottoms and overpants, you should wear another pair of pants. This middle layer can be polypropylene, silk, or wool. Avoid cotton, especially jeans, which soak up water and take forever to dry. If you skip this middle layer and wear only outerpants, you cannot remove a layer unless you are willing to ski in your long underwear.

Mittens are warmer than gloves but permit less fine motor control. Layers let you adjust for temperature fluctuations. Nylon, windbreaking outer mittens shed snow effectively. For snow play, fiberfill-insulated mittens stay warm even if they get wet.

Since much heat is lost through the head and neck, a hat and a hood are musts. Some hats tie under the chin and protect the ears; balaclava-style hats cover chin, ears, and forehead, and generally roll up into a watch cap. On warm days a headband or a baseball cap can be used, but always carry a soft, warm hat, too.

For extra warmth, wear more than one pair of socks (don't forget to take them with you when you buy your boots). To control moisture and prevent itching, wear a wick-drying, noncotton liner sock next to your skin. Carry extra socks, too, as the ones you wear are bound to get wet.

Cross-country ski boots have a sole that extends beyond the boot so that it can slip under the toe hold on a cable binding or into the clip closure of a pin binding. They come in leather (expensive) or with synthetic-coated uppers (less expensive). Look for fleece linings—they offer greater warmth.

Beginners should rent, rather than buy, skis and boots. As your commitment to the sport grows, you might search for secondhand gear. Consider ski swaps, used-boot departments of outdoor stores, and trades with others who cross-country ski.

■ Objective Hazards

Falling rock, collapsing cornices and seracs, storms, hidden crevasses, avalanches, and weak snow bridges are often called "objective hazards," as though we can do nothing to avoid them. There are, however, precautions to take. Moreover, by accepting some responsibility for mountain hazards, we are more likely to be careful, further minimizing the risk.

We should cross zones of rockfall only when the rocks are solidly in place, avoiding the morning thaw and evening freeze; we should allow enough time for new snow to settle and stabilize before we commit ourselves to an avalanche slope; we should rope up when snow hides crevasses, and unrope to move faster when that is appropriate; we should be prepared for freezing temperatures and storms; we should allow time to acclimatize properly, listen to our cautious side a little more, and avoid gambling recklessly.

Avalanche Avoidance

Winter campers must do their research. Read guidebooks, look at maps, talk to rangers, and pay attention to weather forecasts. Take calculated risks only. Boot Hill is filled with the bodies of people who marched arrogantly into battle against Mother Nature. Rule number one is to be alert to areas with high avalanche danger. Contact a ranger for advice on snow conditions. If no ranger is available, the ski patrol at an established downhill resort should have that information.

Snow avalanches are of two main types: 1) loose snow avalanches, which start at a point and gather mass into a fan shape as they fall, and 2) cohesive slab avalanches, which start sliding over a large area all at once, creating a well-defined fracture line.

Both types require a "trigger," which may be a falling rock or cornice, the collapse of a weak layer in the snowpack, a sudden change in temperature or barometric pressure, wind, new snowfall, a nearby jet breaking the sound barrier, or the weight of a hiker.

Of the two types, slab avalanches are more likely to be started by the weight of a climber on a stressed slab that is weakly bonded to the ground or to other layers within the snowpack. An avalanche of either type need only travel a short distance to gain deadly force and mass. People have been buried at the bottom of a thirty-foot slope.

The following information can improve your chances of avoiding, and if necessary surviving, an avalanche.

- Avalanches most often occur on slopes between thirty and forty-five degrees, low-angle enough to allow poorly bonded snow to accumulate to significant depths.

- Slab avalanches most often occur on convex-shaped slopes, though they may occur on concave-shaped slopes if other factors overcome the natural compression on such slopes.

- Snow on north-facing slopes in the Northern Hemisphere (and south-facing slopes in the Southern Hemisphere) receive less sun, so such slopes are often slower to stabilize than other slopes.

- Snow tends to be blown from windward slopes and deposited as slabs on leeward slopes, which are often unstable.

- If surface features such as rocks, trees, or brush are visible above the snowpack in significant quantity, they will help anchor the snow. Once those features are buried, avalanche danger increases.

- If the rate of new snowfall is greater than about an inch per hour, avalanches are more likely to occur.

- If wind is present, the danger increases rapidly. In the absence of new snow, wind is the major contributor to instability. Sustained wind will push loose snow into gullies and slopes on the leeward sides, forming slabs.

- New snow is not necessarily deposited evenly on every slope, so be alert to variations in depth. When six inches of new snow builds up on a slope without sloughing, avalanche conditions are dangerous.

- Storms starting with low temperatures and dry snow, followed by rising temperatures, are a recipe for avalanches. The dry snow at the start forms a poor bond to the old snow or icy surface. On the other hand, if a storm starts warm then gets colder, bonding is improved.

- Wet-snow avalanches occur most often during the first prolonged spring thaw. In the high mountains, however, wet-snow avalanche danger may exist throughout the summer.

- The art of avalanche avoidance requires constant vigilance. As you travel through the mountains, take note of old avalanche paths, especially those that show signs of recent activity, as those slopes will be most likely to slide again.

- If the snow cracks and the fractures travel for some distance, avalanche danger is high.

- If a slope is suspect, dig a snow pit through the snowpack on that slope and examine the various layers of snow. Take a handful of snow from each of the layers and try to form a snowball. If it holds together well, then that layer is probably stable.

- The safest routes follow ridge crests on the windward side below the potential fracture line of a cornice.

- On dangerous open slopes or wide couloirs, climb up and down the edges in a straight line. Switchbacks in the middle are likely to cause an unstable slope to slide.

- Traverse dangerous slopes or couloirs at the top, above the release zone. If you can't cross above the release zone, make an even longer detour if necessary and cross well below the bottom of the slope.

- If you must cross a suspect slope, only one person should cross at a time, with the others waiting their turn in a safe location and watching each exposed climber carefully. Don't assume a slope is safe because one person crossed it safely.

- Roped belays are only useful on small slopes. The force of a major avalanche will make it impossible to hold a victim. Trailing nonwhite parachute cord from your pack, however, may aid any rescue effort.

- While traveling in dangerous areas, unhook the belly strap of your backpack to assure that you can quickly drop it if necessary. Wear your gloves and hat, and secure all openings in your clothing to help prevent frostbite and hypothermia should you be caught in an avalanche.

- If you are caught in an avalanche, get rid of your pack and all equipment, and try to stay near the surface of the sliding snow by "swimming." Try to make it to the side of the avalanche.

- As the snow slows down, keep your hands in front of your face, trying to create an air pocket when the snow stops.

- If you are buried, you will survive longer, hopefully until your partners find you, if you don't panic.

> If you figure to trek through avalanche country, rent at least two beepers.

- Members of a party should mark the spot where a victim was first caught and also the place last seen to aid them in the search.

- After locating and freeing an avalanche victim, treat for suffocation, shock, traumatic injuries, hypothermia, or frostbite, as appropriate.

Bivouacs

If you get caught out after dark without your tent, you may have to bivouac. A forced bivouac with no tent, bivy sack, or snow cave is the least comfortable and potentially most dangerous option, though there is a big difference between one bivouac and a series of them. Each night will likely be damper and colder than the one before.

When choosing a bivouac site, keep in mind that the landscape is ever changing. Thus, you should avoid camping beneath loose rock or in an avalanche chute.

Other tips:

- If the loose rock is snow-encrusted and gets early-morning sun, move out early in the morning before it heats up.

- Look for shelter protected by an overhang, which will shield you from rain and rockfall.

- If you bivouac in a forest, sleep right next to a tree, which will be warmer than out in the open.

- If your perch is precarious, anchor yourself to the land to prevent a fatal sleepwalk.

- If sleeping in talus or loose rock, build a rock barrier to prevent yourself from rolling off.

- If traveling where others have gone before, look for sleeping areas already flattened out. Make a nest out of conifer branches. This is one time when your survival takes precedence over environmental concerns.

- If survival is still an issue, dig a deep snow cave. Both the arduous task of excavating and the hole you create will keep you warm.

- Place your skis upright in the snow, crossing them in the shape of the biggest possible X you can make. X is the international ground-air emergency signal for "Unable to proceed."

To avoid emergency bivouacs, start early and quit early. That will also help you avoid problems like loose rock, avalanches, and afternoon thunderstorms. If you know that it's six hours to your destination and that storms typically roll in around two in the afternoon, you should start before eight in the morning. Add a cushion of time to cover things that might go wrong, because things always go wrong. They may be small things, causing little delay, and so you finish early. So what? Take the rest of the day off.

Another emergency option, if conditions permit, is to build a snow cave. Sheltered from the elements, a snow cave can be an ideal shelter. Winds will not affect you and, with luck, avalanches should roll right over you as well. A snow cave is far warmer than a tent at night, but pleasantly cooler in the heat of the midday sun. The disadvantage of a snow cave is that digging it is tiring, time-consuming work, and it's not always easy to find the soft, deep snow you need. For more information on a snow cave, see the Department of the Army Field Manual #21-76, entitled "Survival."

You can also build an excellent shelter using dead vegetation and other debris. See the section "Making Shelter" on page 218.

The danger of bivouacking can be mitigated by any or all of the following: a bivouac sack (though there may be no suitable ledge on which to put it); a good Gore-Tex sleeping bag; a good jacket with a large hood. In the absence of all those items, hug the one you're with.

■ Surviving Exposure

If you're caught out alone on a cold night, your survival may depend on your ability to generate heat, which is a product of how much work you do.

Climber and backpacker Peter Croft once endured an unexpected bivouac at nineteen thousand feet in Nepal. As he describes it: "The idea of an unprotected bivouac almost four thousand feet above the highest elevation I'd ever slept was scary. I had no idea of my survival potential, but with no down jacket, sleeping bag, or bivy gear, matters seemed pretty serious. Realizing that movement was the key to getting through the night, I started hacking away at an ice slope with my axe. I kept moving all night: shifting positions, rolling boulders down the mountain (cool crashes and flying sparks), doing isometrics. For hours, I tensed the muscles in my feet, calves, thighs, hands, and face, and back down again. Tense and relax, tense and relax, hundreds of times.

"It was a tough night for rest, but what should have been the worst part of the trip turned out to be one of the best parts."

Chapter Eleven

SURVIVAL SKILLS

*To survive it is often necessary to fight, and
to fight you have to dirty yourself.*

—George Orwell

F EW skills are more valuable than the ability to
cope when things go awry. Besides the psychological strength needed to think clearly, you must be
educated in survival techniques. Think of it as an insurance policy,
an antidote against ignorance, which can be fatal when you're going
up against Mother Nature. The misguided have died of hypothermia
less than a mile from help; the misinformed, of dehydration with
water still in their canteens; the ignorant, of starvation with food
growing all around them.

Before you even start the quest for information, work on increasing your sensory awareness. Start paying more attention to detail, big
and small, subtle and obvious, extraordinary and common. Tune in
to all five senses, not just the overused eyes. Experience the power of
sounds, smells, tastes, and textures.

This survival kit is light, so you can routinely carry it whenever
you go off day hiking. It may seem excessive on a sunny day, but
imagine if it suddenly started blowing and raining and you got lost.
Ask yourself: Could you spend the night out with just what's in your
pack?

Survival tip number one is that most accidents start with a series
of seemingly minor mishaps that swell into major misfortune. Say

Make a survival kit and carry it in your daypack. The ultimate kit for the fanatically prepared would include:

- Butane lighter
- Candle
- Matches
- Whistle
- Plastic bags
- Signal mirror
- Map and compass
- Flashlight (with headband and fresh batteries)
- Coins for a phone
- Toilet paper
- Sunscreen
- Lip balm
- Water bottle
- Water filter or iodine tablets
- Swiss Army knife
- PowerBars or trail mix
- Plastic cup and spoon
- Waterproof shell, top and bottoms
- Long johns
- Mittens
- Sunglasses
- Nylon rope
- Space blanket
- First-aid kit
- Hackey Sack (a footbag for keeping warm and passing time)

you're hiking above treeline late in the day. You're getting colder and colder, but you're in a hurry to reach the summit of Mount Rigorous, so you put off stopping to fiddle with your sweater. Before long, your concentration and coordination start to shred, then you stumble and fall, you break your ankle, and now you are faced with real trouble. Stop the progression early and head off the problem.

These are the skills necessary to survive alone in the wild:

- Wayfinding
- Making shelter
- Finding water
- Making fire
- Signaling for help
- Finding food
- Forecasting weather

■ Wayfinding

It would be nice if every backpacker carried a compass and knew how to use it—but it won't happen. That's why using nature to find your way is such a handy skill. Being a skilled wayfinder means being alert and tapping into all five senses. That takes concentration and practice. Try some of the exercises at the end of this chapter to stimulate your senses.

Study the countryside as you move through it. Frequently stop and look backward over the land just traversed. Note how it looks going the other way, keying on dramatic and unusual features. Known as "taking a back bearing," this should be done routinely.

Note your position relative to landmarks. Talk to others about it. As you hike around a ridge or peak, take mental photographs of how it looks from different angles; remember the route you've taken in relation to such landmarks. After you set up camp, walk a circle around it, noting how it looks from all angles.

Involve others in your group in route finding, even if you're just following a trail. Pull out the map at rest stops and discuss the route. Ask children to show you where you are on the map. Help them by comparing real cliffs, rivers, and trail junctions with those depicted on the map.

Direction

Okay, you're lost—or at least you think you are. First and foremost, don't panic. Take several deep breaths, recite a mantra, ease yourself into a yoga position—whatever it takes to stay calm.

If you have a whistle, give it three distinct blasts. Three of anything is the international signal for "Help!" If you get no response, then STOP; this is an acronym for Sit, Think, Observe, and Plan. Some will be comforted by reciting the following ditty aloud—"Camper not lost. Camper right here. Campsite lost."

If others will be searching for you, keep in mind that further wandering will only make it harder for rescuers to find you. Instead of darting all about, mentally retrace your steps. After calm reflection, the right route often miraculously appears. If not, explore the immediate area, marking your original spot and returning to it after your initial search.

Project Hug-a-Tree (www.tbt. com/hugatree) offers basic survival training to schools and clubs. Even if you don't contact them, remember the name—it carries an important message. Hugging a tree when you've lost helps ground you, averts panic, and forces you to stay put. Teach your children this technique.

If you are lost and staying put, the following will help you prolong your survival time:

- Remain quiet unless signaling. Keep your mouth closed to prevent evaporation of moisture.

- Undertake no unnecessary activity. Exception: If you're suffering from the cold, move about to create heat and avoid hypothermia.

- Take advantage of the coolest microclimate available: rest in shade; if possible, elevate yourself some inches above the hot ground.

- Remain clothed. Wear a hat; if unavailable, improvise one. Put a plastic produce bag between your socks and shoes.

- Wear sunglasses. If unavailable and glare is a problem, improvise some slit glasses (or blacken beneath the eyes with oil or soot).

- If water is available, drink often to prevent dehydration. Ration your sweat, not your drinking water.

- Do not drink urine, sweat, or seawater. If you are desperate, you can gain cooling benefits by dipping clothes in seawater or urinating on clothes or skin.

- Do not take salt tablets unless there's plenty of water.

- Do not eat unless there's plenty of water. If water is limited, consume carbohydrates before protein.

Eventually, if staying put fails, you may have to try to walk to safety. You may feel the need, for example, after some time has passed, if rescue does not seem imminent, and water, food, and shelter are lacking.

As you walk, stay alert to signs of water, food, other people, or rescue efforts. Be prepared to signal to rescuers. Unless you know better, move downhill in your search for help. If you find a road, stay on it.

If water is short, avoid walking in the heat of the day. Night walking may deplete water more slowly, but without a moon, you risk walking right off a cliff. Walking in the early morning and evening is a good compromise, offering better visibility and fewer accidents.

Take the easiest route, avoiding obstacles whenever possible. Try to skirt steep gullies and cliffs that can sap energy. If you must tackle a steep incline, take a zigzag or switchback route. Stay in control and conserve energy.

If you're on the other end—you've lost someone—fight the urge to panic. Take a few deep breaths and blast your whistle three times, listening carefully for a response. If you have no whistle, yell. Retrace your steps and mark the last place you saw the lost one. Whistle again; if no response, send for help. Include information about the lost hiker: physical description, clothing, footwear, and the time and place last seen.

Sometimes determining direction is easy. For example, most people standing on one coast or another with the sun low in the sky can roughly gauge east and west merely by recalling that solar verity: "The sun rises in the east and sets in the west." Having established west, face that direction. North is on your right, south on your left.

Of course, most of the time the sun doesn't rise due east or set due west. On top of that, you may be a thousand miles from a coast, lost in the wilds of, say, Kansas, the sun high in the sky. If so, would you be able to tell north from south? If the answer is no, try the stick-and-shadow method. It's easy, and everyone will enjoy it, especially if they're not lost.

Find a flat, clear piece of ground. Drive a three-foot-long stick into the ground. Cut two other sticks about a

All the high-tech gear in the world is no substitute for a little common sense. In the summer of 1996, a hiking couple got lost in the White Mountains of New Hampshire. They had packed a GPS unit and cellular phone, so they called the sheriff's department for help. Although they didn't know the name of the trail they were on, they were able to give rescuers a precise reading of their longitude and latitude. The rescuers gave the couple directions to the nearest trail junction.

When they reached the junction, the couple still didn't know which way to go, so they called the fire department. When rescuers finally found them, they learned that the couple had no map.

foot long and drive one into the ground at the tip of the shadow cast by the three-foot stick. Come back twenty minutes later. Insert the remaining stick at the tip of the new shadow. It will have moved from the first mark. Now find or cut a direction-pointer stick and mark one end with tape or knife marks. Lay it against the two small sticks with the marked end against the second stick. The marked end points east (as the sun moves west, the shadow it casts moves east); the unmarked end points west.

Need to know how long before sunset? Extend your hand at arm's length, thumb up (as though shaking hands). Count the number of fingers between horizon and sun. Time until sunset is ten to twelve minutes for each finger.

If you have any kind of watch, or can determine the approximate time, you can figure direction by recalling that in western America the summer sun rises a little north of due east, lies due south at noon (standard time), and sets a little north of due west. The path of the winter sun lies far to the south, rising south of east and setting south of west.

When stars are visible, look for Polaris, the North Star, which is never more than one degree from true north. It's at the tip of the handle of the Little Dipper, a constellation high in the summer sky, but the easiest way to locate it is to start at the Big Dipper. The two stars located on the outer edge of the cup (farthest from the handle) are called pointers. They point upward to the nearby North Star. Thus the North Star is opposite the open side of the dipper.

Actually, any star can teach you direction. Like the sun and the moon, most stars move east to west across the sky. That's because the Earth is revolving beneath them; the North Star, directly over the North Pole, does not appear to move at all.

To confirm that stars move, drive a stick into the ground, then back up and drive another stick into the ground. Sight along the tops of the two sticks at a star. Keep watching the star. Which direction does it move? If it moves to the left, you are looking north; to the right means you are looking south; a rising star means east, a setting star west. Of course, you only have to remember that a rising star means you're facing east and a left-moving star means you're facing north—the opposites will take care of themselves.

Nature provides plenty of other directional clues:

- Snow is generally more granular on southern slopes.

- Evergreens are bushiest on the eastern side.

- The tops of pines and hemlocks point east.

- Vegetation is larger and more open on the northern slopes, smaller and denser on southern slopes.

- Many plants orient themselves toward the sun. Others, like the compass plant, align their leaves north-south to shade themselves.

- The smell of a wind blowing off the ocean can lead you to shore.

- The path of migrating birds (flyway) offers directional hints. The ancient Polynesians traveled thousands of miles in open waters using flyways to guide them.

- Birds build nests in the most protected places. More nests on one side of an area's bushes or trees suggests which way the wind blows. If you know the prevailing winds, you have a shot at figuring direction.

Distance

With a map and proper techniques, you can answer two important preliminary questions: Can I get there from here? How long will it take me?

Let's say the map tells you that you should follow a trail to a certain point and then cut west into the woods to reach the lake with the big fish. How far is that cutoff point and how long will it take you to reach it? Unless you are wearing a pedometer, an instrument that straps to your leg and measures the distance walked, this figure will be an estimate. Try to raise it to the level of an educated guess.

Knowing how fast you walk will help you estimate how far you've walked. A young, well-conditioned athlete walking swiftly on level ground carrying not too much weight can do about four miles per hour (mph). In mountainous terrain above six thousand feet, the same backpacker will do well to average three mph. The average city-bred backpacker will be closer to two mph. Add kids to the mix and that figure can drop to one mph or less.

You can measure distance by counting footsteps and multiplying by the length of the hiker's stride. All you need to figure stride is a tape measure and a place to walk. Children especially will enjoy doing this.

Lay out the tape measure in a straight line. Start at the beginning of the tape and walk along it with a natural pace, counting your steps. To figure stride length, simply divide the distance walked by the number of steps. If you take eighteen steps to walk fifty feet, then fifty divided by eighteen equals a stride of 2.77 feet, or 33.24 inches.

List some places within walking distance of home and guess the distance. Check your accuracy by counting steps and doing the arithmetic. Hint number one: Count only the right footfall and multiply by two. Hint number two: There are 63,360 inches in a mile.

As a map exercise, take a pipe cleaner and bend it to the shape of the route. Put one end at the start and trace the route with the pipe cleaner. If you are following a trail, bend the pipe cleaner to conform to its twists and turns. Using your thumbnail to mark the point where the pipe cleaner crosses your destination, straighten the pipe cleaner, line it up with the map's bar scale, and read the distance. Add a pessimism factor of 10 percent to account for the curves and switchbacks that don't show up on the map.

You can also measure map distance with the ruler edge of an orienteering compass, though such a straight edge measures the distance the proverbial crow flies, ignoring the inevitable zigging and zagging of trails. Your calculations will be more accurate if you add 20 percent or so to your straight-edge distance.

Let's say that your educated guess is that you should follow a stream for one hundred meters, then cut west into the woods. How to figure one hundred meters?

The easiest, but least precise, way is to know how fast you move over various terrain and then watch your watch. The following chart indicates how many minutes the average person takes to cover one mile. (You may want to adjust the numbers up or down to reflect your own pace.)

Highway	15 minutes per mile
Open field	25 minutes per mile
Open woods	30 minutes per mile
Forest	40 minutes per mile
Mountain	40 minutes per mile

Compass

Historians cannot agree on the compass's precise date of origin, though credit for discovering magnetism in lodestone goes to the Chinese. Early compasses were primitive—a piece of lodestone floating on a cork in a bowl of water. More elaborate early compasses, with magnets shaped like fish or turtles, appeared in Chinese books in the eleventh and twelfth centuries.

It was not until 1260, when that great backpacker Marco Polo returned from China, that Europe had the compass. Before then, Europeans had relied on the sun and the North Star for navigation. By the fifteenth century, marine compasses were widely available in Europe. Refinement continued into the twentieth century.

In 1933 Bjorn Kjellstrom combined a protractor with a standard needle compass, and the modern orienteering compass (O-compass) was born. It is now the most popular recreational and sporting compass on the market. Although the O-compass is more versatile than the old ore-bearing rock suspended from a thong, it's really just as simple in principle. The basis of both is the fact that a small magnetized needle suspended in a housing always swings to point north.

Still, the orienteering compass beats the rock and thong in several ways:

- You can determine bearings from a map without a separate protractor or having to orient the map to north. This means you can set the bearing while shuffling through nature.

- Your direction-of-travel (bearing) is retained by the protractor setting. There's nothing to memorize or write down.

- The ruled scale along the edge of the plastic baseplate makes it easy to figure map distances.

- Liquid-damped needles reduce oscillation in seconds. The system works at temperatures to about forty degrees below zero.

- It's so simple that an eight-year-old can learn its basics in minutes.

Parts of a Compass

An orienteering compass is an amalgam of three basic parts:

1. Magnetic needle. If you keep your compass away from iron objects, the painted end of the needle always points north. This is very reassuring.

2. The housing. It is mounted on the baseplate so that it can be easily rotated. The bottom of the housing is transparent.

- Direction-of-travel arrow. This and any auxiliary direction lines and the longer edges of the baseplate all serve as direction lines.

- Orienting (or north) arrow. The (usually) red arrow at the bottom of the rotating compass housing. The lines parallel to the north arrow are called north-south lines.

3. The baseplate. Made of transparent plastic, with scales along its edges. Interchangeable scales are available on some models.

Using the Compass

Whole books have been written about land navigation, but you can learn the basics in about thirty minutes. First, determine which end of the needle points north. It is usually painted red. Keeping the compass flat, move it until the painted end points to *N*. Congratulations—you've found north. The unpainted end of the needle points south. East and west will quickly fall into place.

Because an orienteering compass is also a protractor, you can sight some landmark in the field and take its bearing, measured in degrees. This is simply the angle between two lines—one pointing north from your position and one pointing toward the landmark. Although accomplished backpackers seldom pay attention to their bearing numbers, taking a bearing is a useful skill, one that when mastered will boost your confidence in compassing.

Taking a bearing in the field is a simple three-step procedure.

1. Point the direction-of-travel arrow at the landmark. Hold the compass level so the needle swings freely.

2. With the baseplate still, rotate the housing until you have the needle in the gate—that is, until the painted end of the needle points to the *N* on the dial.

3. Read the bearing at the index mark. It's nice to remember this number, although if you keep the dial set, you can always read it there.

Maybe you already know the bearing to where you want to go, say sixty degrees, but you need to determine your line of travel—that is, which way to walk. First rotate the housing until the sixty-degree bearing is lined up with the direction-of-travel arrow. Then hold the compass level in front of you and pivot your body until the orienting arrow (the one at the bottom of the liquid-filled vial) lines up with

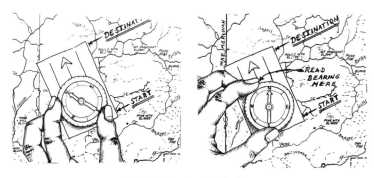

Illustrations by John Kelty

Step One: When using an orienteering compass as a protractor, place compass on the map in such a way that one edge of the compass touches both starting point and planned destination. Step Two: Rotate the movable housing until the orienteering arrow lies parallel to a map meridian. Then at the base of the direction-of-travel arrow, read the bearing of your destination in degrees.

the painted end of the needle. The direction-of-travel arrow now points the way to your destination.

Let's say you've climbed a mountain and want to take a different way down. You want to head for Magic Lake, where the big trout live. You can see it from the mountaintop, and so you take its bearing, which turns out to be 270 degrees (due west). The problem is, reaching Magic Lake means you have to drop into deep forest, obscuring your view of the lake.

You could just start out walking the bearing, but walking a straight line in rough terrain is harder than you realize. Better to sight along the direction-of-travel arrow and pick an intermediate landmark. In deep forest or fog, that might mean a target only fifty yards away.

Once you have moved to that target, sight again and choose another target near the visibility limit; move to that one and repeat the process until you reach your destination.

But let's say you come upon a cliff or a bog, something that forces you to leave your 270-degree bearing line. If you can see across the obstacle, the solution is as simple as one, two, three:

1. Sight along your bearing to some interim object on the far side of the obstacle.

2. Work your way around the obstacle.

3. Walk to the object you sighted.

If you can't see across the obstacle—the cliff is too high, the fog is too thick—then you will have to count steps and maintain proper direction while you skirt the obstacle. First decide if you plan to skirt left or right. Let's say you choose right. While standing on your bearing, make a ninety-degree turn to the right (the right angles of the compass baseplate can help guide you) and walk far enough to clear the width of the obstacle, counting your steps as you go. Then turn ninety degrees to the left and walk until you clear the length of the obstacle. (During this second leg, you are walking

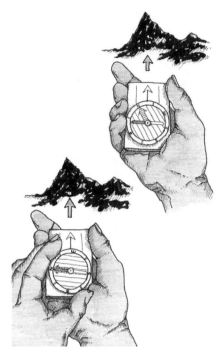

Taking a bearing.
• Point the direction-of-travel arrow at a selected landmark.
• Rotate housing until N on dial and painted end of needle align.
• Read bearing at direction-of-travel arrow.

Illustrations by John Kelty

parallel to your original bearing and can sight a nearby object and use the compass in the normal way to guide you; there is no need to count steps.) Once you have cleared the obstacle, make a ninety-degree left turn and go the same number of steps you took on the first leg. That puts you back on your original line of travel. Turn right, sight a landmark on your original bearing, and be off.

To return home, simply follow a bearing that is 180 degrees from your original bearing. Either add or subtract 180 degrees, whichever keeps your answer between 0 and 360. If you went out on a 270-degree bearing, you will come back along a 90-degree bearing (270 − 180 = 90). If you went out at 60 degrees, you will come back at 240 degrees (60 + 180 = 240). To skip the math, keep your compass set at the original bearing, and return with the direction-of-travel arrow pointed toward your body instead of away from it.

Declination. Your compass needle is actually pointing toward magnetic north. For reasons unknown, our planet has a magnetic north pole that is near, but not precisely at, the geographic north pole. The difference, or error, between these poles is called magnetic declination. It is read as an angle measurement, expressed in degrees. For North America, declinations range from about twenty-one degrees east (in northern Washington) to twenty degrees west (in northern Maine). If that seems backward, consider this example: A zero declination line runs through Wisconsin and then curves slightly southeast through the Florida Panhandle. As you go east of that line, your compass needle, locked on magnetic north, will move to the west of true north. Conversely, as you move west, your compass needle will move east.

Since the magnetized needle in your compass will always point to magnetic north, you must compensate or your readings will not correspond accurately to map coordinates, which are based on true north.

How far off course will you be if you ignore declination? Farther than you might think. For each degree of declination error ignored, you will be off almost eighteen feet per one thousand feet traveled, or about ninety feet per mile. Consider the example of a group of hikers in central Maine, where declination is twenty degrees. For each mile they hike without adjusting their course for declination, they will deviate from their final destination by ninety (feet) times twenty (degrees of declination being ignored), or 1,800 feet. If they hike three miles, they will be off by more than a mile.

Topographic Maps

All maps have three things in common: they are representations of some place, they use symbols, and they use some kind of scale. It's essential that you develop decent map skills. You can start by pulling out state and city maps, which show the land as though it were all one level (*planimetric* maps). Eventually you will want to graduate to *topographic* ("topo") maps, which use contour lines to show the shape of the land, or topography. If topo maps are too complicated for your children, draw them simple maps for a while.

Begin by reading the map's fine print. Find the arrow that indicates north. All topo maps are printed with the direction of true north toward the top of the map. Now find the scale, which usually looks like a ruler. It shows you how many inches (or centimeters) represent a mile (or kilometer) on that particular map. The scale of a map depends on how much area it covers. On a map of the United States, one inch may equal more than one hundred miles; on a topo map of a mountain, one inch might equal only a mile.

Next, look for the legend, which tells you what the symbols on the map mean.

> Study maps regularly, at least a few minutes every other day. Try putting them with your favorite magazines, by your bedside table, or in the john. As you look at a map of an area you know, try to picture how the symbols translate into actual terrain features.

For hikers, backpackers, fishermen, hunters, skiers, and other adventurers, topo maps are essential. You can find them in camping stores or order them from the United States Geological Survey.

At first glance, a topographic map looks like an incomprehensible jumble of squiggly lines, but it's really quite easy to read. Consider the ice-cream cone example. Imagine that you place an ice-cream cone upside down on a piece of paper. You want to draw a map of it, looking straight down, that will show its cone shape.

Draw a line around the base of the cone. That circle is the outside perimeter of the cone. Then measure all around the cone one inch up from the table and slice the cone along that line. Put the partial cone back on the paper and draw around the new base. You now have a circle within a circle. The inside circle represents all the points on the cone exactly one inch up from the table.

If you repeated the process, each time measuring another inch up from the table, you would have several concentric circles. Any point on a line is the same elevation as any other point on that line.

Each of those lines is called a *contour* line. Contour lines connect points of equal elevation, so they never intersect or overlap. You gain or lose elevation when you travel from one line to another. Lines close together indicate steep terrain, while lines far apart show the opposite. Walk along a single contour line and you will be on level ground.

Some other topographic truths:

- The vertical distance between contour lines—the *contour interval*—is given in the lower map margin. For Sierra topos, 15-minute series, the contour interval is eighty feet. That means if you walk from one line to the next, you are climbing or dropping eighty feet. The larger the contour level, the less detailed the map.

- Where contour lines are close together, you will find an abrupt drop, a falls or canyon.

- The closed (or "V") end of a contour line always points upstream.

- U-shaped contours indicate an outjutting ridge of a hill or mountain. The closed ends of the U's generally point downhill.

- Elevations are given periodically on many of the lines. The actual height of many objects—mountain peaks, settlements, trail junctions—is also noted, often marked with an X.

- Topos are commonly available in a 15-minute series, covering an area of about 13 by 17 miles, and 7½-minute series, covering about 6½ by 8½ miles. Map *minutes* are measures of distance, not time. There are sixty minutes in a *degree*, and one degree covers about seventy miles of latitude or longitude at the equator.

Topo Skills Quiz

I. Choose from the lettered answers to complete these statements.
Contour lines that are

1. Evenly spaced indicate_____.

2. Closely spaced indicate_____.

3. Widely spaced indicate_____.

4. Irregularly spaced indicate_____.
   a. Gentle slopes
   b. Varied terrain
   c. Steep slopes or cliffs
   d. Uniform slopes

II. True or False
1. Contour lines crossing a stream form V's that point downstream._____

2. Contour lines sometimes split, intersect, or cross._____

3. The farther apart contour lines are, the steeper the hillside._____

4. An intermittent stream is portrayed as a broken blue line._____

Answers

I.

    1. d   2. c   3. a   4. b

II.

    1. False. Contour crossing a stream valley form V's that point upstream.

    2. False. Contour lines never split, intersect, or cross. However, they may be so close together as to appear to converge, which represents a vertical, or nearly vertical, slope.

    3. False.

    4. True.

■ Making Shelter

I'd rather wake up in the middle of nowhere than in any city on earth.
          —Steve McQueen

The biggest outdoor killer is hypothermia (see pages 269–71), a condition in which the body loses more heat than it produces. If you get lost, making shelter is the most important skill you can have. You can survive for days with only water and an adequate shelter. Besides physical protection, shelters offer a sense of security, a psychological comfort for the lost and frightened.

The first step is to pick an emergency campsite. The ideal campsite has several important features:

- Protection from weather

- Protection from rockfall, flash floods, high tides, insects, harmful animals, and poisonous plants

- Level ground for a bed and fireplace

- Materials for making shelter and bed

- Firewood

- Food and water supply

The ideal shelter should retain heat as well as protect from wind, rain, and snow. Surviving means getting out of the wind, which chills and dehydrates. Natural features (such as caves and hollow logs; the leeward side of ridges, boulders, and overhangs; and deadfalls) may offer temporary refuge, but they can also be dangerous. Given wildlife's own fondness for natural shelters, you may just barge in on a sleeping bear, a nest of bees, or a coiled snake. Moreover, some natural shelters are naturally unstable and may collapse. An added problem is that they offer camouflage, making search and rescue more difficult.

In order to insure survival, you should learn how to construct at least a rudimentary shelter. The simplest man-made shelter, effective against rain but less so against cold, can be made from one decent conifer. Look for a spruce or pine tree with branches growing nearly to the ground. Break off enough lower limbs to allow room to sit against the tree. Use the broken boughs as insulation against the ground, or weave them through the other branches to make a tighter canopy.

If caught in blizzard country with night falling and weather worsening, find the leeward side of a ridge, boulder, or gully. Dig through

> In a pinch, a beaver lodge may offer shelter. After a beaver leaves, his dam often washes away, leaving his house high and dry. Enlarge the opening and you have a tight, waterproof shelter for sleeping. Abandoned beaver ponds usually have a good supply of dead trees lying around that can be used for firewood and shelter repairs.

the snow, if necessary, to hollow out a burrow. Line with vegetation; if not available, use sticks and logs (dirt gets very cold).

If no natural windbreaks are available, make a trench shelter. Dig a rectangular hole in the ground, about eight feet long and three feet wide, with the length of the hole at a right angle to the wind. If vegetation is available, use it for both bedding and roof. If snow is available, build a windbreak, piling it high on the windward side of the trench.

With time and sufficient materials, you can build a working shelter. Many survival books advise building wickiups or lean-tos, but debris shelters are easier. Pick an area that won't get washed out in a hard rain. It should be away from any rocks and trees that might fall, with good drainage, far from poisonous plants, and not over an anthill or animal hole.

Keep in mind that the air temperature under a thick stand of evergreens is up to ten degrees warmer than it is in open areas and that thick trees help break the wind, reducing the windchill factor. On the other hand, a thick forest is shielded from the sun and may be perpetually damp. The best place for a shelter is usually the transition area between forest and field.

Now find a boulder, a fallen tree, a stump, or some other object about three feet high. You have just completed one wall of your shelter. Next, find a stick several inches in diameter and five or more feet long. Lean one end of the stick on the object and rest the other end on the ground. That's the shelter's center ridgepole.

Next, collect a few bushels of smaller sticks to lean on both sides of the ridgepole, perpendicular to it. This forms the roof of the structure, with the ridgepole as the peak. Near the boulder, stump, or log, on the side away from the wind, leave an opening for a door.

At this point, crawl inside your shelter to make sure it is large enough. It should permit movement without kicking out the sides. If so, finish the outside by piling on a thick insulating

Building a shelter is strenuous work, and it's easy to move so quickly that you perspire heavily. Then when you stop, your body gets badly chilled, which can be life-threatening without a fire. Work at a moderate pace and minimize sweat.

layer of twigs and dried leaves. Add another layer of small branches to hold the insulation in place. Finally, taking a lesson from animals, stuff the inside with dried leaves, pine needles, or ferns, loosely filling the shelter from top to bottom. Need more insulation? Evergreen boughs make a comfortable bed.

With the shelter complete, you should be able to crawl inside feet-first and, if need be, survive warm and dry for days. After you're done, restore the environment to its natural state by breaking down the shelter and scattering it.

■ Finding Water

Many people think of finding food first, water second. But humans can actually live much longer without food than without water. According to the Backpacker's Law of Threes, you will die if you go longer than:

three minutes without air

three hours without shelter from a storm

three days without water

three weeks without food

Water is critical at any time of the year. Dehydration, which can strike even in the winter, worsens other outdoor ailments, such as hypothermia and frostbite. Lack of water also makes us more susceptible to the cold.

The water table is often close to the surface and can be located by digging in the following places:

- At the base of cliffs where more than a little vegetation is thriving.

- At the base of large sand dunes on the steep or shady side. If you hit wet sand, cease digging; if conditions are right, water will seep out of the sand into the hole you created. The primary water should be fresh; if you dig deeper, the lower water may contain salt.

- In dry mudholes, sinks, and at the outside bend of riverbeds.

- Anywhere the ground is damp or muddy.

- In low spots favored by indicator plants, which grow only where they can obtain water: sycamores, cottonwoods, cattails, salt grass, greasewood, willows, hackberries, and elderberries.

Obtaining water from the soil is possible if you do the following:

- Dig a hole in damp or muddy sinks, allowing water to seep in.

- Wring mud through a shirt or cloth to force out water.

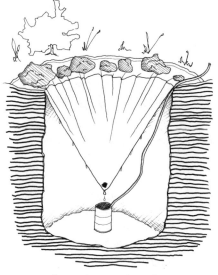

Illustration by John Kelty

- Construct an evaporation still, which requires a little equipment but almost no building skills. You need a container (usually a bucket), a plastic drinking tube, and a six-by-six-foot piece of clear plastic.

Dig a three-foot hole and place the container at the bottom of it. Arrange the drinking tube so that one end sits in the container and the other end extends outside the pit. Stretch the plastic sheet over the hole and hold it in place with dirt, which seals the hole off from the outside air. Place a rock in the center of the plastic to weigh it down until it sags to within two inches of the container.

The sun's warmth will penetrate the plastic and warm the soil in the hole. Moisture from the soil evaporates, then condenses on the underside of the plastic, where it runs down the cone and drips into the container. The water can be sucked right through the plastic tubing without disturbing the still.

Green plants placed in the pit will increase water production. It is best to locate stills in damp areas, lowlands, at the base of hills, in dry riverbeds, or in rich soil at the bottom of gullies.

Other sources of water include these:

- The dew from rocks and plants. In many arid parts of the globe, primitive peoples arise before dawn to collect dew. The easiest way is to mop gently with a handkerchief or shirt, then wring it into your mouth or a container. If cloth is not available, you can use a handful of dry grass. It is possible to mop up more than a pint an hour using this technique.

- If you're desperate (why else would you be mopping up dew?), you can cut and peel a cactus and suck out the moisture. The taste is vile, but it will slake thirst. Though dew is generally one of the safest water sources, don't mop from poisonous plants or chemically sprayed vegetation.

- In the Southwest, much of the desert is dotted with uplifted sandstone ridges that divide the land into valleys and drainages. These exposed areas of stone absorb little moisture, and even a skimpy rain can cause water to collect in tiny rock pockets. To find it, you must abandon your instinct to look in low land; instead seek high ground. Check side canyons, narrow clefts, and white sandstone ridges. Such pockets can sometimes hold water for months after a rain.

More Water Tips

- Animal tracks may lead you to water.

- Birds can sometimes be seen circling over, or heading toward, water holes, especially in the morning and evening. Listen for their calls and watch their flights.

- When you find water, mark it on your map with the date. Build a valuable history of water sources in your favorite areas.

- Beware of stagnant water bearing no signs of life. If the water has crawling or wriggling creatures, it probably is not deadly poisonous, though it may harbor harmful microorganisms. Animal tracks near water holes are a good sign, unless there are a lot of skeletal remains.

- Consider all water polluted, even if it looks good. Giardia does not discolor the water; it just makes you sick. Simple diarrhea or vomiting can dehydrate a body quickly, leaving the victim worse off than if he had stayed away from water altogether.

- Water polluted by animals or debris tastes bad, but it is harmless if purified or treated.

- Let muddy water stand overnight. Run it though a grass filter or several layers of cloth, or allow it to seep through the soil into a hole dug about a foot away.

- If the water supply is limited, walk slowly and avoid the midday heat. Eat little or not at all, as digestion depletes the body's water reserves.

- Sucking on pebbles and chewing gum slake thirst but do nothing to stave off dehydration.

- Drinking blood or urine increases dehydration, although soaking clothing in urine will cool the body and stem sweat loss.

- Store water in the stomach. People have died from dehydration with water still in their canteens.

■ Making Fire

Besides providing light and heat, a fire can aid in cooking, signaling, purifying water, and feeling more secure.

Many people learn fire skills as they're growing up. Outdoor author Tom Brown believes that a child of eight should be able to make a fire using primitive means. Whatever the learning pace, here is a logical order for children to earn merit badges in fire skills:

- Wood Gatherer

- Careful Observer of Adults Building and Maintaining Fires

- Assistant Fire Maintainer

- Chief Fire Maintainer

- Assistant Fire Builder

- Chief Fire Builder

Fire mavens should know all of the following and more:

- How to use matches safely. Stick matches are best for teaching kids.

- When it is appropriate and legal to have a fire. If possible, take your children to the site of a forest fire and show them the destruction.

- How to find dry wood under logs or around the base of trees.

- How to use a knife to expose dry wood inside of wet wood.

- How not to find wood, except in emergencies, on live trees.

- How to find the best size for kindling.

- How to break wood against rocks or stumps so it fits in the fire.

- How to avoid burning poison oak, ivy, and sumac.

- How to construct a tepee fire.

- How to position wood in the flames to maintain the fire.

- How to moderate the flame and create proper coals for cooking and roasting marshmallows.

- How to select a fire site that is distant from trails, waterways, standing rocks, and overhanging limbs; protected from the wind; relatively free of ground vegetation; neither beneath tree branches nor too close to a shelter; and, except in emergencies, in an established pit.

- How to put out a fire and camouflage the remains.

When it's time to build a fire from scratch, use a stick or rock to scratch out a fire hole, a shallow depression about twelve inches deep and two feet across. Clean the immediate area of vegetation (we've seen fires travel several feet through rich, loamy soil). Ring the hole with rocks to contain the fire. Use dirt, rocks, or wood to build a wall on the windward side of the fire. That will protect the flame from the wind, reflect heat, and conserve wood.

Everyone who is old enough should have in their survival kit a means of starting a fire. Matches are a terrific invention. They consistently beat striking rocks or rubbing two sticks together, two very challenging friction methods for starting a fire. Most people forced to rely on friction for a flame—without first having practiced and perfected the technique—will do better waiting to be struck by lightning.

No matter where you get your spark, you will need tinder. This can be last night's math homework, but if you want to perfect fire skills, practice with nature's own tinder. It can be found in many forms, including dead grass or dry twigs (shredded between the fingers), the inner bark of dead trees, dry moss, evergreen needles, downy feathers, abandoned nests, dried animal dung, cattail fluff, and oily birch bark. Other tinder candidates: paper, clothing, bandannas, and burnable trash. Ideally, tinder should be finely shredded but not powdered.

> If you want to master a primitive friction technique for starting fires, practice the hand-drill method. For more details, see "Survival," Department of the Army Field Manual #21-76.

Over a carefully placed ball of, say, shredded twig bark, pile tiny dry twigs, tepee style. A tepee's flame is hot and efficient and holds up well in rain. The twigs should be close enough to feed off one another, but not so close that oxygen fails to reach the core. Light the tinder in more than one place. If a prolonged flame is needed, try lighting a well-placed candle stub.

If you can't find an overhang and rain threatens the life of your young fire, cover it with bark slabs, being careful not to smother the flame. As the fire builds, gradually increase the size of the sticks. Don't drop or throw sticks on the fire—it sprays sparks and hinders air flow—but rather lay them on the fire carefully, maintaining the cone shape. After branches an inch or so in diameter are burning, you can hunt for bigger pieces. Increase the size of the fire until it

The Paiute Indians used to transport fires over long distances by ingeniously wrapping coals in a core of finely shredded bark, around which they wrapped more shredded bark, then several layers of bark strips. The finished package, resembling a cigar two feet long and six inches wide, could hold a live spark for up to twelve hours.

will burn logs six inches or more in diameter. Those will hold a fire for hours. If they can't be cut short enough, push the ends into the fire as they burn.

Know your woods. Softwoods, like pine and fir, start a fire more easily than hardwoods, like oak and birch. But they burn more quickly and, being full of pitch, have a tendency to spark.

Once a fire is made, it must be maintained. You can keep it going through the night by building up a deep bed of hot coals and banking them with ashes and a thin layer of dirt. You can also lay two green logs across the fire bed so that flames dart up between them. If they get a good start before the other wood burns out, they will smolder through the night. The key is to keep the wind from the coals. If it rains, cover the banked fire with bark, a flat stone, or something waterproof.

Some more fire tips:

- You can buy waterproof matches at an outdoor store, waterproof them yourself by dipping the tips in wax, or carry two dozen regular wooden ones (break and alternate ends) in a plastic 35mm film canister. This handy little container will keep matches dry even if you fall in a lake. Damp wooden matches can usually be dried by stroking them twenty to thirty times through your dry hair.

- Candle stubs can be a big help, especially if the wood is wet. They can sit in the fire timber for a long time, drying out the wood.

- You can direct sunlight through a magnifying glass (or any convex lens) to start a flame in tinder.

- Softwoods produce more light than hardwoods do.

- Use reflectors for added warmth.

- Use flames for boiling and baking, coals for frying.

- When leaving a fire for good, douse it with water, then douse it again.

- When using something other than a permanent fire site, scatter ashes and work them into the soil to remove all traces.

- Before building a fire on bare rock, put down a two-inch layer of sand or soil to prevent charring the rock. Scatter the protective layer when you are done. Archaeologists uncovering the remains of ancient civilizations have found rocks still smudged from fires that burned thousands of years ago.

Some wet-weather fire tips:

- Matches must be kept dry not just from water but from dampness, too.

- If it looks like it might rain, gather tinder and kindling for several fires and stash them under something waterproof.

- Split open wet logs to get to the dry wood inside.

- A disposable butane lighter should be good for a thousand lights even in wet weather.

- Use a fire starter (a petroleum gel) to prolong the flame so that the tinder has a chance to catch.

- If the damp tinder is slow to ignite, blow gently on the spark until it bursts into flame.

- In some parts of the country, you can find pitch wood—dead pine that is warted with dried sap. The sap burns easily, making it a natural fire starter.

■ Signaling for Help

> What's wrong with dropping out? To me, this is the
> whole point: one's right to withdraw from a social
> environment that offers no spiritual sustenance,
> and to mind one's own business.
> —William S. Burroughs

Pose this exercise in creative thinking to your friends and family:
"If you were lost in the wilderness, how many different ways could
you signal rescuers?"

Here are some suggestions; there are no doubt others.

- Build a smoky fire, taking special care when fire
  risk is high. Clear an area and burn green boughs,
  which create a lot of smoke and are less likely to
  spread. If you can't keep a fire going, set it up but
  wait to light it until you hear a low-flying aircraft
  (a 747 at thirty-five thousand feet won't be much
  help).

- Lay out bright-colored clothing or camping gear on
  a hilltop or in a clearing.

- Rearrange the natural features of the landscape into
  some unnatural geometric form, if it doesn't take
  too much energy.

- Blast your whistle three times. Three of anything
  (gunshots, lip pops) is the universal signal for distress.

- Use a mirror to reflect sunlight. A regular hand mirror will do, but a signal mirror with a sighting hole
  in it is best. Used by the military, they are available
  at surplus stores.

  If you do use a regular mirror, hold your hand
  in front of it and catch the reflected light. This will

give you a rough idea of the direction of the most intense flashes and allow you to adjust your aim.

No mirror? Improvise. A piece of broken glass covered on one side with dark mud will make a usable mirror; a can lid can be polished until it is like a mirror, and it's easy to punch a sighting hole in the center. A wet log slab can be a signal mirror, as can a slab of ice. With some chrome reflective tape from an auto-parts store, you can turn any hard surface into a signal mirror.

Officials at Newfoundland's huge Gros Morne National Park, seeking to avoid costly search and rescue operations for lost hikers, are issuing radio collars to every group of backcountry travelers. The radios, which weigh ten ounces and have a range of twelve miles, are identical to the ones used to track caribou. No, you don't have to wear it around your neck.

Even though it may seem futile, flash your mirror repeatedly throughout the day. It takes little effort, and in open areas the flashes can be seen for long distances. Flash toward the sound of an aircraft, even though you cannot see it.

- Aircraft in sight? Flash a flashlight three distinct times. If not, especially at night, wave it around. Someone may see it.

- Wave a bright-colored jacket on the end of a stick.

- Climb a tree or mountain and tie something eye-catching up high so it will wave in the wind.

- When snow covers the ground, stamp out SOS and fill the depression with leaves and branches to make the message more visible. Try to make the letters at least twenty feet long.

- Pile rocks or logs in the pattern of a cross at least twenty feet long.

- Stand with both arms raised, palms open. In football this means touchdown, but in search and rescue it means, "I need help." Don't go halfway: Holding up one hand means, "I don't need help."

- Pound on a hollow log, a rock, or a metal object with sticks. It will make quite a ruckus and can be kept up for a long time to guide rescuers. Audio signals will be the most effective for the first day or two; after that, when aerial rescue is more likely, concentrate on visual signals.

- Use the International Ground-Air Emergency signals. Make the following symbols large, using whatever is available: aluminum foil, clothing, rocks, or tree limbs.

Unable to proceed:	X
Require doctor:	I (single straight line)
Need food and water:	F
No:	N
Yes:	Y
All is well:	LL
Am going in this direction:	use arrow

▪ Finding Food

Although most of us get crabby if we miss a meal, we can actually survive weeks without food, much longer than without water. On the other hand, if you are physically, stressfully involved in staying alive, you'll be burning a lot of calories and survival time may be reduced. Foraging alone can be a full-time job, carrying the risk that the hunt will burn more calories than the meal provides.

If water is scarce, eat nothing, for digestion of food demands extra water; normally, someone fighting a water deficit does not feel hunger. If there is enough water, and you're desperate, almost every animal may be considered edible if properly prepared. He who concentrates exclusively on larger game will starve, so use the entire food chain. Adaptability is important, as are certain skills.

There's a telling moment in the movie *Jeremiah Johnson* in which Robert Redford is making a futile attempt to catch a fish with his hands while a skeptical Indian looks on. He was finding out what Hollywood had kept secret for so long: Obtaining food in the wild is hard.

Edible Animals

The pursuit of edible animals is a special challenge. Slow-moving beasts tend to be small, perhaps requiring dozens to make a meal; larger, meatier game is often too fast or too powerful for easy capture. What to do?

Starting at the bottom of the food chain, insects can provide an important emergency source of food. Found in profusion after hatching, they have high nutritional value and can add substantially to a meager meal. They must always be cooked, though, as they carry parasites. Insects can be roasted and dried, ground into meal, and served in soups and stews. Consider grasshoppers, locusts, crickets, katydids, cicadas, and ants. Grubs and caterpillars can be added to soups and stews, but avoid fuzzy ones, as some are poisonous.

Of the reptiles and amphibians, frogs are probably the best food source. They are easily caught and are sometimes numerous in marshy areas. Lizards may require too much effort for the return, though a capable slingshotter can have some success. A well-thrown rock can also stop small game. The best tool for snake hunting is a sharp, fire-hardened stick. Like all reptiles and amphibians, snakes should be skinned and eviscerated before they are cooked. That should quell your appetite for a while.

Jeremiah Johnson notwithstanding, you can catch fish by hand, as well as by spear, trap, or hook. Hooks can be fashioned from twigs, bones (including fish skeletons), nails, or thorns. Fishing line can be adapted from plant fibers, wire, the inner bark of some trees, a leather belt cut into strips and tied together, or unraveled clothing. Before you start taking apart your clothes, however, search the area for discarded fishing line. Ten feet on a long pole should suffice.

When trying to snatch a fish, move your hand slowly through the water until it is below the fish's belly, then quickly scoop it onto the bank. Watch grizzlies to improve your technique.

Some animals, such as rabbits and deer, are quick but lack endurance and can be run down and caught by hand. Prefer to outthink your animals? Make a noose out of string, rope, or fishing line and place it around an animal's hole or burrow. When the animal begins to emerge, jerk the string and tighten the noose around its neck. You also can put bait under a heavy, flat rock propped up by a stick. Tie a line to the stick; when your prey goes after the bait, pull the string, drop the rock, and trap the animal.

Pay attention to birds of prey. Sometimes you can scare them away from their catch of the day. As for preying directly on birds, the small ones usually require more effort than they're worth, and the larger ones require unusual dexterity or a sophisticated knowledge of traps and snares. Occasionally, by using fishing line, birds can be caught at a water hole or where seeds have been scattered. Attach one end of a very fine line to a fixed object and place the rest of it in a loose tangle on the ground. The hope is that a plump, tasty bird will become entangled in the line, permitting capture by hand. Once in a new moon, you might bring down a distracted, possibly retarded, bird by throwing a stick. Quail and chuckers, which prefer to scurry rather than fly, can sometimes be herded, especially in narrow canyons.

If you seek animals for food, consider the following:

- Bird eggs, regardless of the stage of embryo development, are good to eat.

- Lizards are all edible, although you should be careful of the Gila monster's bite.

- Snakes of all species are good to eat.

- Tortoises and porcupines are slow moving, easy to kill, and good eating (if you remove the shell or quills).

- Meat may be cooked on a stick over a fire, simmered in a stew, or wrapped in green leaves, aluminum foil, or mud, then nestled in coals and baked.

- Any extra meat can be preserved by making it into jerky. Take lean meat, cut it into thin strips several inches long, then hang it in the sun for two or three days until completely dried. The jerky will keep indefinitely as long as it is dry, and may be eaten soaked, cooked, or as is.

If you seek animals for food, beware of the following problems:

- Some animals, particularly rabbits, have been known to carry tularemia, a disease transmittable to man. If an animal acts sickly or its liver is spotted, do not eat it.

- Rabies is another concern. Beware of wild animals that seem abnormally fearless of humans, though not all animals that fail to run from people have rabies.

- Skin a frog before eating it (and you thought you'd never use tenth-grade biology); avoid toads, which have glands in their skin.

- Rodents may harbor plague-carrying fleas.

- A few animals, like skunks and peccaries, have scent or musk glands that will taint the meat unless removed immediately after killing.

- Don't allow the hair of an animal to contact the meat; it may give the meat a strong taste.

Edible Plants

People have died amid plenty because they couldn't "stomach" wild foods, a bad trait if there ever was one. There are plenty of edible plants in the wild; unfortunately, there are also a bounty of inedible ones and some poisonous ones. You must know plants to tell the difference. In other words, before you can know edible plants, you must know plants in general.

Make botany a fun family project. Stock your library with field guides on plant identification. Take a class on the subject. Each time you venture into nature, open your guides and identify some plants. When you have improved your identification skills, concentrate on wild edibles. Focus on one plant at a time. Identify it, compare it to look-alikes, harvest it, take it home, and prepare it with a regular meal.

Unless you are experienced, stay away from mushrooms; also avoid plants that secrete a milky sap, for they are often poisonous.

Roots

Finding edible roots is usually easy, though digging them out can be difficult. The best wilderness tool for that task is a "digging stick," a stave of hardwood about three feet long and one inch in diameter. After the bark is removed, the stick is hardened by several scorchings (not charrings) in a fire, then its end is sharpened into a chisel shape by rubbing it on a coarse rock.

Roots can be dried for future use, steamed in a steaming pit, ground into flour on a smooth rock, roasted whole like baked potatoes, boiled, or mashed on a flat rock and eaten like mashed potatoes.

Seeds

When seeds are ripe they can be captured in large quantities in a basket, cup, or open shirt. Plants like amaranth that form seeds in clusters can be stripped of those seeds by hand. Some flower seeds, like those from the nutritious sunflower, can be picked by hand or rubbed from the head on a flat stone.

Seeds must be threshed and winnowed to remove chaff and stems. One can winnow small amounts by taking a handful at a time and blowing away the chaff, or by tossing them in the air and catching them in a blanket or shirt.

Most seeds are tastier and more nutritious when ground into flour or cracked for mush than when eaten whole. Place a handful of dry seeds on a flat stone and grind with the flat side of a loaf-shaped rock. Place the stone on a blanket or shirt to avoid losing seeds.

Consider concentrating on the following four wild, edible plants. Branch out only after you have achieved some expertise. Oaks, cattails, grasses, and pines are pervasive in North America and are easy to identify, with almost no poisonous look-alikes.

Oaks

Oaks, which produce acorns, are everywhere. They range from scrubby plants to huge trees and are easy to identify. Young children tend to call lots of nuts "acorns," so be careful with identification.

The acorns of all North American oaks are edible, though some are bitter. You can remove the bitterness by leaching. Afterward, shell the nuts and mash the meat. Soak the paste in water for two hours, drain, and soak again and again. The paste is ready when it has lost its bitter taste.

Cattails

One need not starve where cattails grow. They are edible from root to top. In fall and winter, the rhizomes (thick roots) can be peeled and cooked like potatoes or dried and pounded into flour. In spring and early summer, the young shoots can be eaten raw or cooked, and the immature flower spikes can be boiled and eaten like miniature ears of corn.

It is hard to confuse the cattail with any other plant, so eating it is safe. Be careful harvesting these bog-loving plants, as your survival may depend on staying dry.

Grasses

New shoots of grass, up to six inches tall, can be eaten raw. Mature grasses contain cellulose, which is difficult to digest. You can chew these grasses and spit out the pulp or steep them in hot water for thirty minutes and make a tea. That way you get the nutrition without the cellulose. Most grass seeds are edible, but because a few are toxic, cook all seeds.

Pines

Widespread throughout North America, pines are easy to recognize and supply nutritious food. Some evergreens are toxic, so it's important that you learn to identify pines.

To make a tea high in vitamins A and C, break the needles into tiny pieces and steep them in warm water for thirty minutes. Pine nuts are found within mature cones—open them by placing them near a fire. A delicacy in many cuisines, they are edible raw, roasted, or ground into flour. Even the inner bark and tiny rootlets of a pine tree are edible in a stew or soup.

■ Forecasting Weather

> For many years I was the self-appointed inspector of snowstorms and rainstorms, and did my duty faithfully.
> —Henry David Thoreau

The ability to predict weather is valuable for wilderness campers, but for backpackers it can be life-or-death. Decisions like "Do we make a stab at the summit or pitch the tent?" often hinge on weather forecasts.

Unless your hiking partner is a professional forecaster, you'll have to wing it in the backcountry. Even when you're car camping, you may be beyond the reach of radio stations and newspapers. If so, you will have to be your own forecaster. Here are several ways to improve your powers of prognostication:

- Watch the sky and chat about what you see. Practice identifying clouds and interpreting their significance. Be aware of changes in temperature, humidity, and winds. Encourage discussions on anything that falls from the sky or billows up from the ground. Go to the library or the Internet to answer difficult questions.

- Buy some weather gadgets and make observations at about the same time every day. Cheap tools include an indoor/outdoor (or minimum/maximum) thermometer, a rain gauge, and possibly an anemometer, which measures wind speed. Chart your rainfall and your daily high and low temperatures. Practice converting Celsius temperatures to Fahrenheit and vice versa; the formula is $F = \frac{9}{5}C + 32$; the Fahrenheit temperature equals nine-fifths the Celsius temperature plus thirty-two.

- Record your own forecasts of the weather for twelve and twenty-four hours hence. Check your accuracy and analyze your mistakes.

- Peruse the weather page of your daily newspaper. Learn the symbols and compare yesterday's weather map with tomorrow's and next week's.

- Watch television weather, complete with computer graphics and satellite photos. If you subscribe to cable TV, you probably have access to twenty-four-hour weather information.

- Use a computer and an on-line network to obtain information from the National Weather Service.

- Listen to the radio. The National Oceanic and Atmospheric Administration (the parent organization of the National Weather Service) maintains a network of 380 radio stations across the United States that broadcasts on the VHF FM band in the 162.40 to 162.55 MHz range.

- Take a barometer or altimeter into the wilderness. Used for measuring air pressure (the altimeter translates the pressure into elevation), both can help the backcountry weather prognosticator.

  Air can't be weighed, but its pressure can be measured with a barometer, calibrated in "inches of mercury." At sea level, a barometer should register close to the standard pressure of 29.92 inches of mercury. If it's significantly higher or lower, an area of high or low pressure is nearby. Take note of dramatic barometric changes. If the reading suddenly plummets, a major low-pressure area is fast approaching. Prepare for a storm, possibly a severe one.

  Be alert to incidental signs of dropping barometric pressure: a "trick" knee, headache, sleepiness, birds roosting, or bees returning to the hive.

- Ask questions. Challenge your children or friends with thought-provoking questions and give them enough time to find the answer.

  For example:

  1. Why are there clouds? (condensation of water vapor)
  2. What causes winds? (differential heating of the Earth)
  3. Why is the sky blue? (refraction of light)
  4. Why is it summer in Australia when it's winter here? (the tilt of the Earth)

Understanding basic weather principles, like the ones discussed below, will help you make intelligent decisions when you're out backpacking.

1. Air expands and rises when warmed. As the sun warms the Earth's surface, "bubbles" of air rise. As long as a bubble is warmer than the surrounding air, it will continue to rise. As it rises, nearby air moves in horizontally to take the place it vacated. That horizontal movement is called wind.

2. As warm air rises, it cools. If a humid mass of air is cooled enough, the water vapor in it condenses into water droplets that reflect light, forming a cloud. Cool those droplets even more and they get heavier, eventually falling as precipitation.

3. Mountains tend to create updrafts, resulting in high precipitation on the windward slopes and dry conditions on the lee side. The dry air that continues flowing down the lee side compresses and becomes warmer. Most of the deserts of North America lie in the so-called "rain shadow" (usually on the east side) of a mountain range.

4. During stormy weather, locations many miles distant will have similar temperatures, humidities, and winds. When skies are clear, however, local conditions may vary a lot. Microclimates form. Local winds develop in response to differences in surface heating. An understanding of microclimates can be a big help when you have to break for lunch or pitch a tent.

5. Wind speed increases with elevation, so that any time of the day it's windier on the mountaintop than down below. However, wind speed near sea level usually increases as the day goes on, while on the mountaintop it decreases. At night, as the ground cools and conditions stabilize, winds decrease at lower levels and increase on a mountain.

6. In apparent contradiction of the principle that warm air rises, it is often colder at the bottom of a depression (like beside a mountain lake) than up on a slope. At night, the ground cools, as does any air around it. The cool air near the slope's surface flows downhill and collects in the valley bottom. That pushes the warmer air hanging over the middle of the valley up and outward. On a clear, calm night, the temperature in a small depression may be twenty degrees lower than on a nearby slope.

You also must take into account the local climate, the long-term prevailing weather conditions of a region. If you know the climate where you'll be camping, you can make educated guesses about its weather at a particular time. Climate is influenced by several factors. Latitude determines the amount of sun an area receives. Hiking near the equator, you'll get lots; at the poles, you'll go six months with almost none.

Elevation affects both temperature and precipitation. Mountain camping? Expect cooler and wetter climes. Proximity to an ocean or large body of water moderates temperatures. Continental areas are generally drier, with greater temperature extremes.

The slope of the land is important. In the Northern Hemisphere, south- and west-facing slopes will be warmer than north- and east-facing ones. At noon on a sunny day, a south-facing slope may be ten or more degrees warmer than a nearby north-facing slope.

Dark, rough surfaces absorb more of the sun's rays than light, smooth ones. Other things being equal (they seldom are), dark, rough surfaces will be warmer than smooth, light ones.

Some climates are easier to forecast than others. In the tropics, you can expect humid heat. Near the other end of the spectrum, a hiker doing the Appalachian Trail in winter can count on cold followed by snow followed by cold. If you hike the Sierra's John Muir Trail in summer, be prepared for hot days and cold nights, a possibility of rain, with snow unlikely. Conditions can change quickly and dramatically.

Campers and hikers should be alert for weather fronts, which are the contact points where two air masses clash. A warm front means that the leading edge of a moving air mass is warmer than the air mass it is overtaking and replacing. Stratus clouds are usually associated with this type of front. A cold front means that cold air is replacing relatively warmer air. The result is anvil-shaped cumulonimbus clouds moving in from the west or northwest, bringing violent, though brief, thunderstorms.

The mean temperature is technically the average of all temperatures day and night. More typically, it is the average high and low temperatures for the day or month. If you are planning a camping vacation, check out month-by-month mean temperature and precipitation totals for your prospective destinations.

Precipitation or rainfall, measured in inches, is often listed as an annual total. For campers, it's more valuable to know the month-by-month totals. In California's Mediterranean climate, for example, you can count on almost no sea-level rainfall in the summer. In Ireland, on the other hand, you can figure on approximately the same amount of rain (lots) every month of the year.

Pay attention to the direction and intensity of winds, important clues in the prediction of weather. Wind also plays an important role in our well-being. Windchill is a measure of the cooling power of temperature and wind on your skin. Moving air has a chilling effect on the human body that makes the thermometer temperature seem lower. On a hot day, the cooling effect of air brushing against our bodies is pleasant. As the temperature drops, however, windchill can be dangerous. For example, a temperature of five degrees Fahrenheit (F) combined with a light breeze of ten miles per hour equals a windchill temperature of minus fifteen degrees F. This is a potentially critical drop (and one not measured by a conventional thermometer), for frostbite occurs much sooner at fifteen below.

Become a cloud watcher, if you aren't already. Clouds offer important clues to what weather will do. Cirrus clouds are the highest in the sky. They are indistinct, fuzzy clouds, composed of ice crystals, and are associated with fair weather, but only temporarily. Appearing as much as a thousand miles ahead of a front, they typically provide a few hours' to two days' warning of an approaching storm. If you see cirrus clouds, keep an eye on the sky for cloud buildup.

Stratus clouds come in waves, layers, or bands. When the waves are regular, expect fair, cool weather; when the waves become irregular or break up into a buttermilk sky, a storm is probably brewing.

Cumulus clouds are lumpy and billowy with flat bottoms and puffy tops. Normally, they indicate fair weather. If, however, they billow upward, mass together, and darken into towering, anvil-shaped cumulonimbus clouds, a thunderstorm is imminent.

The temperature at which water vapor in the air condenses and dew (drops of water) begins to form is called the dew point. Air can hold only a certain amount of water vapor at a given temperature. When the temperature falls, excess vapor condenses onto everything from plants to cars. Because dew forms on cold, clear nights, it is a sign of fair weather.

Another factor to watch is the relative humidity, or the amount of moisture (water vapor) in the air compared with the total amount it can hold. Because warm air holds more water vapor than cold air, a relative humidity of 75 percent on a warm day is moister than a relative humidity of 75 percent on a cold day.

Humidity can affect activities and health. When humidity approaches 100 percent, it may be difficult to get small twigs to burn. On the other hand, relative humidity below 20 percent can make dead grass highly flammable. High humidity saps strength ("it's not the heat, it's the humidity"), and some experts believe dryness may promote the growth of certain viruses. A moderate level, say 30 to 50 percent, is thought to be the most healthful and comfortable.

> How can any man be sad and watch a sunset?
> —Bela Lugosi

According to Don Haggerty, author of *Rhymes to Predict the Weather*, the three most important variables to watch in predicting weather are barometer reading, cloud progression (rising or lowering ceiling), and wind shifts (veering or backing). It also doesn't hurt to know a few weather rhymes and what they mean:

Red sky in the morning, sailor take warning; red sky at night, sailor's delight. Fair weather involves high-pressure cells that are composed of dry, stagnant air filled with dust and haze. When the sun is low in the sky, the dust causes light to be refracted (bent), making visible the red end of the spectrum. If the sunset is fiery, then a high-pressure pocket of air lies hundreds of miles to the west (the direction of the prevailing winds in the Northern Hemisphere), and has yet to arrive. A scarlet dawn indicates that high-pressure air has passed eastward, increasing the chances that the following weather will be wet.

Hens' scratchings and mares' tails make tall ships carry low sails. "Hens' scratchings and mares' tails" refers to those wispy, high-altitude cirrus clouds that typically follow tranquil weather and often indicate a low-pressure air mass is on its way. Watch the sky, and if a lower, thicker mass of clouds rolls in behind the mares' tails, remember that *"the lower they get, the nearer the wet."*

A backing wind says storms are nigh; a veering wind will clear the sky. A "backing wind" is one that is shifting counterclockwise (say, from westerly to southwesterly), while a "veering wind" is one that is shifting clockwise (southwesterly to westerly). In the Northern Hemisphere, prevailing fair-weather winds tend to blow from the west or north, foul-weather winds from the south, southeast, or east. If you notice the wind backing, expect worsening weather. In evaluating winds, trust cloud movement more than ground air.

If with your nose you smell the day, stormy weather's on the way. You hear people say, "Smells like rain today." Extra humidity helps transmit smells, and plants give off oils that are absorbed by soil, then released into the air when humidity exceeds 80 percent.

Smoke rising high, clears the sky; when smoke descends, good weather ends. Air temperature gets colder with elevation. (The rate at which it gets colder is called the lapse rate.) If the area is dominated by a high-pressure system (lapse rate is high), the temperature will drop quickly with elevation, and smoke will rise nicely. Low-pressure air has a low lapse rate. Smoke starts to rise, but the low lapse rate fails to propel it neatly upward. It flattens out, spreading like a blanket over the ground.

When the dew is on the grass, rain will never come to pass. A clear night will lower temperatures enough for humidity to condense as dew. If you find morning dew on the plants, expect fair weather. But *when grass is dry before the morning light, look for rain before night.* This is especially true if the warming trend is caused by an increasing cloud cover.

Ring around the moon, rain by noon; ring around the sun, rain before night is done. The most common halos are high cirrus clouds, which portend bad weather twelve to eighteen hours hence.

When stars begin to muddle, the Earth becomes a puddle. If your view of the stars becomes blurred, you either need glasses or bad weather is likely. Excessive twinkling, particularly if the stars appear blue, suggests increased humidity and/or high winds disturbing the upper atmosphere. Humid air absorbs red and green light, but lets shorter-wavelength blue pass through.

When the air gets light, the glass falls low; batten down tight, for the winds will blow. The "glass," of course, is a barometer, which measures air pressure. Stormy weather arrives in low-pressure air masses, resulting in a lower barometer reading.

Rainbow to windward, foul fares the day; rainbow to leeward, damp runs away. With the damp air of a rainbow upwind, what you see is what you will get. When it is leeward, you've already got it, and the storm may have passed.

Swallows flying way up high means there's no rain in the sky. In the high air pressure that accompanies fair weather, insects are carried aloft, as are the swallows that feed upon them.

After the rain, good weather
In the wink of an eye
The universe throws off
Its muddy clothes.

    —Ho Chi Minh

Resources for Weather Forecasting

Rhymes to Predict the Weather by Don Haggerty (Spring-Meadow Publishing)

The Weather Companion by Gary Lockhart (John Wiley and Sons)

Chapter Twelve

OUTDOOR HEALTH
AND SAFETY

Before supper walk a little;
after supper do the same.

—Latin proverb

THIS chapter focuses on the accidents and afflic-
tions that can befall you in the wilderness. The
same type of list could be drawn up for accidents
around the home. Most of these bad things will never happen, but,
like the Boy Scouts, you should be prepared.

That means learning all you can about wilderness first aid. It also
means carrying a well-equipped first-aid kit and having a working
knowledge of what's in it. If you plan to spend much time in the
wilderness, you should have training in CPR (cardiopulmonary resuscitation), setting broken bones, and suturing cuts. It would also
help to be familiar with the problems covered in this chapter.

After reading this chapter, consider the areas you most need to
work on and focus on them. For more information, I recommend
NOLS Wilderness First Aid by Tod Schimelpfenig and Linda Lindsey
(Stackpole Books).

To test your readiness, imagine emergency scenarios in which you
must perform capably. For example: You are hiking along a trail when
suddenly you happen upon a fellow backpacker who has tripped and

fallen. His femur is poking through his skin and he's screaming in pain. It's late in the day, so besides setting the break, you must prevent hypothermia. Can you handle it? Or say you respond to cries for help from a nearby campsite and find a child bitten by a rattlesnake. She fainted, then fell into a campfire, suffering second-degree burns. What do you do? The answers are in this chapter.

■ Accidents

Accidents can occur for a variety of reasons, such as bad or wrong equipment, rapid change in weather, or "operator errors" like getting lost overstepping one's ability, inexperience, and incompetence. Operator error is by far the most common cause of accidents.

If you help an accident victim:

- Note the state of consciousness of the victim.

- If the person is unconscious, make sure the air passage is not blocked by the tongue or vomit. Keep the patient on his side or front.

- Safeguard the unconscious or thrashing patient from any further fall.

- Stop any bleeding by using pressure with a handkerchief or first-aid dressing. Cover open wounds with a clean, light dressing.

- Make the person as comfortable as possible, keeping him dry, insulated from the ground, with no more movement than is necessary.

- Use a temporary splint or some other means of immobilization, in the case of a broken limb.

- Keep the victim warm, using extra clothing, a survival bag, or whatever. Unless internal injuries are suspected, hot drinks can be given; but in cases of exposure, warming a person too quickly can be dangerous.

- Try to attract attention by shouting, whistle blasts, use of flashlight or distress flares, mirror to the sun, smoke signals. The Alpine Distress Signal is six long blasts, or six flashes of light, repeated at one-minute intervals.

- If the wait for rescue is likely to be long, try to construct some type of shelter.

- If it is impossible to fetch help, continue trying to attract attention.

- If the injured person has to be left alone while you get help, you should do two things before you leave: 1) Take note of the exact location of the injured person, paying particular attention to any landmarks, and 2) Use a fixed object to put a belay on the injured person to prevent his staggering off semiconscious.

> When bandaging an open wound, avoid using Kleenex-type tissue to stem bleeding. Medicos, before treating the wound, will have to pick out disintegrated pieces of tissue.

■ Altitude Sickness

As you gain altitude, the air gets thinner—the amount of oxygen in a given volume decreases. Cheated of it, the body is plagued with chemical imbalances. The first stage, called acute mountain sickness (AMS), is unpleasant but not life-threatening. Temporary symptoms, usually a throbbing headache and nausea, can be endured. Susceptibility to AMS seems to be greater in those under forty, and there's no way to predict someone's highest comfortable altitude. Few people have trouble below eight thousand feet, but two-thirds of those who summit 14,410-foot Mount Rainier suffer some symptoms.

Everyone needs time to adjust to such conditions, no matter how often they have been to high altitude. Afterward, when they descend to sea level, that hard-won acclimatization is lost in a few days. At very high altitudes (over fourteen thousand feet above sea level), pulmonary and cerebral edemas—water accumulation in the lungs or the brain—are more likely. They are less common than AMS (striking 1 to 2 percent of hikers and climbers above twelve thousand feet), but far more serious. Early symptoms may include a hacking cough, shortness of breath, and coordination problems. Later may come a bluish skin color and a phlegm-producing cough. In some cases, an edema victim can lapse into a coma or die without warning.

Prevention

- Ascend gradually. If ascent is less than a thousand feet per day, the condition is unlikely to occur.

- Maintain a high-carbohydrate, low-fat diet.

- Make intermediate stops to allow the body to adjust and minor symptoms to pass.

- Drink lots of water.

- Avoid alcoholic beverages.

- Don't try to overpower altitude.

- Descend immediately if you feel particularly ill.

Treatment

If the symptoms are mild, rest and wait. Induce vomiting, if that feels right. (One time-tested method is to clean a fish. If you're teetering on the edge of nausea, cutting open a trout will just about guarantee vomiting.)

If the symptoms are severe, including a cough and a loss of coordination, descend a couple thousand feet.

■ Bee Stings

What can attract bees and increase the likelihood that you'll be stung? Brightly colored clothing, floral prints, perfumes, skin lotions, and sweet foods at a picnic. Still, if you treat honey bees and bumblebees with respect, they will return it in kind. In four decades of outdoor life, I have never been maliciously stung by a bee (I have stepped on a couple). On the other hand, I have occasionally been dive-bombed by their aggressive cousins, yellow jackets, wasps, and hornets.

If you are among the 3 percent of the population that is hypersensitive to bee venom, even one sting can cause nausea, irregular heartbeat, circulation problems, a lump in the throat (breathing problems), faintness (a drop in blood pressure), and, for about forty people a year, death. Fortunately, most people suffer only localized swelling, pain, and itching that disappear after a few days.

The risk of a serious reaction naturally increases if you are stung by multiple bees. That can happen if you disrupt a nest or hive, some of which are close to the ground. One sting can make you more vulnerable to a second, as it releases a chemical that attracts subsequent attackers.

Beware of the infamous killer bees, which have invaded parts of the South and Southwest and are headed north. Unlike docile European honey bees, the Africanized "killer" bees are aggressive and swarm and sting in mass. They look like common honey bees, and their venom is no more potent, but they travel in large packs and seem to enjoy the thrill of the chase. Backpackers should avoid all bees, especially around a hive.

Are children at greater risk from bee stings? Apparently not. Life-threatening reactions usually occur in people over thirty.

Treatment

Quickly remove the stinger. A bee's stinger is barbed, meaning the bee can't pull it out after stinging you. Don't use tweezers or your fingers to try to remove a bee stinger; it has a sac at the exposed end

Brothers Rob and Rich White had a memorable encounter with bees that shows how animals seldom threaten us if we don't threaten them. "I was twelve and Rich was ten," Rob said. "One day we were hiking and came upon a swarm of bees right in the middle of the trail. No easy way around. I remembered hearing that bees wouldn't sting you if you avoid sudden movement, so we tried it. I led and Rich followed, inching our way through the swarm, and didn't get stung."

"Another time we weren't so lucky," Rich put in. "We were picking berries and reached into a place we couldn't see. It was a bees' nest. We got stung plenty."

that can pump more venom into you if squeezed. Instead, scrape the sac away with a fingernail, knife blade, or credit card, then remove all the stinger.

Wash the site thoroughly. Apply ice, then some itch inhibitor like calamine lotion or Derma Pax. According to the *University of California at Berkeley Wellness Letter* (August 1993), a paste mixture of meat tenderizer or baking soda and water may offer relief. Others say that meat tenderizer is useless and that you should rub a cut clove of garlic on the site.

A more traditional treatment includes an ointment containing an anesthetic, such as benzocaine, and an over-the-counter antihistamine, such as Benadryl or Chlortrimaton, to help reduce swelling.

Emergency bee-sting kits are available that include a syringe of epinephrine (adrenaline). The device has a spring mechanism that automatically triggers the injection when pressed against the skin. If you know you or your children are allergic to bee stings, acquire a kit and carry it whenever you go outdoors. Long-term treatment for the highly sensitive includes regular desensitizing shots.

■ Blisters

A hiker's feet are the first line of defense. Unfortunately, they are often the weak link. Consider that on a seven-mile hike your feet will pound the ground about fourteen thousand times, often on rough, uneven terrain in unfamiliar boots. Such an effort will expose the slightest chink in your defense. The result: blisters.

Foot blisters are caused by friction. The movement of skin against a sock, for example, sends thick outer skin back and forth over a thin inner layer. The layers separate and fluid rushes into the space between the layers. If untreated, the skin covering the fluid may break, exposing highly sensitive skin and increasing the risk of infection.

Prevention

- Toughen your feet before a big hike by walking a lot. Wear the boots in which you will hike, especially if they are new. Go barefoot sometimes.

- Make sure the fit of your boots is snug but not cramped (see chapter 5, "Footwear," for fitting boots). Check them each time you put them on for dirt and rocks.

- Wear the correct kind, number, and thickness of socks to assure proper fit. Smooth out any wrinkles before putting on boots. Watch for hikers whose socks are slipping into their boots.

- Keep feet dry with foot powder and sock changes. Everyone should carry at least one change of socks. While hiking, hang the damp pair from your pack to dry.

- At rest stops, prop your feet up higher than your heart to reduce swelling and increase circulation.

- Upon arriving at the campsite, remove boots, massage feet, and slip into sandals or soft shoes.

- Be alert to the first signs of rubbing. Stop early and check "hot spots."

- Some people swear by duct tape, which is slick and so thin as to have little effect on boot fit.

Treatment

A hot spot is the first sign of trouble. Tender to the touch, it is the early stage of a full-blown blister. Treat with tape, Second Skin, Moleskin, or Nu Skin, which can be used to coat the friction area and protect it against further rubbing.

If the rubbing is in the toe area, put a thin lining of adhesive felt inside your boot so your feet don't slip forward. You can also stuff in a small piece of foam to help absorb impact.

Do not open a blister unless it is the size of a nickel or larger and there is danger of it rupturing or interfering with walking.

If you do plan to open a blister, wash your hands and wash the skin with soap. Sterilize a pin or needle over a flame, holding the end of the pin with a cloth, then let it cool. Puncture the base of the blister, not the center, and let it drain. Gently massage the remaining fluid out. Apply an antibiotic ointment, then cover with a light bandage, a piece of gauze, or a thin foam pad with a hole in the center.

> For years the self-adhesive bandage Spyroflex has been used by hospitals as a burn and wound dressing. Now backpackers can use it as blister prevention and treatment. Like duct tape, Spyroflex is thin and slick, almost eliminating friction as a blistering agent. Unlike duct tape, however, it breathes and controls moisture to help promote healing.
>
> Each Spyroflex Blister Kit includes antibiotic cream, cleansing pads, and sterilized Spyroflex patches to be applied directly over open wounds. Contact Advanced Medical at (800) 886-3040.

Leaving the blister uncovered and going barefoot, if practical, speeds healing.

Check daily for signs of infection—reddening, swelling, or pus. See a doctor if infection occurs.

▪ Bloody Nose

We are more susceptible to this when camping, especially at higher elevations. As the air turns dry and dusty, the urge to pick your nose can be overwhelming, even for those taught that it's a mortal sin. The result is tissue irritation and, often, a bloody nose.

Prevention

A damp handkerchief or bandanna regularly dabbed in the nose keeps things moist and manageable. If you must blow your nose, do it gently.

Treatment

Sit up so that gravity will lower pressure in the veins. To keep blood from running back into the throat, tilt your head forward a little.

Pinch the fleshy part of the nose (between the bridge and the nostril) with your thumb and index finger for five to ten minutes. Applying ice probably won't help, since it's really pressure, not temperature, that stops the bleeding.

After the bleeding stops, don't blow your nose too hard or too often. Sneeze through an open mouth. Apply a little petroleum jelly with a fingertip or a small cotton swab just inside the nostrils several times a day for a week to keep membranes moist.

■ Broken Bones

Use gentle, persistent traction to set the bone in its proper alignment and minimize soft tissue damage. Immobilize the set bone with a splint or sleeping pad. If the fracture is compound (bone poking through the skin), immobilize but don't try to set it. See a doctor.

■ Burns

In the wilderness, burns can be caused by stoves, pots, boiling water, or falling in the campfire (sunburn will be treated separately).

Apply the "rule of palms" to determine the extent of the burn. The palm of your hand, representing about 1 percent of the body surface area, can be used to estimate the percentage of body area burned.

The severity of such burns depends on the intensity of the heat and the length of exposure. For example, water at 120 degrees F will burn skin in five minutes; water at 140 degrees F will do the same damage in five seconds.

First-degree burns injure only the outer skin—the epidermis—causing it to turn red, as in most sunburns. Second-degree burns result in blisters and may be swollen for several days. Third-degree burns make the skin look charred, leathery, gray, and dry, but may not be painful if nerve endings are destroyed.

Treatment

If necessary, remove the source of the burn. If clothing or hair is on fire, stop, drop, and roll. Remove clothing and jewelry, which can hold heat and continue to burn.

Myth: Aloe can heal burns.

Fact: There is no solid evidence that aloe helps heal burns or cuts. Aloe vera is a popular houseplant, and people often treat minor burns by snapping off a leaf and applying the juice to the affected area. Many users report that this provides relief and promotes healing. Recently, however, a FDA group reviewed the scientific tests done on aloe derivatives and concluded that there is no solid evidence of any benefits.

Next, cool the burn. Treat minor burns with cold-water applications. Weather permitting, a cool, wet T-shirt or clean cloth can be applied to a burn in which there is no broken skin. Clean the area with soap and water, and apply a topical anesthetic. Also, you can reduce pain by blocking the burned area from air with plastic wrap or plastic bags. Remove the block after three hours.

Second- and third-degree burns mean broken skin; do not use ointments, sprays, or any home remedy on these. In case of a third-degree burn, do not remove adhered particles of clothing. Instead, bandage over the burns, clothing pieces and all. Elevate burned hands, feet, or legs. If the face is burned, maintain an open airway with the patient sitting up. You may apply cold packs to cool the body, but not directly to third-degree burns.

Victims of severe burns often go into shock from fluid loss. If the victim is conscious and not vomiting, you may give water or a sports drink. Seek medical help as soon as possible.

▪ Cuts

How to deal with the little cuts and scrapes of everyday life? Most small wounds don't need much doctoring.

Think of cuts as falling into one of three categories:

Level 1: No blood, no problem. Chuck on the chin.

Level 2: Slight bleeding. Apply pressure to the injured area with a gauze pad, paper towel, or clean cloth and, if necessary, elevate the injured area above the heart. For a cut foot or leg, the patient can lie down and prop his leg against a tree; hold a cut hand above the head.

Level 3: Larger cut, more blood. Draw the edges of the wound together with the fingers before applying pressure. If bleeding persists, squeeze the pressure point for the blood vessel feeding the cut. Elevate the wound. If that doesn't stop the bleeding, tape the edges of the wound together with a butterfly bandage.

As soon as bleeding is under control, wash the wound with soap and water or irrigate. Once cleaned, blot the area with a clean cloth and bandage. If the wound is minor, especially on a protected part of the body, leave it unbandaged. Larger wounds may require a gauze pad held in place with adhesive tape.

Those antiseptics our moms gave us—Mercurochrome, iodine, Merthiolate—are no longer recommended. They tend to trap bacteria in the wound. The drier the wound, the less chance of infection. A wet bandage inhibits healing by providing an environment favorable to bacteria. If a wound is small and is kept clean, the body's own immune system can adequately dispose of any bacteria that may be present. Be wary of any product that claims to "speed" or "promote" healing.

■ Dehydration

Humans are reservoirs of water. The brain is cushioned by fluid, joints are lubricated by fluid, blood is 90 percent water, and every biochemical reaction requires water.

Dehydration is the cause or a complication of many mountain ailments. It contributes to hypothermia, heat illness, altitude sickness, and frostbite. It worsens fatigue, decreases the ability to exercise, and reduces mental alertness. End-of-the-day headache, weariness, and irritability are often preliminary signs of dehydration.

We can survive much longer without food than without water. As effort increases, so does the need for water. Exercise causes water loss through sweating, breathing, and metabolism. If it is not replaced, a fluid deficit results. With a 2 percent fluid deficit, we experience mental deterioration, nausea, loss of appetite and energy, an increased pulse rate, and a 25 percent loss in efficiency. A 12 percent fluid deficit means a swollen tongue, inability to swallow, sunken eyes, and neurological problems. A fluid deficit of 15 percent is potentially lethal.

Prevention

Drink, drink, drink—especially water. Force fluids before a big hike, even if you're not thirsty. Drink because you know you should. During a long hike, sipping water frequently is preferable to gulping vast amounts during long rest stops. Drink after hikes, too. Urine color is a helpful indicator: darker urine is an early signal of dehydration.

Develop the water habit in daily life. Carry a water bottle and skip soft drinks. Two quarts of water a day should be the minimum, and three or four are better.

Treatment

Force fluids. In severe cases, you may have to evacuate the victim.

■ Diabetes

Diabetes, a disease in which the pancreas produces insufficient insulin, resulting in excessive sugar in the blood or urine, should not keep you from enjoying the wilderness. It does, however, require care and planning. If you're going to exercise, then overeat. Before a long hike fill your pockets with nuts, trail mix, and dried fruit. Munch frequently. If the diabetic loses consciousness, sprinkle sugar under the tongue, or use one of the commercial gels made for this purpose.

■ Frostbite

Unlike hypothermia, which affects the whole body, frostbite acts on local areas such as fingers, toes, and ears. It happens when tissue is frozen. Severe tissue damage from frostbite can lead to gangrene and even require amputation, although this is not as prevalent as it once was because clothing is now better.

The following can contribute to frostbite:

In the 1970s, I backpacked a lot with my friend Jay, who is diabetic. As he was young, lean, and fit, the disease didn't prevent him from hiking twelve mountain miles with forty pounds on his back. But more than once, usually after we had reached camp, he descended into insulin shock. He eventually came to understand that backpacking burned more calories than he was replacing. The result could be frightening.

One drizzly afternoon, after a long hike, I was building a fire while Jay was digging a trench around the tent (trenches were in vogue then). After nursing a tentative blaze to life, I went to speak to Jay and found him eating...dirt. Like a drunk, he wore a goofy grin on his face and had only spasmodic control of his limbs. I'd seen the symptoms before, so I quickly administered a candy bar and two cups of sugary lemonade. Thirty minutes later, he was shaky but recovered.

—S.B.

- Low temperatures

- Windchill

- Moisture

- Poor insulation

- Contact with supercooled metal or gasoline

- Constriction of blood flow from tight jewelry, boots, gaiters, or cramped position

- Dehydration

There are three categories of frostbite—simple (frost nip), superficial, and deep.

Treatment for Frost Nip

Gently warm the affected area. Place your hands under your armpits. For other parts of the body, place your hands over the affected area, blow warm air on it, or immerse it in warm (100- to 108-degree) water. A burning sensation during recovery is normal. Never rub snow on frost-nipped areas—this promotes further chilling and can damage tissue. Never expose frost-nipped skin to direct heat, such as a campfire or stove.

Simple frostbite is physiologically similar to a first-degree burn. Upon rewarming, the layer of frozen skin becomes red. After a few days, the dead skin will peel, just like a sunburn.

Treatment for Superficial Frostbite

Superficial frostbite affects deeper tissues, injuring a partial thickness of skin, similar to a second-degree burn. The skin, which appears white and waxy, will feel frozen on the surface but have a normal pliant texture.

As long as there is no chance of subsequent refreezing, immediately begin rewarming the affected part by immersing it in warm (100- to 108-degree) water. If bathwater is unavailable, cover the victim's body and keep it warm during and after treatment. Handle the affected area carefully. Blisters will likely appear within twenty-four hours.

Treatment for Deep Frostbite

The most serious frostbite is deep or third-degree. The skin has the feel of frozen meat. Its surface changes from blotchy white to grayish-yellow to grayish-blue. Deep frostbite should not be treated in the field. Walking out on frozen feet does less damage than partial rewarming followed by refreezing. As with superficial frostbite, try to keep the area frozen until rewarming can be carried out correctly. Act quickly, though, for the longer tissue is frozen, the more damage it sustains. Don't break the skin; that increases the chances of infection. As the tissue thaws out, it is further prone to infection, which usually calls for antibiotics.

■ Giardia

Contaminated water is believed to account for most infectious diarrhea in the wilderness. This is a remarkably recent phenomenon. In the 1950s, when we first started backpacking, one of life's great pleasures was drinking straight from a cold mountain lake or stream. As recently as 1977, the Sierra Club backpacker's guide lauded drinking directly from wilderness water as one of the "very special pleasures" of backcountry travel. No more. Today, primarily because of a protozoan called *Giardia lamblia*, that is a type of wilderness Russian roulette.

Giardia lamblia is a microscopic cyst that causes a parasitic disease called giardiasis, but commonly called giardia. Giardia is spread by fecal-oral transmission, meaning it is shed in feces that find their way into water that finds its way into a new host. Infection can occur from swallowing as few as six microscopic cysts. Giardiasis used to be called "beaver fever," which almost certainly misplaced the blame for the problem. After all, beavers were around long before giardia, and today the disease is prevalent in areas that have never been home to beavers.

Humans are the more likely villains. We support the theory that winter cross-country skiers who relieve themselves in the snow are at least partly to blame. In the spring the snow melts, forming giant sluiceways that carry the parasites into the water supply.

In the old days—before about 1978—water that looked good and was moving fast was considered safe. Today, according to the Centers for Disease Control in Atlanta, no surface water is guaranteed free of giardia. It has been discovered in mountain headwaters and at Vasey's Paradise in the Grand Canyon, close to where water springs forth in utter purity from ancient aquifers deep in the limestone. Technically, as soon as water falls from the sky or bubbles from an underground spring, it may be unsafe.

Slow to heed the warnings that began cropping up in national parks in the late seventies, Steve contracted giardia in 1980. Although he lived, there were times when he wondered whether it was the right thing to do. It was an unpleasant, at times debilitating, disease that produced the following symptoms:

- Chronic diarrhea, commencing seven to ten days after ingestion.

- Abdominal distention, flatulence, and cramping, especially after meals.

- Symptoms lasting seven to twenty-one days, followed by periods of relief, then relapses.

Prevention

- In addition to giardia, there may be viruses or bacteria in water. Always assume wilderness water is contaminated, and use one of the three basic methods of disinfection—filtering, boiling, or chemical treatment.

- In the wild, away from established toilets, dig an environmentally sound toilet hole six to eight inches deep, well above the high-water line of spring run-off, and far enough from surface water—two hundred feet is usually recommended—to prevent feces from washing into any surface water.

- Educate children and newcomers to the wilderness on the importance of proper toilet holes.

- Ritualize hand washing after squatting and before handling food.

- If possible, use only tap water for drinking. If not, carefully boil, filter, or chemically treat your drinking water. Years ago, the choice was limited to boiling or chemicals (iodine or chlorine). Both have serious drawbacks.

Boiling takes time and fuel and leaves you with hot, flat-tasting water. It is, however, highly effective. Contrary to previous thinking, boiling immediately kills all diarrhea-causing microorganisms. According to Dr. Howard Backer, a lecturer at U.C. Berkeley, any water is adequately disinfected by the time it reaches its boiling point—even at twenty-four thousand feet, where water boils at 135 degrees Fahrenheit. One strategy is to boil your water just before bedtime, then pour it into drinking containers that you can use as hot-water bottles in your sleeping bag. Secure the tops.

Chemical treatment means adding halogens to water. Chlorine is the choice for municipal water, and iodine has been used by the military for the past century. For backpackers, the choice has long been between Halazone (chlorine) or Aqua Potable (iodine). Chlorine doesn't kill giardia, while iodine kills viruses, bacteria, and protozoa cysts. However, it tastes bad (chunks of orange peel in the water after the pills dissolve will help), causes allergies in some people, and is not recommended for babies, small children, or nursing mothers. In addition, as we now know, iodine doesn't kill *Cryptosporidium*, which is a supercyst with an extremely durable shell. The only way to extricate it from your water is by either boiling or filtering.

Treatment

If untreated, giardiasis can last for years. If you think you have giardiasis, you should see a doctor for a stool test. Unfortunately, diagnosis can be elusive and drug treatment can be hit or miss.

If you do have giardiasis, three prescription medicines are available for treatment: Atabrine, Furozone, and Flagyl. Flagyl is the most effective, but it can be hard on the stomachs of small children. No one medicine is 100 percent effective, so it may be necessary to try a second course of treatment using a different medication.

If diarrhea is a symptom, drink lots of fluids.

■ Hantavirus

Rodents have long been known to carry deadly hantaviruses. A new strain, recently recognized in the Southwest and dubbed "Four Corners Disease," can infect anyone who breathes. The primary carriers are deer mice, piñon mice, brush mice, and western chipmunks.

When a human inhales microscopic airborne particles of dried, virus-laden mouse urine and feces, the result can be severe flulike symptoms: fever, achy muscles, headache, and cough. The lungs eventually fill with fluid, followed by respiratory failure. So far, half of those diagnosed have died. There is no evidence of human-to-human transference.

Prevention

The Centers for Disease Control offers these guidelines for anyone hiking or camping in the Southwest:

- Don't pitch your tent or lay your sleeping bag near a rodent burrow. Use a tent with a floor.

- Store food and garbage properly so it won't attract rodents.

- Disinfect all water.

- Don't use an enclosed structure unless you know it has been cleaned and disinfected.

Heat Illness

In a temperate climate, a person loses two to three quarts of water per day, half of it in urine. In the desert, water loss climbs to eight to twelve quarts in sweat, one in urine, and almost a quart exhaled. Since much of this lost fluid is concentrated in the blood, the blood becomes abnormally thick unless the water is replaced.

Drinking plain water is the best way for the average person to replace lost fluids. Excessive loss of sodium and potassium (electrolytes) occurs only after severe and prolonged sweating. Otherwise, a normal diet will replace the minerals lost in sweat. Remember, though, when you're exercising hard, your thirst mechanism lags behind your need for fluids. In other words, by the time you're thirsty, you're already dehydrated. Always drink before, during, and after exercising.

The three stages of overheating are, from bad to worse, heat cramps, heat exhaustion, and heatstroke.

Treatment for Heat Cramps

Cramps, characterized by severe, spasmodic contractions of one or more of the large muscles of the legs, is caused by sweating away body minerals during heavy exertion. Try rest, gentle massage, stretching, and lots of drinking. Now is the time to replace minerals with a sports drink. Ice comforts painful muscles and reduces inflammation. For the common calf cramp, straighten out and support the affected leg, grasp the foot at the toes, and pull slowly and gently. Never pound or twist a cramping muscle.

Treatment for Heat Exhaustion

Heat exhaustion is caused by the body's inability to dissipate heat. It too involves the loss of electrolytes during strenuous exercise, usually in a hot, humid environment. Symptoms include dizziness, faintness, fatigue, nausea, and vomiting. The victim's skin becomes pale and moist, but heart rate and temperature are normal.

Treatment includes rest, mineral replacement, and water. Apply wet cloths to the victim and fan vigorously. When the victim feels better, activity can be resumed.

Treatment for Heatstroke

This most serious heat condition is also caused by the body's inability to dissipate heat. The onset of heatstroke symptoms can be rapid, with the victim quickly losing the ability to help himself. Complaints are weakness, fatigue, headache, vertigo, thirst, nausea, vomiting, muscle cramps, and faintness. Body temperature is between 102 and 104 degrees F, and the skin is hot and usually dry. Pulse and respiratory rate are elevated, while urine output is nil. Altered brain function—confusion, delirium, ataxia, even loss of consciousness—is a sure sign that heat exhaustion has degenerated into heatstroke. Shortness of breath, diarrhea, and seizures may also arise.

Treatment must be immediate. Stop all activity and protect the victim from the heat source, usually the sun. If no shade is available, make some. Remove the victim's clothing, apply wet cloths, and fan vigorously. If water is limited, sponge the victim, especially around the armpits, groin, and neck. Give liquids only if the victim is conscious and able to swallow. Continue cooling until body temperature returns

---

Risk Factors for Heat Illness

- Overweight
- Overdressed
- Fatigued
- Dehydrated
- Alcohol consumption
- Medications
- Exertion
- High humidity
- High temperature
- Not acclimatized

to normal. Do not administer aspirin or stimulants. After the condition has stabilized, get the victim to the doctor as soon as possible.

■ Hypothermia

This is a dangerous cold-weather condition in which the body can no longer generate enough heat to compensate for heat loss. It is one of the two risks (frostbite is the other) of exercising in the cold. You are most susceptible to hypothermia if you are wet, injured, or not moving about enough to stay warm. It can happen in minutes or take hours. Children and the elderly are at greatest risk.

It doesn't have to be freezing cold for hypothermia to strike; in fact, it's most common when the temperature is between thirty and fifty degrees F. Far more insidious than temperature are wind and moisture, which can penetrate clothing and remove the insulating layer of warm air next to the body. For example, a fifteen mile-per-hour wind makes thirty degrees feel like ten degrees. This is the windchill factor.

Hypothermia can strike on even the sunniest summer day. Fifteen minutes in water as warm as sixty degrees can turn lips blue and cause uncontrolled shivering, symptoms that kids tend to ignore but parents should not. If your child's skin begins to look bluish, towel the tot off, put clothes on, and set in the sun until toasty.

A friend, Tim, had a frightening brush with hypothermia: "We were two couples, camping at about eight thousand feet in the Sierra. It wasn't that cold—maybe fifty degrees—but there was a storm moving in. I suggested to my friend Jeff that he move their tent to higher ground, near ours. I went back to our tent to wait, but he didn't show. It started to hail, so I ran down to see what was wrong. Jeff was basically out of his mind, wandering around in a daze. We had to lead him back to the car. It was only a half-mile away, but it occurred to me that he would have died if I hadn't been there. He's six-foot-two and 185 pounds, and his wife couldn't have helped him out by herself. Back at the car, we changed his clothes and turned on the heat. He was all right in about thirty minutes, though pretty depressed. It was scary."

Strong, uncontrollable shivering may be a sign that the patient's body temperature has dropped to a hypothermic level, the mid to low nineties. Warm the victim, yes, but don't try to immediately stop the shivering because it's the most effective warming mechanism your body has. Shivering raises your metabolic rate fivefold.

Mild hypothermia generally involves little loss of acuity or coordination, though the victim may have trouble managing buttons, zippers, or laces. Profound hypothermia alters mental status. The victim may become belligerent or uncooperative and dispute your diagnosis of his condition. Muscle rigidity replaces shivering. Movements become erratic and jerky. If untreated, the victim will die from cardiac arrest or other complications.

Prevention

Hypothermia is easier to prevent than to treat. Preventatives include a balanced diet, plenty of fluids, controlling sweat, and dressing for the weather—that is, covering head, neck, and hands, and wearing clothes that insulate even when wet.

It's also important to be smart and know how hypothermia strikes. For example, the biggest danger of hiking Utah's warm desert canyons isn't heat exhaustion, but hypothermia from the cold streams that wind through the sinuous sandstone canyons.

Treatment

Treatment should begin immediately. Insulate the victim from the ground up—have him lie on a sleeping pad or bag. Get the victim out of the elements and remove any wet clothing. Protect him from any further heat loss, especially from the head and neck. Give warm, nonalcoholic beverages.

To accelerate warming, place wrapped warm rocks or hot-water bottles around the victim. Treat gently when removing clothing and giving care; sudden movement may force cold blood from the limbs into the core of the body. Do not rub or squeeze the extremities to stimulate circulation; it can damage tissue. If possible, place the victim in a sleeping bag in between two warm people. Continue warming until you can get the victim to a doctor.

■ Lightning

Thunder is impressive, but lightning is the real show. It streaks across the sky at sixty thousand miles per second, lasts but a few thousandths of a second, and withers anything in its path. Cattle banding together for protection against rain have been struck and wiped out en masse. A flock of 504 sheep was abruptly eradicated by a lightning bolt in Utah's Wasatch National Forest. Every year in the United States alone, hundreds of people are killed by lightning, more than by snakes, spiders, bears, bees, and mountain lions combined. Three times that many are injured, and untold numbers have the bejesus scared out of them.

Prevention

Here's a guide for estimating how far away lightning is: When you see a flash, start counting until you hear thunder; every five seconds equals about a mile.

- If you are indoors, stay there and get to the center of the room. Don't venture outside unless absolutely necessary.

- Don't handle metal objects, such as fishing rods or tent stakes.

- Don't handle flammable materials in open containers.

- Get out of the water if you're swimming or off the water if you're in a small boat.

- Seek shelter. If no buildings are available, take refuge in a cave (but not near the mouth), ditch, canyon, or cluster of small trees.

Getting hit by lightning has become a standard of comparison, for example, "You have a better chance of being hit by lightning than meeting a girl who likes you." Actually, the risk of being struck by lightning exceeds most other outdoor risks. That's because there are about sixteen million annual thunderstorms. That's an average of forty-four thousand storms building up, exploding, and dissipating daily, which works out to 360,000 lightning streaks every hour, or about 8,640,000 per day. As you read this sentence, about eighteen hundred lightning storms are hitting Earth. That seems incredible to denizens of the temperate zones, but probably not to the people of Java, who hear thunder 231 days a year.

With such pervasive distribution, lightning has been seen by almost every person on the planet—past and present. Columbus called it "holy fire" and regarded it as a good omen. Martin Luther said his decision to become a monk originated with a lightning strike. He considered it a call from heaven.

- When there is no shelter, avoid the highest object in the area. You're better off crouching in the open than near an isolated tree.

- Avoid hilltops, open boats or fields, lone trees, wire fences, exposed sheds, and any elevated electrically conductive objects, like transmission towers or transmitters.

- In a grove, stay away from the tallest trees.

- Get off your bike or horse.

- If you are caught in the open, crouch. Better yet, stand or sit on something dry and non-conducting, such as a foam pad or sleeping bag.

- If you begin to feel an electrical charge—your hair stands on end, your skin tingles, you glow in the dark like a black light—immediately drop to the ground.

- Watch the weather for cloud buildup. In the mountains, the afternoons are generally more dangerous than the mornings. Get below the timberline if you see a storm building.

Treatment

A lightning bolt can create heat up to fifty thousand degrees for up to a tenth of a second. With such a short duration, severe burns are uncommon; more likely, a victim will suffer ruptured eardrums, cardiac or respiratory arrest, or brain or spinal cord damage. Breathing may stop while the heart keeps beating. Artificial respiration may be necessary. Be prepared to commence CPR immediately, even if the person appears to be dead. People frequently survive direct hits of lightning.

Some, like Roy C. Sullivan, the Human Lightning Rod, have survived more than one. Roy was struck seven times during his thirty-plus years as a ranger in Virginia's Shenandoah National Park. The first bolt struck him in a lookout tower in 1942, the second while he was driving a truck. One incident cost him an eyebrow; others ripped off a toenail, knocked him unconscious, set his hair on fire, and tossed him from his car.

> A Canadian couple camped north of Toronto had a shocking experience. They were hugging in their tent, waiting out a thunderstorm, when a lightning bolt hit. It struck a gold medallion around the man's neck, then emerged through his eyes, ears, and nose. Amazingly, both survived. They suffered only first-degree burns and, no doubt, a barrage of ribbing about their "hot date."

At one point, Sullivan had twelve lightning rods surrounding his home but no sense of security. "Lightning has a way of finding me," he said. "I have a feeling I'm going to be struck again someday."

All things being equal, your chance of being hit by lightning in any year is about one in six hundred thousand. Sullivan is a reminder that all things are not equal.

■ Lyme Disease

Lyme disease, so called because it was first identified in Lyme, Connecticut, in 1975, is transmitted by certain species of ticks. Worldwide, only the mosquito transmits more disease than the tick.

Before a tick becomes engorged with blood, it looks as innocuous as a mole or a blood blister. The male is black and the female is dark red and black. While an adult is about one-tenth of an inch long (three times that when filled with blood), an immature tick (nymph) is about the size of a pinhead.

Tick eggs hatch into larvae that are nearly invisible. The larvae become infected by feeding on white-footed mice in the East, lizards or jackrabbits in the West. The larvae molt and become infected nymphs; the nymphs are the chief threat to humans—70 to 90 percent of all cases of Lyme disease are caused by nymphs.

Nymphs and adults both like to hang out on low vegetation and transfer to whatever or whomever brushes by. They don't fly or jump. Dogs or cats can carry ticks.

Lyme disease poses a double bind for doctors; many people who have it don't know it, and many others are convinced they have it but don't. The disease is hard to diagnose because its symptoms vary from person to person. No symptom appears in all cases, and there's no predictable sequence of symptoms. The blood tests for Lyme disease are only about 60 to 70 percent reliable. Still, three general phases have been identified:

Phase one: Three to thirty days after the bite, a white-centered red ring may appear, possibly at the site of the bite, possibly somewhere else. You may also develop classic flu symptoms, such as headache, fatigue, muscle and joint ache, chills, and low fever. You may skip the rash and just get the flu symptoms, or you may have none of these symptoms but still carry the disease. If you do have symptoms, they may disappear after phase one, or more severe symptoms may develop, sometimes months later.

Phase two: About 20 percent of untreated victims develop neurological or cardiac disorders within weeks or months of the bite.

> Many years ago, when our son Richard was two years old, we were camped at Green Lakes, north of Mono Lake, when I noticed a tick on Richard's back. It was half-buried in his skin. Our friend Clay came to the rescue with some strong war-surplus mosquito repellent. He dabbed some on the rear end of the tick, which caused it to back out in a hurry. Dick says that people have used stove fuel in a similar manner.
>
> —N.K.

These range from heart rhythm abnormalities to impaired motor co-ordination and even partial facial paralysis.

Phase three: About half of untreated people develop chronic or recurring arthritis after a dormant period of up to two years. The knees are almost always affected.

More and more cases of Lyme disease are reported each year. The Centers for Disease Control reported 4,574 cases in 1988 and 7,400 cases in 1989. Nevertheless, there is no reason to panic or avoid the outdoors. Instead, take precautions.

Prevention

- If you're in tick country, wear a long-sleeved shirt with buttoned cuffs; tuck the shirt into your pants and your pants into your socks. Sure, you look like a geek, but Lyme disease makes you *feel* bad, not just look bad.

- Wear light-colored clothing. It's easier to spot ticks on white or gray pants than on black ones.

- Use insect repellent with DEET on your body and clothing (see "Mosquito Bites" on page 276).

- In an overgrown area, try to stay near the center of the trail.

- Do an occasional body check for ticks. Have some-one check your back and head.

Treatment

Lyme disease is treatable and almost always curable, especially in its early phase.

If you find an embedded tick, use forceps or tweezers to grab the tick's head close to the skin and gently pull it straight out. Do not burn the tick off, do not use Vaseline, do not twist the tick and break the head off in the skin.

If you want to know whether that tick was infected, preserve it

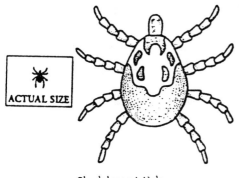

ACTUAL SIZE

Black-legged tick

(dead or alive) in a moist paper towel or cotton ball (so its precious bodily fluids don't dry out), and put it in your freezer until you can take it to a lab. Tests can now determine whether a tick was infected. If so, you should immediately commence antibiotics. If caught early, treatment lasts about six weeks and is virtually foolproof. Waiting can cause treatment to last more than a year, and even then it's not always effective.

If you develop the characteristic ringlike rash, see your doctor, who should prescribe antibiotics. If you have only the flulike symptoms, a blood test may or may not reveal Lyme disease. You may want to shop around until you find a doctor who will prescribe antibiotics, but the medication can have physical side effects, and overuse of these drugs can produce resistant organisms.

■ Mosquito Bites

> Mosquitos were using my legs for filling stations.
> —Cornelia Otis Skinner

All the world's insects weigh about the same as all the world's humans, and mosquitoes make up a disturbingly high percentage of that total. In buzzing hordes and do-or-die kamikaze attacks, they spoil more peaceful moments for backpackers than all other annoyances combined. Mosquitoes are numerous, voracious, and willing to sacrifice their own lives for one last shot at your juicy self.

Prevention

- Learn the enemy's habits. In the mountains, mosquitoes breed in pools formed by melting snow; below four thousand feet, most prefer to breed in the water-filled nooks of trees. Obviously, snow melts earlier in the lower elevations, so expect mosquitoes earlier there as well.

The mosquito's life span is short; in any area, the mosquito problem seldom lasts more than a few weeks. Call ahead to park or tourism officials to find out if the area you intend to visit is under attack.

> Before the invention of DEET in 1954, you had a choice of home remedies with which to combat the mosquito scourge. Some soaked pipe tobacco in water and spread the solution over their skin. Others plastered themselves with mud. Or consider this repellent recipe proffered in an old camping text:
>
> Mix 2.5 pounds of lard with 0.5 pound of tar. Stir in 3 ounces of citronella oil and 1.5 ounces of pennyroyal. Spread evenly.

- Know your limitations. You can't kill them all or outrun the little beggars; lured by your warmth and expired carbon dioxide, they move in for the attack. Even if they don't strike (only the females bite), their incessant whining in your ears may drive you to the nearest Holiday Inn.

- Wear the right clothes. Most heavy nylon is mosquito-proof, as are loose-fitting thick cottons. Keep head, neck, and ears covered with hats, bandannas, and hoods. Don't forget gloves and thick socks. If the problem is serious, wear head netting. Some people believe that earth tones have a calming effect.

- Smell right. Avoid deodorants, soaps, shampoos, and laundry detergents that act like a big dinner bell to mosquitoes. Airing clothes outside for several days may help.

- Stay calm. Agitation creates movement, heat, and sweating, all of which compound the problem.

Mosquito Facts

Number of species in North America: 160. In the world: nearly 3,000

Ratio of mosquitoes to humans in the United States: 42,000 to 1

Percentage of its body weight a female mosquito draws in blood during an average meal: 200

Batches of eggs laid by a female mosquito in her lifetime: 10

Number of eggs laid per batch: up to 500

Number of hatchlings an acre of stagnant water can yield on a summer day: 4 million

Average life span of a mosquito: 3 to 4 weeks

Flight speed of mosquitoes: up to 8 miles per hour (with no tail wind)

Range of a mosquito seeking a meal: up to 50 miles

Estimated number of people who annually use a bug repellent containing DEET: 200 million

Thanks to _Backpacker_ magazine

- Take advantage of rain, wind, cold, and blazing sun, when mosquitoes tend to find shelter.

- Make smoke, any sort of smoke. Lay green or damp vegetation on your fire, but know that the cure may be worse than the mosquitoes themselves.

- Go camping with someone who is more attractive to mosquitoes than you are. Mosquitoes, like humans, seem to like some people better than others. Body temperature, skin color, personal odor, and levels of lactic acid in the blood all may be factors.

- Rub your body with orange peels, a remedy lacking the support of the mainstream medical community.

- Use a chemical repellent containing DEET (diethyl metatoluamide). Apply it sparingly to skin and liberally on clothes. DEET is absorbed through the skin—48 percent of an application is absorbed within six hours. The most common side effect is a rash, but occasionally anxiety, behavioral changes, lethargy, and mental confusion have been reported. If using a spray repellent, aim the spray at your hands, then rub it on your face. After applying DEET, wash your hands or keep them away from your eyes and mouth. With young children, don't use a repellent with more than about a 30 percent concentration of DEET.

If you are using sunscreen or other lotions along with DEET, apply them first. Putting DEET on the top layer means it's less likely to be absorbed through the skin. Don't use DEET under clothing, where it's in full contact with your skin but has little effect on insects. Never use DEET or any other repellent over cuts, wounds, or irritated skin. Once out of harm's way, wash all DEET-treated areas of your skin with soap and water; launder all DEET-treated clothing.

If you prefer an alternative to DEET, try Na-trapel, which contains citronella. Some praise Avon's Skin-So-Soft as a repellent, but the lotion has little staying power and the oil, which is more effective, smells perfumy. Scarfing garlic and vitamin B has some adherents, but it doesn't work for everyone.

If your trip's timing is bad, repellent can go quickly, but one four-ounce bottle per person per week is usually more than enough.

■ From 3M comes Ultrathon, a repellent cream advertised to keep biting insects away for twelve hours. A "controlled release formula" slowly releases DEET (33 percent), so it supposedly works longer. Besides mosquitoes, it's effective against ticks, flies, chiggers, gnats, and fleas. Both the aerosol and the cream leave a greasy feeling, which no doubt allows it to stand up well to rain and sweat.

- Look on the bright side. While mosquitoes are merely annoying in the United States, elsewhere they are downright deadly. Thousands of people die every year in Africa, Asia, and Central America from such mosquito-borne diseases as malaria, yellow fever, and dandy fever.

- Bring along a pig. In Italy, it is said that he who sleeps with a pig in the room will be free of malaria. Perhaps the pig's higher body temperature makes it more attractive.

Treatment

Don't scratch. We can offer no better outdoor advice. Some people are mad scratchers, which results in quarter-sized welts followed by hideous scabs followed by scars. For many, the welts go away if they refrain from scratching for the first hour.

Anti-itch medications like Campho-Phenique, Afterbite, or calamine lotion may help reduce itching.

■ Mushroom Poisoning

Recently nine people in northern California were rushed to the University of California at San Francisco Medical Center after consuming a wild white mushroom called *Amanita phalloides*, or death cap. Eventually one of them died.

The mushroom, which resembles several varieties of its safer cousins, has been proliferating in northern California during the past two years. Mycologists say that death caps used to be rare in northern California but now are sprouting year-round, everywhere from forests to backyards.

Prevention

Prevention couldn't be easier: Don't eat any wild mushrooms, picked by anyone, from anywhere except the produce department of your local supermarket. According to Chester Laskowski, president of the Mycological Society of San Francisco, the poisonous mushrooms "are not that difficult to recognize," but it's apparently easy for amateurs to confuse phalloides with a variety of mushroom called volvariella, which is favored by people who like Asian cuisine. Moreover, when the death cap is young, or in the "button" stage, it displays few of the characteristics that distinguish it from other mushrooms.

Death cap
Illustration by Jade Lew

Other characteristics of the death cap:

- Often distinguished by a shiny, metallic-green top, it lacks the small lines near the edge common to other mushrooms.
- It tastes good but has a strong smell.
- It grows in many regions of the world, usually in the fall or rainy season. In California and the Northwest, the mushroom is now being found at all times of the year. The *Amanita phalloides* mushroom is believed to be responsible for as many as 95 percent of the fatal mushroom poisonings around the world.

Treatment

Death cap mushrooms produce an extremely potent toxin that binds proteins in liver cells. The illness may not appear until six to twenty-four hours after the mushrooms have been eaten, but then the toxin can quickly destroy the liver. The first symptom is severe diarrhea, but by that time liver damage is already under way. In severe cases, a liver transplant is called for.

If you suspect you have eaten a poisonous mushroom, contact the nearest poison control center.

Overuse Injuries

Wilderness hypothermia, dehydration, and lightning hits are quite rare compared to the number of overuse injuries. They are brought on gradually by the wear and tear of a repetitive activity, say, hiking with weight on your back. In one survey of athletes, overuse injuries outnumbered acute injuries in every sport except basketball and skiing.

An acute injury is almost always caused by one incident. An overuse injury may have no obvious cause, apart from a sudden increase in activity. A perfect candidate for an overuse injury is the fifty-weeks-a-year worker who embarks on an ambitious two-week backpacking trip. The result, too often, is a dull pain in the knees or ankles that recurs intermittently, then more frequently. You have pushed your body beyond its abilities. Tissue has developed microscopic tears that cause pain and swelling.

The most common overuse problem is tendinitis—inflammation of the fibrous cords that anchor muscles to bones. Tendons are especially vulnerable, because the force of muscle contractions is transmitted through them. People who exercise regularly are actually more at risk because of the powerful forces transmitted by their well-developed muscles. Perhaps that's why children seem to suffer less. Tendon inflammation is characterized by pain, swelling, warmth, and redness.

Tendinitis can be deceptive. It may hurt at the start of exercise, diminish, then return sharply once you've finished. For hikers and backpackers, knees, feet, and Achilles tendons at the back of the ankle are most at risk.

Prevention

Start slow and build up gradually. Apply heat to vulnerable parts of the body before exercise and ice afterward.

Treatment

The standard therapy is RICE—rest, ice, compression, and elevation. Apply ice to the tender area for twenty minutes right after you finish your hike; repeat every two waking hours. Cooling decreases nerve conduction and pain, constricts blood vessels, limits inflammation, and reduces cellular demand for oxygen. Don't exceed the twenty-minute limit, lest you damage skin and nerves. If you are car camping, put ice cubes or crushed ice in a towel or plastic bag and press gently on the affected area. If you are backpacking, use an instant cold pack or immerse the injury site in a lake or stream. Also do the following:

- Stay away from heat, especially at first. It may offer symptomatic relief, but it will increase the inflammation.

- Regularly take an over-the-counter anti-inflammatory, such as aspirin or ibuprofen (Advil).

- Rest or at least reduce your workout. Actually, research suggests that "active rest" is better than stopping. Besides, if you are midway through a hundred-mile backpacking loop, you can't very well stop; you can, however, slow the pace and reduce the stress on the affected area.

- Massage the tender area to increase blood flow and promote healing.

Poison Ivy/Oak/Sumac

Many a child grows up believing they are immune to poison plants. Turns out, between 75 and 85 percent of all humans are potentially allergic to them. Poison oak, ivy, and sumac contain an irritant called urushiol (uh-ROO-she-all), a sap found in the roots, stems, and leaves. Urushiol is the fiercest allergen known; a drop the size of a pinhead could cause a rash in five hundred people.

The only way it can travel through the air is if it's carried in smoke. Urushiol doesn't affect dogs and cats, but they can bring it home in their fur.

Prevention

- The best way to escape the wrath of poison oak, ivy, and sumac is to know what the plants look like and stay away from them. Keep in mind the rhyme "Leaves of three, let it be" (though if you take that too literally, you'll miss out on some good berries). The poison plants may cling to the ground or grow up the trunks of trees or along fences. They may look like shrubs, bushes, small trees, or vines. Leaves may be dull or glossy with saw-toothed or smooth edges. In autumn, the leaves may turn orange; in summer, poison ivy has white berries.

Poison sumac

Poison oak

Poison ivy

Illustrations by Jade Lew

- The big three haven't yet taken root in Nevada, Alaska, or Hawaii. California has no poison ivy but does have plenty of western poison oak, which is rampant from Mexico to Canada. The rest of the United States and southern Canada is home to poison ivy and eastern poison oak. Poison sumac is found in bogs and swamps in the eastern United States.

- If you think you've touched poison plants, wash the area like Lady Macbeth. If you have urushiol on one hand and scratch your back or touch your face, you can spread it.

- Beware of vines entangled in your firewood; they may be poison ivy, which can elude identification when the leaves are gone. Even touching dried-out poison ivy can cause a rash. Inhaling fumes from a burning plant can cause extreme respiratory irritation (a major hazard for firefighters).

- If you are in heavy poison plant country, wear gloves and other heavy clothing. Lightweight garments are inadequate, as urushiol can penetrate them.

- Don't eat a poison ivy or oak leaf to "desensitize" your skin; it won't work and it may make you sick.

Treatment

- If you believe you have brushed up against urushiol, put on clean gloves and carefully remove your clothing. Wash everything in strong detergent; wipe off your shoes.

- Wash your body with soap and cold water, ideally within fifteen minutes. Hot water opens the pores, allowing the oil to penetrate the skin more easily.

- If you become rashy, try not to scratch. Scratching won't cause the rash to spread, though it can lead to infection. The blisters don't contain urushiol, so you can't pass the rash to another person. However, if you have the oil on your body before the rash develops, you can pass it by touching someone.

- Cold saltwater compresses, cool baths, calamine lotion, baking soda, and over-the-counter cortisone cream offer relief. The best product we've found for drying up the blisters is Derma Pax. Even if you do nothing, you'll probably be rid of all traces in less than three weeks.

- Be happy. With thousands of plant species in North America, it could be worse.

Shock

Shock is the body's response to injury, serious illness, overwhelming blood loss, infection, or dehydration. It happens when the blood supply to the vital organs, the skin, and the muscles is decreased. When the blood flow to the intestines, kidneys, heart, and brain falls far enough, collapse follows. Severe shock leads to death when the heart stops. Symptoms of shock include pale, cold, clammy skin; shallow, irregular breathing; rapid but weak pulse; dilated pupils; beads of perspiration; weakness; nausea; and thirst. Loss of consciousness may follow.

Treatment

Shock demands immediate medical attention.

- Have the patient lie down. In case of vomiting, turn the head to one side to keep the victim from inhaling the vomit.

- Loosen tight clothing, particularly near the head.

- Keep the victim warm but avoid sweating.

- Speak soothingly, striving to instill confidence and keep spirits up.

- Light, rhythmical massaging is comforting; holding the hands or feet can be reassuring.

- Do not give water if the victim is unconscious, nauseated, or if medical help will arrive within thirty minutes. If medical help is more than thirty minutes away, give only sips.

- If the victim stops breathing and the heart stops, cardiopulmonary resuscitation should be started immediately. CPR should be learned by everyone. Classes are available through the American Heart Association and the Red Cross.

■ Snakebite

The risk of snakebite is greatly exaggerated by most people. Although there are about eight thousand bites from venomous snakes in the United States each year, many are inflicted upon professional snake handlers, and only twelve to fifteen people die each year from these bites, mostly the young, the old, and the infirm. Most snakebites occur when a snake is antagonized or inadvertently stepped on.

There are only four poisonous snakes in all of North America: rattlesnake, copperhead, cottonmouth (water moccasin), and coral.

Prevention

- Stay away from snakes, and they will stay away from you. Like most wild animals, they want no part of people.

- Wear shoes and, if practical, long pants, a long-sleeved shirt, and gloves, especially when gathering firewood.

- Be careful when turning over a rock or fallen branch.

- Don't reach or step into dark places.

- Don't gather firewood at night in snake country.

- Don't alarm a sleeping snake nor tease an awake one.

- Carefully shake out sleeping bags and clothing before use.

Treatment

- Carry a snakebite kit. Read the instructions at the time of purchase, and again before heading out, rather than waiting for an emergency.

- If you are certain the snake that bit you was non-venomous, treat the bite like any other wound.

- If bitten by a poisonous snake, symptoms usually appear within minutes: a metallic, rubbery, or tingling taste in the mouth and possibly a burning sensation at the bite site. Within one hour: swelling, pain, or tingling at the bite. After some hours: skin discoloration, blood blisters, chills, fever, muscle spasms, decreased blood pressure, headache, and blurred vision.

- If those symptoms arise, seek medical help as soon as possible. In the meantime, immobilize the bitten body part and keep it below heart level.

- If a foot or leg has been bitten, the patient should be carried.

- If the bite is on the hand, remove rings. Most snake-bite wounds will cause swelling.

- Don't apply ice. This can drive the venom deeper and damage tissue if left in place too long.

- Avoid tourniquets. They shut off arterial blood and can result in loss of the limb.

- Cutting a wound and sucking out all the poison should be done only if you are the star of a TV western or if you are hours away from medical help (and only then if you have a suction cup, can start treatment within five minutes, and are trained in the procedure).

Spider Bites

There are over thirty thousand spider species in the world. All are carnivorous, but there's nary a one that would choose your fleshy arm over a juicy fly. The most dangerous spider in North America, the black widow, kills only four to six people a year in the United States, despite its sinister name. The brown recluse is also poisonous. Fatalities are rare, but bites are most dangerous to children, elderly, and those in poor physical condition.

Spiders are blamed for a lot of bites they don't commit. Shy and retiring by nature, they decline the opportunity to hang out with people and will bite only when brushed against or when someone blindly reaches under a log or into a dark hole. The bite of a venomous spider is barely noticeable, but it's usually followed by redness and swelling, then numbness, then large-muscle cramps. The abdomen may become hard and painful. Weakness, nausea, breathing difficulties, vomiting, and anxiety are common. The pain generally peaks in one to three hours, and symptoms begin to regress after several hours. Poisoning is more likely to be fatal to children or to people with hypertension or coronary problems.

Often the victim has not seen the spider and does not realize the cause of his illness (though two tiny red marks identify the bite). That can mean the occasional blown diagnosis, the most common of which is appendicitis. If doctors suggest taking out your appendix, raise the possibility of spider bites.

Prevention

Don't brush against spiders or reach blindly into dark holes.

Treatment

- Clean the wound with antiseptic soap.

- Ice (or clean snow) may be used on the bite.

- Keep the victim quiet.

- If symptoms develop, get the victim to a doctor. Antivenin is readily available.

■ Sprains

The most common hiking injury is an ankle sprain. Sprains are partial or complete tears or ruptures of ligaments, the elastic cords designed to prevent excessive motion. The sprained ankle is to the backpacker as the knee injury is to the football player—common and debilitating.

The severity of sprains varies greatly. Most amount to nothing more than a fleeting twinge. The worst ones require the victim to be immobilized.

Prevention

- Wear good hiking boots and socks for ankle support. You may feel as light as Mercury in running shoes or sneakers, but they offer no protection when your ankle decides to move sideways on uneven terrain. There are hiking boots for toddlers.

- Watch your step. If you miss one, keep your balance, shift your weight slightly forward, and seek a safe landing zone for the next step.

Treatment

- To limit swelling and permit healing, the standard treatment is rest, ice, compression, and elevation. Aggressively treating a mild sprain with RICE—rest, ice, compression, and elevation—for a day or two might keep you from having to cut short your trip. When you do start walking again, provide support for the injured joint with tape, elastic brace, or Ace bandage.

- If you suspect a severe sprain or fracture (the area becomes black and blue) immobilize the injury.

■ Sun Injury

A sobering six hundred thousand cases of skin cancer are diagnosed each year in the United States, almost all due to overexposure to the sun's ultraviolet (UV) rays.

Sun protection can be a big issue when you're camping. First, you tend to spend more time outdoors; second, if you're in hills or mountains, the air gets drier and thinner as you climb, making you more susceptible to sunburn. The thin atmosphere at, say, ten thousand feet above sea level does a poor job of filtering out the particular UV rays that tan and burn.

Many people who tan easily and rarely burn shun sunscreen. It may be the biggest mistake of their lives. Scientists now tell us that a golden tan is prima facie evidence of skin damage.

Prevention

Exposure to UV rays is cumulative. The exposure your daughter gets at age ten can harm her at forty. The damage accumulates and can't be undone. A tan protects her from sunburn but not necessarily from skin cancer.

The most important time to defend against skin damage from the sun is during childhood. Research indicates that the more sunburns you had as a youth, the greater the chances of skin cancer. So protect yourself and your children. The following tips will help you accomplish that:

- The first precaution is to minimize the amount of time your skin is exposed to the sun. Shade yourself with a hat; one-third of all skin cancers occur on the nose and another 10 percent on the lips. They now have scalp screen—for young and old.

- Keep infants and toddlers out of the sun as much as possible. If you use a carriage or a stroller, make sure it has a hood; if you're backpacking your child, consider an umbrella clamped to your pack frame.

- Try to schedule your outdoor activities before or after midday. The sun's rays are most intense from ten A.M. to three P.M. Intensity also increases as you gain altitude or get closer to the equator.

- If you are on medication, consult your doctor about possible adverse reactions to sunlight. Antibiotics, for example, can exacerbate a sunburn.

- For children and the fair of skin, use a sunscreen with a sun protection factor (SPF) of 15 or higher.

> An SPF rating measures only a sunscreen's ability to block the rays that burn. Ultraviolet light also contains nonburning rays that penetrate deeply and are now believed to cause cancer. The most commonly used ingredients in sunscreens—PABA (para-aminobenzoic acid) derivatives such as padimate O—effectively absorb UVB rays, but let through the longer-wavelength UVA rays. Look for products containing dibenzoylmethane compounds, which offer the fullest protection against such rays. Because no SPF rating exists that speaks to UVA protection, two sunscreens with the same SPF can offer markedly different protection against UVA rays.

Sunscreens are oils, lotions, or creams containing compounds that filter out UV rays. Because sunscreens are regulated by the Federal Drug Administration (FDA), you can trust the labels. The all-important SPF tells you how long a sunscreened person can stay in the sun compared to that same person with no sunscreen at all. Each person's base figure depends on location, time of day or year, and skin type. In the tropics a fair-skinned person who freckles can endure only about ten unprotected minutes; sunscreen with an SPF of 15 will extend that safe time to two and a half hours (fifteen times ten minutes).

- Apply the protection thirty to forty-five minutes before going out, to allow it to soak in.

- Apply it generously and often. Studies have shown that people tend to apply only about half the sunscreen the FDA used to determine SPF. Thus SPF 14 effectively becomes SPF 7. It takes at least an ounce to cover the average adult.

- If you swim or sweat, use waterproof or water-resistant sunscreen. By law, products labeled "water-resistant" must protect at their SPF level even after forty minutes in the water. Those labeled "waterproof" must protect after eighty minutes in the water. Bring a watch.

  Waterproof sunscreens are also sweatproof. That's a huge plus, especially when hiking with kids. It means when they exercise, the stuff doesn't run into their eyes and mouth.

  According to a study in *Pediatrics*, only 9 percent of teenagers always use sunscreen and 33 percent never do. Those with family histories of skin cancer are no more likely to use sunscreen than other teens.

- Do you have a bottle of sunscreen of undetermined age? Toss it. Unless the label says otherwise, sunscreens last about three years.

- Don't forget the lips. They don't tan but they do burn. Lip balm with SPF 15 or more is available. Blistex 30 doesn't melt in a hot car or pocket.

- If you or your kids have fair skin, red or blond hair, and light eyes, cover up with long pants, long-sleeved shirts, and hats.

  Fabrics, too, can be rated for SPF. In clothing, tight, opaque weaves are better protection than loose weaves, dyed fabrics are better than undyed. One researcher rated a cotton T-shirt as having an SPF of 5 to 7.4, lower if it's wet. According to the *UC Berkeley Wellness Letter* of August 1993, another researcher rated a cotton-polyester T-shirt at 12 to 20. On the upside, dark blue denim, according to an English study, has an impressive SPF of 1,000.

  Clothing with SPF ratings is coming on the market. Because such products are classified as health devices, claims must be approved by the FDA. Such garments are intended primarily for people with conditions like lupus or melanoma that make them especially sensitive to the sun. But if the ozone layer continues to deteriorate, they may someday become the height of fashion.

- Long-billed hats can halve the eyes' exposure to UV rays. Neck drapes attach to some hats to protect vulnerable ears and neck.

- Wear sunglasses. Even on cloudy days, 60 to 80 percent of UV light can reach your unprotected eyes. Around bright granite and snow, you risk burning your corneas, an affliction known as snow blindness. Symptoms typically don't appear until eight to twelve hours after exposure. The eyes, red and painful, feel like a sandbox. Sunglasses with side blinders decrease the UV radiation received by the eye and prevent snow blindness. If someone loses a pair of sunglasses, you can improvise with two pieces of cardboard with slits cut in them.

Treatment

Just because your skin isn't red while you're outdoors doesn't mean you're not sunburned; a sunburn is most evident six to twenty-four hours after exposure.

If you do get sunburned, the best remedy is to soak the affected area in cold (not iced) water or to apply cold compresses. This is the same treatment as for first-degree burns. This removes heat from the skin, provides some immediate pain relief, and eases the swelling. If you or yours are sunburned all over, try an oatmeal bath. If you're backpacking, you might actually have the oatmeal; you're on your own for the bathtub. Sprinkle a cup of dry instant oatmeal (or corn-starch) in a tub of cool water and soak for a while. The oatmeal soothes the skin and reduces inflammation.

If the burn is severe, try a first-aid spray containing benzocaine, a topical anesthetic. Benzocaine can sensitize the skin, leading to al-lergic reactions to other medications in the "-caine" family. Don't use other "-caine" anesthetics for sunburn, for they are readily absorbed into the bloodstream if the skin is broken and may cause a toxic reaction.

Greasy substances such as butter, baby oil, or after-sun creams seal in heat, so avoid them. Cooling lotions containing menthol or camphor can ease symptoms, but they can also cause allergic reac-tions, especially in children.

■ Swimmer's Ear

Just as you needn't be an athlete to get athlete's foot, you needn't be a swimmer to get swimmer's ear, also known as "jungle ear." It's an infection brought on when water containing bacteria or fungi gets trapped in the outer ear canal. Swimming is the most common cause, but you can get water in your ears from showering or washing your hair.

Prevention

The longer water remains in your ear, the likelier it is that any microorganisms will breed. There are simple steps to prevent swimmer's ear:

- After swimming or washing your hair, shake your head to remove trapped water.

- Dry your outer ear well with a towel or soft cloth.

- Still feel that bubbling sensation? Tilt your head, cup your hand over your ear, and gently press on the ear until the pressure forces the water out.

- If you are prone to ear infections, use antiseptic eardrops, especially after swimming in a lake. You can buy them at any drugstore, or you can make them yourself by mixing equal parts of white vinegar and rubbing alcohol. Put one or two drops into each ear with a dropper. This will restore the natural acid balance of the ear canal and kill the bacteria. If alcohol irritates your skin, use vinegar diluted with water. If your ear continues to itch, use the drops three times daily.

Treatment

Ordinarily, antibiotic drops and irrigation of the ear canal will cure the problem. However, if the ear swells and becomes painful, if the triangular piece of cartilage becomes sore to the touch, or if you have a discharge, seek medical care.

I have two doctors, my left leg and my right.
—George Trevelyan

There are no accidents whatsoever in the universe.
—Baba Ram Dass

■ Safety

Despite the occasional high-profile assault of a thru-hiker on the Appalachian Trail, statistics suggest that you are a lot safer on trails than you are on pavement. In 1991, for example, there were 24,703 murders in a total U.S. population of 252.2 million people, but only 17 of the 267.8 million people who visited national parks were victims of homicide.

Still, hiking alone in unfamiliar territory can make you feel as nervous as Ichabod Crane pursued by the Headless Horseman, especially if you're a woman. Not to mention parking your car in strange places and leaving it for days on end. Chances are nothing bad will happen to you while you're in the wilderness, but you'll have more fun and be more relaxed if you heed the following tips:

> People are usually their own worst enemy in the backcountry. A survey of 700 accidents in Wyoming's Grand Tetons found that 699 of them were the result of "pilot error."

- Before you go, contact a local hiking club or park or forest district office to find out what types of crimes, if any, have been committed where you're heading.

- Find out ahead of time the locations (and telephone numbers, if any) of occupied ranger stations, backcountry camps, and businesses near highway crossings.

- Tell someone back home where you're going, including the name and location of the trailhead, your intended route and campsites, and any cross-country treks you might take. If you need more flexibility, provide alternative routes.

- Consider taking self-defense classes. Studying the martial arts can enhance awareness and confidence.

- Carry a whistle on a string around your neck and know how to use it. A loud, shrill blast is penetrating—and painful—and more likely to scare away an attacker.

- To avoid that lonely Ichabod Crane feeling, hook up with other hikers.

- Adopt a positive, alert attitude and a confident stride. Send the message that you can take care of yourself.

- Learn to trust your instincts, especially if you feel uneasy about another person, a campsite, a shelter, or anything else that raises the hairs on the back of your neck. Such intuition is a subconscious warning flag.

- Avoid overused campsites near roads or trailheads. By camping even a mile off the beaten path, you leave most urban-type crime behind.

- Don't be shy about asking for help. If you're spooked by someone making a crude sexual remark, ask another group of hikers if you can join them.

- Be careful where you park your car. Most wilderness trailhead parking is comparatively low risk. Avoid parking in lots near bars or restaurants, which could draw late-night visitors.

- Remove valuables from your car before leaving home. At the trailhead, leave the glove box open and, if possible, remove the radio and fold down the backseat to the trunk to show there's nothing there. Better yet, have a friend drop you off and pick you up.

Chapter Thirteen

FITNESS

As a nation we are dedicated to keeping fit and parking as close to the stadium as possible.

—Joe Moore

SERIOUS backpacking demands a cardiovascular system strong enough to supply oxygen and nutrients to muscles that may be needed for several hours. Those muscles must be trained to function efficiently, using aerobic sources of energy, but they also need the anaerobic power necessary to surge up hills, leap over dead falls, and scale rocks. To accomplish this, tendons and ligaments must be supple and strong enough to hold joints together as ankles twist and turn. Muscles, tendons, ligaments, and bones must be fine-tuned and coordinated with your nervous system.

Fitness, however, is a hazy concept. The President's Council on Physical Fitness calls it "the ability to carry out daily tasks with vigor and alertness, without undue fatigue, and with ample energy to enjoy leisure-time pursuits and to meet unforeseen emergencies." Yet physical fitness means something quite different to dancers, weight lifters, and hikers. Even within the hiking world, it's a relative term: You may be fitter than you were last year, fitter than your partner, but still out of shape compared to your twenty-five-year-old self. There is no clear-cut point at which you are "fit."

It is clear, however, that if fitness is the goal, then exercise is the means. Physical fitness is made up of four basic elements: muscular strength, muscular endurance, flexibility, and cardiovascular endurance. Each is measurably improved with regular exercise.

For basic health—and efficient backpacking—cardiovascular endurance is the most important element. It is the sustained ability of the heart, blood vessels, and blood to work together to transport oxygen to the cells, the ability of the cells to use that oxygen, and the ability of the blood to whisk away waste products. Since every cell in the body needs oxygen to function, this is a basic measure of fitness.

Many of the problems commonly associated with aging—lower metabolism, increased body fat, decreased muscular strength and flexibility, loss of bone mass, and slower reaction times—are really often signs of inactivity, and they can be minimized or even prevented by exercise. Even if you have been sedentary most of your life, it's not too late to start benefiting from exercise. A study of seventeen thousand Harvard alumni found that "sedentary men who become more active might reduce their risk of death by 24 percent."

Cardiovascular endurance is enhanced by exercises that force the body to deliver ever larger amounts of oxygen to working muscles. To achieve this, the exercise must be sustained and it must work the large muscle groups, such as the leg muscles. At the beginning of exertion, your muscle cells draw on quick energy sources within their own cells. These are obtained without oxygen, and thus short-term efforts like sprinting and weight lifting require scarcely any breathing. Such quick, intense activities are called *anaerobic*, a word derived from two Greek words, meaning "without air."

When exercise lasts longer than a minute or two, as in distance walking, running, cycling, swimming, rowing, and skiing, the muscles get most of their energy from processes that demand extra oxygen delivered to muscles and tissues. Hence, these activities are known as *aerobic*, meaning "with air."

Regular aerobic exercise will tune your cardiovascular system, allowing your heart to pump more blood and thus to deliver more oxygen with greater efficiency. Muscles, too, become more efficient, able to use that increased oxygen. This is part of what is called the aerobic training effect. Because your now stronger heart pumps more blood per beat, your heart rate, both at rest and during exertion, decreases.

To achieve a training effect, you should make aerobic exercise at least an every-other-day habit. Dr. Kenneth Cooper, who has been called "the father of aerobics," asserts that we can achieve basic cardiovascular fitness in as little as twenty minutes every other day. If you exercise more than that, says Cooper, you're doing it for reasons other than cardiovascular fitness. Like perhaps hiking the Pacific Crest Trail.

To get the most from aerobic exercise, you should strive for a range of intensity called the training heart rate (THR). To calculate THR, figure your maximum heart rate (MHR) by subtracting your age from 220, then figure both 60 and 80 percent of that to establish the lower and upper end of your THR.

If you are forty years old, for example, subtract 40 from 220 for an MHR of 180.

$$180 \times 0.60 = 108$$
$$180 \times 0.80 = 144$$

So you want your heart rate while you exercise to be between 108 and 144 beats per minute.

Don't become a numbers nerd. Once you're an experienced exerciser, you may no longer need to take your pulse; you will simply know how it feels to work out at your training heart rate. Two exceptions: highly competitive athletes tracking their progress, and people who need to be cautious due to age, illness, or years of inactivity.

■ Working Out

> The beginning [of exercising] is the most difficult.
> The rewards are almost nonexistent and the sacrifice required is measurable.
> —Fred Schumacher

Unhappy businessmen, I am convinced, would increase their happiness more by walking six miles every day than by any conceivable change of philosophy.
—Bertrand Russell

Whether you're a weekend backpacker or a nationally ranked runner, you should have some kind of fitness program. To obtain maximum benefits, consider the following principles when designing your program.

Individuality

You are wise to take guidelines from others, but remember that you are a unique individual. Your potential is genetically determined and environmentally realized. Age and physical maturation are also factors. Although backpacking is a wonderful activity for children, training for it will be less effective with prepubescents who must channel much of their energy into growth. Many children's coaches limit strength training and prohibit their charges from running more than three miles.

Your current fitness level will greatly affect your rate of improvement. If you're out of shape when you start, you will progress rapidly. Once you become more fit, greater effort is required to see slight improvements.

Lifestyle can also affect your ability and willingness to train. Working sixty hours a week can be fatal to a serious training regimen. Stress can also cut into your workout. A diet rich in fat and low in complex carbohydrates and vitamins probably won't support the energy level required to train. Long-term sleep deficit will have the same effect.

Motivation is also highly individualistic. Those who are internally motivated participate for self-fulfillment; those who are externally motivated thrive on the attention they receive from others.

Knowledge of Results

Keeping track of accomplishments—whether it's how much weight you lift or how fast you run the mile—can provide the positive reinforcement needed to persevere.

Progressive Overload

Pushing yourself beyond ordinary limits overloads the body and causes it to adapt, or improve. This overload—running farther or faster, lifting more weight—should be increased by small increments to produce adaptive buildup rather than destructive breakdown. Overload can be applied to all three elements of training—frequency, intensity, and duration—but strive to increase duration and frequency before intensity. This will provide a sound aerobic base upon which to build strength. As you adapt to new levels of fitness, you must increase frequency, duration, and intensity to continue to overload the system.

Adaptation

If you tax your body to the limit, it responds by raising the limit. It adapts. Want more speed and strength? Run fast or uphill for short distances. The body responds by producing more muscle fiber filaments, more enzymes to break down glucose. Want more endurance? Run long distances at a higher intensity. Your body will produce more mitochondria and enzymes to burn carbohydrates aerobically; it will store more glycogen to help you burn fat longer. More agility? Expose the body to a variety of maneuvers, including running through the woods dodging tree branches and roots. Over time, the nervous system will develop a larger repertoire of responses, and each response will be quicker.

Rest

Overloading temporarily weakens the body. Muscle filaments break down, enzymes are depleted. It is during the rest phase that rebuilding takes place. Give your body enough time between workouts for recovery. If you overload it too soon, you risk injury or illness, leaving you in worse shape than before. Inside your body, rest time is not idle time.

In the beginning, rest may mean taking a whole day off; later, it may mean alternating a heavy workout with a light one.

Reversibility

Although rest is essential, it shouldn't last too long. If you eliminate the demands you place on your body, it will return to a lower level of fitness. If you want to stay fit, you must continue to place the same, or higher, demands on your body. If you stop completely, aerobic losses will approach 10 percent per week; strength will also decline, though not as fast. Maintain fitness during the off-season by participating in activities that place demands on the body similar to what is needed for backpacking.

Specificity

For maximum efficacy, training must be specific to the activity you wish to perform. If you want to be good at going up steep hills with weight on your back, practice going up steep hills with weight on your back.

Variety

Vary your workouts to provide motivation and maximize fitness improvements. Hiking the same trail at a constant pace will leave you stranded on a fitness plateau.

Warmup and Cool-Down

Do not give short shrift to the warmup and cool-down. An effective warmup increases circulation, improves flexibility, and increases the temperature of the muscles, all of which help protect against pulls. It should last five to fifteen minutes and gradually increase in intensity.

The mistake many people make is to begin the warmup with passive stretches. Cold muscles are not ready to be stretched; they respond with a silent scream. As an alternative, begin with brisk walking for two to five minutes; this will warm tissues, making stretching easier and less risky.

After a workout, the muscles are engorged with blood. If exercise ceases abruptly, that blood will pool in the muscles, reducing blood flow elsewhere and causing a buildup of lactic acid in the muscles. In extreme cases, deprivation of oxygen to the brain can cause fainting.

Intense exercise should always be followed by a cool-down that includes walking and stretching.

Flexibility

The latest research confirms the effectiveness of short, moderate exercise sessions. It seems that nine weekly ten-minute sessions offer the same cardiovascular benefits as three weekly thirty-minute sessions. That's good news for beginning exercisers, who may find it easier to stick to shorter, more manageable workouts. Turn your coffee break into an exercise break. Try ten minutes of brisk walking before work, ten minutes of stair climbing or a quick run at lunch, and ten minutes of rope jumping or cycling in the evening.

Long-Term Training

Make fitness a lifetime goal, exercise a lifelong habit.

How do Americans exercise? Here are the most popular fitness activities of 1995 compared to those of 1987, according to a nationwide survey conducted for the Fitness Products Council. These figures are the number (in millions) of Americans who participate at least twice a week in the activities.

	1987	1995	Percentage change
Fitness walking	10.2	17.2	+69%
Free weights	6.3	11.4	+81
Running	7.9	9.5	+20
Stationary cycling	7.0	9.4	+34
Treadmills	0.5	7.0	+1300
Resistance machines	3.2	6.2	+94
Swimming (fitness)	6.6	4.9	−26
Cycling (fitness/touring)	4.8	4.6	−4
Stair-climbing machines	0.3	3.8	+1167

■ Nutrition

The recommended diets for athletes and other active individuals are, with minor adjustments, the same as for all healthy people. One difference is that active people expend more energy than sedentary people, so they need to consume more calories. How many more calories depends on age, body size and type, metabolism, type of activity, and level of training.

> Don't confuse body fat and excess dietary fat. Body fat is the stored form of dietary protein, carbohydrates, and fats. Even lean people have more than enough fat stores for energy production.

Calories come from carbohydrates (sugars and starches), protein, and fat. A gram of fat yields more than twice as many calories as a gram of protein or carbohydrate (about nine to four). Moreover, researchers have found evidence that the body may convert dietary fat into body fat with greater ease than it converts carbohydrates into body fat. For example, if you consume one hundred excess carbohydrate calories, twenty-three of those calories will be used simply processing those foods, and thus only seventy-seven of them can be stored as body fat for reserve energy. On the other hand, consume a hundred excess fat calories and only three calories are burned processing and storing them.

Less than 30 percent of your daily calories should come from fat (some nutritionists advise less than 20 percent), with less than 10 percent coming from saturated fat. Besides being a health risk, a high-fat diet will impair the performance of an endurance athlete. Avoid fatty foods before exercise, as they can take three to four hours to digest.

Here are some other nutritional tips that will help you maximize your athletic potential:

- *Eat breakfast like a king or queen, lunch like a prince or princess, and dinner like a pauper.* According to the United States Department of Agriculture, Americans consume 42 to 45 percent of their total daily calories at dinner. The foods eaten at dinner contribute a significant amount of nutrients to the diet, but also a whopping percentage of the day's fat, cholesterol, and sodium.

- *Eat less.* Studies of societies whose members live the longest reveal this common characteristic: They eat light meals and almost no meat. Also, don't be afraid to eat alone. Researchers have found that meals eaten with other people contain 44 percent more calories than meals eaten solo.

> If you want to take weight off and leave it off, have fun. Studies indicate that increasing the amount of gratification and enjoyment in daily life (unrelated to eating) can help assure the success of a weight-loss plan. Most of the pleasurable activities in an overweight person's life are related to eating. Normal-weight people have a wider spectrum of enjoyable activities, such as hobbies or work.

- *Cut down on fat.* Americans eat way too much fat— nearly 40 percent of their total calories come from fat. The new FDA-mandated labels include both total calories and fat calories, so it's easy to calculate the percentage of calories derived from fat. Try to keep that figure below 30 percent.

- *Cut down on fast food.* One out of five Americans (fifty million) eat in fast-food restaurants on a typical day, and many rely on them to provide them with a quick, hot lunch. But chances are, they are short-changing themselves nutritionally. Between 40 and 55 percent of the calories in most fast-food meals come from fat, mostly in the form of saturated fat, the kind that raises blood cholesterol levels. Burgers and fries are also high in sodium, and you can easily consume the

> The average American gains seven pounds between the ages of twenty-five and thirty-four, with women gaining slightly more than men.

entire maximum recommended daily allowance of sodium (2,400 milligrams) in one sitting. In addition, fast food is low in fiber and calcium and high in calories.

▪ Rest

Rest is necessary to allow your muscles time to recover, rebuild, and refuel for the next workout. Here are some tips to expedite recovery:

- Keep a training journal. Record your workout experiences, including both objective and subjective information. Besides distance, time, and heart rate, you might note degree of difficulty and how you felt during and after the workout.

- Cool down and allow your heart rate to return gradually to normal. After you finish a run, continue at a brisk walk for three to five minutes.

- Drink lots of water before, during, and after a workout. As little as a 6 percent loss of water in the body can damage muscles and slow recovery.

- Stretch thoroughly, particularly calves, hamstrings, and Achilles tendons.

- Eat enough carbohydrates to replace calories and restock glycogen stores. Each mile, whether walked, jogged, or run, burns about one hundred calories, the equivalent of a good-size apple or banana.

- Follow hard days with easy days or rest days. Strength is developed not during exercise but during rest, when muscle tissue rebuilds.

■ Injury Recovery

Although by some accounts less than one-tenth of 1 percent of emergency room business can be attributed to backpacking, it's a rare backpacker who hasn't suffered at least sore muscles and joints. According to orthopedic surgeon Elizabeth Regan-Lowe, trail injuries happen "because people haven't conditioned their bodies to fit their goals." The basic prescription for healthy hiking is fitness and common sense. Stay fit all year round. Don't try to *get* fit on your annual two-week backpacking trip.

When coming back from an injury, it's sometimes difficult to know when to rest and when to work out. The first question you need to ask is, How much does it hurt? There are four general classifications of injuries:

First degree. No limitation of motion, but a low-grade pain at the start of a workout that diminishes as the exercising progresses. Afterward, the pain returns. *Advice*: Warm up thoroughly before you try anything hard. No other change in routine is required.

Second degree. Pain persists during the workout, but there is little effect on form. *Advice*: Eliminate the workouts that cause pain to increase, usually the races, steep hills, and long hard runs.

Third degree. Minor pain on easy workouts; more severe pain on longer or harder ones. *Advice*: Alternate jogging and walking. Start slowly and don't push it. When you feel the pain coming on, slow to a walk.

Fourth degree. Pain is so intense that it is impossible to move without disturbance of form. *Advice*: Replace walking or running with another, more benign aerobic activity, like biking or swimming.

In general, work gradually toward lesser degrees of pain—from fourth to third to second to first. Be patient.

■ Trail Endurance

Even if you work out regularly, it's unlikely you will get as much exercise as you do backpacking. If you hike just seven miles a day, carrying a pack uphill and downhill, you will probably breathe hard for at least three hours and burn more than a thousand calories. Here are some ways to ensure that your endurance endures:

- Stay hydrated (see "Dehydration" on page 260 for details).

- Pace yourself. Find a rhythm that lets you glide along for hours.

- Acclimatize (see "Altitude Sickness" on page 251 for details).

- Hike light. Carry nothing you can do without.

- Get out of yourself. Instead of dwelling on your achy feet or how far it is to camp, daydream the miles away. Hiking is an ideal time to let your mind wander.

- Sleep well. One poor night's sleep probably won't affect your hiking performance, but repeated ones will. If it's a problem, don't skimp on proper sleeping gear.

- Walk during the cool of the day. Because heat is the number-one energy zapper, avoid hiking on hot summer afternoons. Start early and break when the sun is high in the sky. If you must brave the midday sun, stay shaded under a wide-brimmed hat.

- Eat often. Small, carbo-laden snacks are the best way to maximize energy.

- Remain goal-flexible. Don't be a slave to your plans or expectations. If you must reach point B by nightfall, start early enough so you don't feel rushed.

- Tune in to your environment. Feel the warmth of the sun, the caress of the breeze, the cry of an unseen bird. If you know something about the geology, botany, or history of the area, you will almost certainly get more out of being there. Interested people are energetic people.

Chapter Fourteen

ANIMAL LORE

*Human beings are the only animals of which I am
thoroughly and cravenly afraid.*

—George Bernard Shaw

WITH the belief that the more we know about nature, the less we have to fear, we present here profiles of a few of the animals you might see, or wonder about seeing, on your next backpacking trip.

■ Black Bear

If you learn nothing else about wildlife, be clear on the differences between black bears and grizzlies. Early white settlers in America made no such distinctions. Forged by fear and need, they held a strictly utilitarian view of bears, regardless of species. Its hide was used for clothing and bedding, its rich meat for food, its fat for frying and healing ointment. Hunting and logging decimated bear populations and habitat until twentieth-century game laws gave them protection, permitting a partial comeback.

Normally solitary and retiring, black bears live in dense thickets, caves, and tree hollows. In their natural state, they eat nuts, berries, insects, and small mammals. Only recently have they developed a taste for freeze-dried backpacking food.

The wild animal that kills the most bears?—the porcupine. If its quills stick in a bear's tongue, the bear can starve to death.

Excluding polar bears, who are rarely encountered by backpackers, North America's bear family (*Ursidae*) is divided into two groups—black bears and brown (grizzly or Kodiak) bears. Color is an unreliable guide, as black bears range from black to cinnamon and browns from pale gold to almost black. A better clue is geography. In the United States, if you encounter a bear outside Alaska or Yellowstone or Glacier National Park, overwhelming odds are it's a black bear. Black bears are about half as large as browns and a fraction as cranky. In the recorded history of Yosemite National Park, no human has ever been killed by a black bear.

California's black bear population is flourishing. According to estimates of wildlife biologists, there are seventeen thousand to twenty-four thousand animals in the wilds, which may be more than when settlers first arrived in the state. The reason: Black bears haven't had a natural enemy since the California grizzly became extinct in the 1920s.

The North American black bear spends the winter in near hibernation, sleeping away the better part of seven months. Female bears rouse themselves long enough to give birth to one to three cubs, each weighing a mere eight to ten ounces. They remain in the den with their sleeping mother, nursing and dozing until spring.

Black bears would no doubt do well in an animal decathlon. They are fast (up to thirty-two miles per hour), powerful (able to break into a car trunk), agile (able to climb a quaking aspen in seconds), and capable swimmers. They are also intelligent, curious, and always hungry. Proper food storage on our part is essential to assure the continued wildness of these magnificent creatures. Moreover, because chronically troublesome bears are sometimes exterminated, keeping your food from bears may save their lives.

Yosemite officials suggest the following precautions around bears:

- Use food lockers where available. Keep them closed and latched except when putting in or taking out

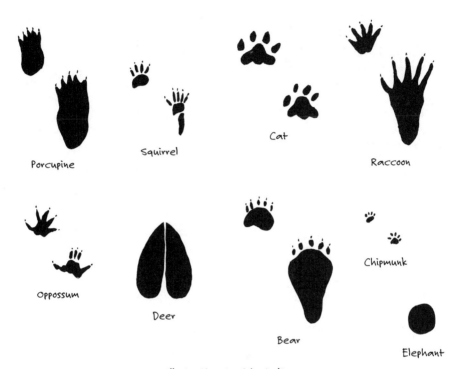

Illustrations by John Kelty

food. Though bears tend to be most active in the evenings and at night, they may be roaming about at any hour and may even enter your camp when you are present, though that is rare.

- If you are car camping and lockers are not available, all food and food containers should be stored in the trunk of a vehicle. In a vehicle with no trunk, cover food and food containers and keep them out of sight, and keep all windows and vents closed.

Between 1960 and 1980, black bears injured more than five hundred people in North America; 90 percent of the injuries were minor. Grizzly bear attacks accounted for fewer than two hundred injuries between 1900 and 1980. Why such a discrepancy if grizzlies are more aggressive? Because most wilderness recreation takes place in black bear country, and they outnumber grizzlies by more than ten to one.

In thirty-seven years of wilderness backpacking, I have fed bears only once. Camped at Vernon Lake, on the edge of Yosemite National Park, a notoriously bad bear area (the defiant bears from heavily populated Yosemite Valley are relocated nearby), we hung our food in a tree, but neglected to counterbalance it. One night we were awakened by a loud thrashing, a few guttural growls, and a thump—our food bag hitting the ground! On only our second day out, a black bear and her cub were clawing at our food stash.

We leapt from our sleeping bags, screaming, pounding pots, and throwing rocks, all to no avail. Black bears can usually be driven from camp by such scare tactics—right up to the time they poke their snouts into your food bag.

Like most mistakes, losing our food was a learning experience. The morning after the heist, we followed bear tracks and scat, picking up a discarded soup mix here, a granola bar there. No freeze-dried dinners survived, however; the bears had eaten those. They had been packaged in distinctive red tin foil, which regularly appeared in the bear scat. A world-class digestive tract.

—S.B.

- Do not store food in a tent or in the open. Seal it in containers to minimize odors.

- Store toothpaste, suntan lotion, insect repellent, cosmetics, and tasty vitamin C as you would food.

- Keep a clean camp. Deposit all garbage in bear-resistant containers before going to bed or leaving camp. Wash the dishes immediately after use.

- In the backcountry, counterbalance two sacks (sleeping-bag stuff sacks are ideal), containing all food and related items, over a tree branch so that they hang at least fourteen feet above the ground, ten feet from the trunk, and five feet below the branch.

- Do not allow bears to approach you or enter your camp. If one approaches, bang pots, clap hands, or throw rocks or pine cones from a safe distance, all the while yelling at the bear. Never try to retrieve food taken by a bear.

- Do not feed or approach bears. This may seem obvious, but some misguided parents have tried to put children on the backs of bears for photos.

- Do not get between a bear and her cubs. Most black bear attacks are motivated by what the mother sees as a threat to her cubs.

■ Grizzly Bear

In 1804, as Lewis and Clark moved west through Wyoming, they heard recurring tales—tall tales, they assumed—of a huge bear with a massive head and ferocious manner. They were skeptical because they were well acquainted with the black bear and found him inoffensive and easily felled with a well-placed shot. They soon had another opinion about the grizzly, with Lewis writing: "The wonderful power of life which these animals possess renders them dreadful. . . . We had rather encounter two Indians than meet a single brown bear."

Besides size—a large grizzly weighs about 850 pounds, a large black bear closer to 400—grizzlies differ from black bears by their longer claws, whitish ("grizzled") hairs on upper parts, and a high shoulder hump, which is actually a knot of powerful muscles that drives the front legs.

The grizzly was given the scientific name *Ursus horribilis*—the "horrible bear"—by a man who had never seen one and who relied on the testimony of another man who, though he too had never seen one, boldly wrote that the grizzly "is the enemy of man and literally thirsts for human blood." This unfortunate hyperbole, along with the fact that people are occasionally mauled by browns, all but doomed the grizzly in the lower forty-eight.

> When humans clash with grizzly bears, the bears invariably lose. In the first eighty years of the 20th century, grizzly bears killed fourteen people in the lower forty-eight states. During just five of those years—1968 to 1973—180 grizzlies were exterminated, most within or near national parks.

Grizzlies do kill people, about one every other year, but with the possible exception of tigers, there is little evidence of any "man-

REI's bear bells are designed to be strapped to your bootlaces when hiking through grizzly country. $3 a bell. REI mail order: (800) 426-4840

eating" animals. However, bear attacks are lurid by nature and make good news, infuriating antigrizzly forces. In response to two deadly bear attacks in south-central Alaska in July 1992, seventeen bears were exterminated.

While it was once the most abundant bear, ranging from Alaska to northern Mexico, hunting and habitat destruction have reduced the grizzly's range to Alaska, western Canada, and six tiny enclaves in the West, including Glacier and Yellowstone National Parks. The last grizzly in California went down in 1924. Since Lewis and Clark explored the West, the brown population in the continental United States has declined from about one hundred thousand to fewer than one thousand. About five thousand to ten thousand brown bears still prowl the huge state of Alaska.

If you travel to grizzly country:

- Be alert to bear signs, such as scat, claw marks, and prints.

I once met a graduate student working for a leading grizzly expert. The expert was a professor, and for years he had preached, "When attacked by a grizzly, don't run. Play dead." Then one day, in Yellowstone, the professor was in fact attacked by a grizzly. Ignoring his own advice, he did what came naturally—he ran. The beast also did what came naturally. He caught and mauled the professor. "He's still into grizzlies," said the student.

—S.B.

- When selecting a campsite in bear country—especially grizzly country— avoid camping right next to a trail or stream, as bears favor those areas when searching for food.

- Sleep in a tent.

- Do not feed any bears, deliberately or accidentally. The bear you feed becomes a little less self-sufficient, a little more dependent on humans. In the absence of trees or man-made protection, you can place your food on top of a large rock, which may be too slippery for the grizzly to climb.

- Never surprise a bear—they hate surprises. In grizzly country, make noise on the trail. Sing songs, tell stories, recite Tibetan chants or bad poetry, or tell stories. Tie a bell to your pack or periodically blow a whistle.

- Never charge a grizzly.

- If you do spot a grizzly, circle around it in a wide arc, staying downwind, for bears have an excellent sense of smell. (Just assume they do everything better than you do.)

Even though the grizzly has been federally protected since 1975 (when it was listed as threatened under the Endangered Species Act), populations are steadily decreasing in the lower forty-eight. The Sierra Club blames it on federal land management agencies that have refused to halt development infringing on grizzly habitat. Fewer than a thousand grizzlies remain in the lower forty-eight, with most in Montana, Wyoming, Idaho, and Washington.

- Consider traveling in a large group. No bear attack has ever been recorded on a party of six or more. Glacier National Park is considering a rule restricting hiking in certain areas to parties of four or more.

In the unlikely event of a grizzly attack, quickly choose one of two alternatives:

- Climb a tree to a height of thirty feet or more. Grizzlies do not climb as well as black bears. Don't worry if you don't climb well; fear is a powerful motivator.

- Play dead and hope the bear stops seeing you as a threat. Recommended dead positions are lying on your stomach with hands behind the head or lying on your side in the fetal position, knees tight to chin.

Chipmunk

A chipmunk is a ground squirrel, distinguished by a bushless tail and stripes on its back that extend to its face. Unlike tree squirrels, which use their bushy tail for balance as they run and leap, chipmunks would find such a tail a liability when diving into burrows.

Although they will climb trees, mostly to escape predators and find food, chipmunks spend most of their time at or below ground level. They dig extensive burrows up to twelve feet long and three feet deep, which usually include a nest, dump, latrine (they are fastidious), pantry, and some concealed entrances and exits. They generally use the same burrow year after year, with regular remodeling. The digging is seldom evident above ground.

The pantry can hold up to half a bushel of nuts and other foods, all carried there in the chipmunk's remarkable cheeks, which hang like saddlebags on both sides of its neck. One patient researcher counted thirty-seven hundred blueberry seeds in the pouches of a chipmunk that looked as though it had a bad case of mumps.

When chipmunks get worried, they freeze. They can remain motionless for a long time, relying on acute sight and hearing to escape danger.

Lacking seeds or nuts, chipmunks will adapt. They've been known to eat mushrooms, moles, grasshoppers, small frogs, salamanders, and small bird eggs. Their elaborate grooming may be a clever defense against predators that rely on scent to find prey, or it may be a reaction to the ticks and fleas that bedevil the animal. Indeed, bubonic plague has been found among chipmunks, leading National Park Service authorities to recommend avoiding all rodents.

Coyote

A member of the dog family, the coyote, with its pointed muzzle, long ears, slender legs, and rhythmic gait, bears a strong resemblance to the wolf and dog. It is distinguished by a long, bushy tail that droops when it runs.

It's rare to see coyotes in the wild but not so to hear them. Their unique howl is a symbol of the Wild West. Their yipping is followed by a long, quavering wail that chills your blood the first time you hear it. Often other coyotes respond, resulting in a group sing that is a lullaby to some and disturbing to others. Relax and enjoy it, and convey that response to your children. There is no danger, it probably won't last long, and it sure beats the caterwauling of alley cats.

Mammals, including carrion, generally make up about 90 percent of the coyote's diet. They also feed on fruit, insects, and barnyard animals. It is the last that provokes the ire of humans. Stockmen hate coyotes with the passion early settlers reserved for wolves. In 1915, the federal government began slaughtering coyotes and wolves. In the next thirty-two years nearly two million coyotes were exterminated.

A coyote may not get any respect, but it has not only survived but thrived while the wolf has been all but exterminated. One of the few predators to extend its range in the twentieth century, it now roams from northern Alaska to Costa Rica.

Coyotes have many qualities we admire:

They are smart. At bumblebee nests, the coyote will wave its tail until bees swarm out to investigate, then stick in its nose and eat the honey.

They are tough. More than one coyote caught in a steel trap has been known to drag the contraption for miles, even pausing to capture a gopher or two en route. If it cannot pull loose from the trap, it may gnaw off its own paw to escape.

They are fast. Coyotes have been clocked at close to fifty miles per hour in a short sprint, and thirty to thirty-five over longer distances.

They are devoted to family. The male will bring food to its pregnant wife, play with the pups, teach them to hunt, even present itself as a decoy to lure men and hounds away from the family lair.

They are resourceful. Coyotes have been known to work collectively on a deer kill, and some have mated with domestic dogs. They will raid garbage cans if necessary.

Though they are extending their range, they represent no threat to campers, unless you ride into the wilderness on sheepback. As John Muir once said, "Coyotes . . . are beautiful animals, and, although cursed by man, are beloved by God. Their sole fault is that they are fond of mutton."

■ Deer

The deer is the large mammal that you and your kids have the best chance of seeing in the wild. By "deer" in North America we mean either white-tailed or mule deer, although elk, moose, and caribou also belong to that family of hoofed animals that shed their antlers each year.

Dusk and early morning are the best time to see deer; during the day, they lay low and digest their food. In national parks, where they are protected, they will often browse for twigs or buds on the edge of your camp. If you wish to prolong their stay, sit still and observe; if you must move, go slowly; enjoy the quiet grace of these animals.

Only male deer have antlers. Contrary to myth, you can't tell the age of a deer by the size of the antlers or the number of tines. Antler development depends on nutrition, not age.

Deer tend to move to lower elevations before winter and back up to higher elevations in spring. They rut in autumn, when males battle for, and associate briefly with, females. Spotted fawns, usually twins, are born in spring. Young females may stay with their mother for two years, but males leave in the first year.

Don't feed deer. The salt, sugar, and preservatives in human food can make them sick. If deer become too dependent on humans for food, they stop foraging. Also, losing their natural fear of humans can be fatal when they migrate to lower elevations outside of national parks and become easy targets for hunters. Although deer seem tame, they are actually wild and unpredictable. A few years ago a five-year-old boy was killed by a deer in Yosemite. He was feeding the animal with his parents' blessing when it bolted, raking him with its antlers.

■ Insects

Iridescent dragonflies, spectacularly patterned butterflies, and dainty little ladybugs are all fascinating examples of insects. About seven hundred thousand species so far have been identified worldwide.

Although most insects are neither helpful nor harmful to humans, we waste little love or respect on them. According to a University of Arizona study cited by Sue Hubbell in her *A Book of Bugs*, 90 percent of respondents said they were either "acutely afraid of" or "heartily disliked" insects. Excluding the universally loved ladybug, less than one percent of Americans say they like bugs. We spend $3.5 billion a year in the United States on chemical warfare against them. How effective is it? Despite their size, there are three hundred pounds of bugs out there for every pound of person.

Children are usually fascinated by bugs; they know what it's like to be small. You can help them appreciate their incredible complexity. Share with them the dragonfly's astonishing eyes, each a glittering mosaic of thousands of tiny facets; the defensive odor of the stinkbug; and the camouflage technique of the walkingstick. Marvel at the complex society created by ants and bees and wonder at the metamorphosis of beetles and butterflies, who go through four distinct life stages—egg, larva (caterpillar, worm, or grub), pupa, and adult.

■ Mountain Lion

Also known as cougar, puma, and panther, the mountain lion is moderately plentiful in the West, scarce across the Midwest, and rare as mango trees in the East. The Florida panther is the most critically endangered large mammal in North America.

This lithe cat comes in shades of reddish brown, golden brown, and dull gray. Its throat and chin are white. Weighing up to 120 pounds when mature, it is big because it is the most adept large carnivore in North America (bears, less choosy, are omnivores), a specialized killing machine. The mountain lion's teeth, claws, speed, and elusiveness are designed to bring down fresh meat. Deer really make a lion drool. Usually solitary and nocturnal, the mountain lion hunts by stalking and rushing or by pouncing from trees and overhanging rocks. Like other large cats, it usually kills by biting the neck of its prey.

Cougar attacks on humans can be serious but are quite rare. During the past century, more than seven hundred people have been killed by lightning for every one killed by a mountain lion. A young girl was seriously mauled in southern California in 1986, apparently by a lion raised in captivity and released into the wild. In April 1992, a cougar pounced on a Sacramento man dressed in camouflage crouching next to a turkey decoy and blowing a turkey call.

Following such an attack, there is a wave of sentiment to wipe out the cougar population. But California biologist Paul Beier, who has examined records of unprovoked cougar attacks in the United States and Canada between 1890 and 1990, brings some reason to the argument. He found fifty-three documented attacks, of which thirty occurred in Canada's British Columbia, and only nine were fatal. Nine human fatalities in a hundred years. Not many compared to the forty or so people who die each year from bee stings, or the eighty from lightning strikes, or the forty thousand slaughtered on the highways each year.

Despite its record for good behavior, the mountain lion has long been viewed as little more than vermin, something to be unthinkingly exterminated. The prevalent attitude was summed up by Theodore Roosevelt, who wrote, "Lord of stealthy murder, facing his doom with a heart both craven and cruel." With such a reputation, an animal that once prowled the entire continent was soon reduced to a few wild spots in the West, usually in rugged high country.

Actually, not only do mountain lions rarely attack people, but researchers have also concluded that they will never overpopulate the countryside because of their territoriality and that they do not threaten big-game herds. They prey on the young, the old, and the sick, leaving alone those of breeding age.

Environmentalists and animal lovers have won widespread protection for cougars, and every state except Texas now regulates the killing of the animal. The government thinks cougar numbers are increasing, but many environmentalists believe this is illusory because their increasing contact with humans is due to more homes being built on land where the big cats once lived by themselves.

If you'd prefer not to see any large cats, make noise as you hike in cougar country. Keep your pets and kids close by (better yet, keep your pets out of the backcountry). Control food odors and other enticing smells. Mountain lions are intimidated by height, so get as big and scary as possible. Take off your pack and put it in front of you. Spread out your jacket like wings. Hoist your children onto your shoulders. Speak in a loud, firm voice. Avoid direct eye contact by looking off to the side, monitoring the cat's movements in your peripheral vision.

If the lion continues to threaten, throw rocks, tree limbs, or tent poles, or jab with a walking stick. If attacked, try to stay on your feet. Don't run or play dead, but rather stand firm, yell, and fight back. This would be a good time to use that canister of hot-pepper spray you carry. Above all, be aggressive. Lions aren't used to their prey poking them in the eye or kicking them in the groin. Most people who have resisted a lion attack have lived to tell about it.

▪ Opossum

The opossum is North America's only marsupial (pouched mammal). Thirteen days after breeding, it bears litters of up to eighteen premature kits, each no larger than a honeybee. Weighing little more than an ounce total, the whole brood could fit comfortably inside a large serving spoon. The young are so immature their skin is translucent, their internal organs visible. Immediately after birth, the tiny creatures begin wriggling up into Mom's pouch in search of a life-sustaining nipple. As Mrs. Possum only has twelve nipples, the race is a textbook case of survival of the fittest. The twelve winners remain attached to a nipple for a month or two, then move onto Mom's back, which is home for another few weeks. At the tender age of three months, they are sent off to make their way in the world.

As their fifty teeth (more than any other North American land mammal) develop, the young switch from mother's milk to an incredibly diverse diet of insects, birds' eggs, grain, mushrooms, fruit, and carrion. Such versatility permits them to live close to humans and assures the success of the species, if not the individual. While opossums have extended their range almost a million square miles in the past fifty years, the individual in the wild rarely lives to see its third birthday. One reason: They are good climbers but slow afoot and easy targets for cars.

Opossums are distinctive looking, with their pink nose and pointed snout, but they often go unnoticed because they are passive and mostly nocturnal. And, yes, an opossum will defend itself by "playing possum"—curling into a limp heap and entering a catatonic trance that can last as long as six hours. Though an attacker may poke, bite, or pick it up, the opossum will not move. As most predators prefer to eat only what they kill, this tactic often saves the opossum's life. Many scientists believe the animal is too stupid to do this deliberately, but instead faints from fear, its nervous system overloaded to the point of temporary paralysis.

■ Porcupine

Contrary to myth, porcupines cannot shoot their quills. They don't need to; they are formidable enough as it is. If this nocturnal rodent perceives you as a threat, it will turn its back, raise about thirty thousand quills, and rattle them like swords. If you don't get the hint, this twelve-pound walking pincushion will start backing toward you. If you're fool enough to stick around, it will swing its tail with enough force to embed hundreds of quills in your skin. The fight is over and the porcupine has won. Don't feel bad. You were stupid, yes, but quills have even been discovered in polar bears.

Removing the hollow quills is excruciating, but leaving them in can be fatal. Body heat and moisture cause them to expand, and muscle movement forces them deeper into the skin, anchoring each shaft and assuring that if the quills are removed, flesh will be, too.

A few hardy humans regard roast porcupine as a delicacy, but one does not eat a quilled animal without risk. Doctors once operated on a man complaining of severe stomach pains, only to find that his intestine had been punctured by a quill consumed in a porcupine sandwich four days earlier. The man died.

Although porcupines have keen touch, hearing, and smell, they are extremely nearsighted. They feed on bark, twigs, leaves, and buds, and Steve once had a porcupine take a bite out of his Ensolite pad.

▪ Raccoon

These cute little ring-tailed, bandit-faced beggars are transcontinental in range and live in rural, suburban, and forested areas from southern Canada to Central America. They are, in short, everywhere.

They usually make their dens in hollow logs or holes in trees, but they may also inhabit deserted buildings. They prefer woods near streams or lakes, which can supply much of their food. This often puts them close to humans, who also like to live near water. That doesn't seem to bother the raccoons. They boldly approach people for handouts in campgrounds and backyards.

Raccoons have long been noted for "washing" their food before eating, but revisionist scientists claim that this behavior reflects the animal's natural habit of finding food in water.

Raccoons are omnivorous in the extreme. When not in search of handouts, they will forage at night for frogs, crayfish, fish, birds, eggs, fruits, vegetables, and insects. Because they are cute and unperturbed by human presence, people go out of their way to feed them. That can be a fatal mistake.

Though they often appear friendly and passive, raccoons can be surly. Family fights are common, sometimes degenerating into a group brawl, complete with snarling, clawing, and biting. Although the male is polygamous, the female won't take just any mate. Once she has made up her mind, she refuses to have a relationship with another male that season. Raccoons mate in the winter and babies are born about nine weeks later. Dad takes no part in raising the family.

With their mother's help, the young quickly learn the art of survival. She leads them to water, where they learn to catch fish and explore for frogs and water insects. They search for grubs in rotting logs and eggs in birds' nests. They learn how to catch grasshoppers and mice. In late summer and early fall, they sample wild grapes, manzanita berries, elderberries, and other fruit. They carry most of their edibles to water and wash or dunk them before they eat.

During the training period, the mother raccoon must be on the lookout for hungry bobcats and cougars. However, she is a fierce defender of her young and few enemies will confront her. Mom stays with her brood through the first winter, after which she goes her separate way.

■ Skunk

This skunk story was sent to _Backpacker_ magazine by Bill Dvorak of Dvorak Expeditions: "We were taking a group of city kids from Denver out into the backcountry. For many of them it was their first trip and they didn't always follow the rules. I told them not to bring food in the tent, but one girl stuck a big bag of M&Ms next to her pillow for a snack. About midnight, a skunk got in the tent and the counselor, still awake next to the girl, froze with fright. She watched it climb over the sleeping girl, tear open the bag of candy, and proceed to sit down on top of her and eat the whole bag. She said later she didn't know if she should chase it out and risk being sprayed or just roll over and hope it went away. She rolled over and, sure enough, it did go away."

While rattlesnakes, black widow spiders, and grizzly bears get heaps of hype, far less attention is paid to the unique defense system of striped and spotted skunks.

Skunks generally live in burrows, though spotted skunks might live in deserted barns or hollow trees. Both breeds are nocturnal and employ odor as a defensive weapon. By the time a skunk finally sprays, you have already had several warnings. It begins with a little stamping of the front paws, quickly escalating to hissing and shaking the head from side to side. When at last the skunk raises its tail (the spotted skunk does a reverse handstand with a high degree of difficulty), it is too late for reason. Head for the hills.

If you get a bad jump, the skunk may just hit you between the eyes with a steady stream of mercaptan, a potent glow-in-the-dark fluid. Up to a distance of a dozen feet, it has the accuracy of a Western gunslinger. Once mercaptan soaks into fur, hair, or skin, it not only makes the victim sick but also can cause temporary blindness. Humans typically become teary-eyed and nauseated.

If you or your pet does get sprayed, you can buy an over-the-counter de-skunking solution at a pet store, but nothing neutralizes skunk odor better than bathing in tomato juice. Those stinky clothes, though, will have to be buried or burned; washing will never remove all traces of odor.

■ Snake

Nothing provokes a startled response in a hiker faster than the sight of a snake—any snake. Intellectually, we know or should know that most snakes are benign. In North America only the rattlesnake, the copperhead, the cottonmouth (water moccasin), and the coral snake are venomous. Yet slithering reptiles—legless lizards, really—are universally reviled.

Snakes are distinguished mostly by what they don't have: legs and eyelids. There are no vegetarian snakes. They are among the most successful creatures on earth and inhabit every continent except Antarctica. There are more than twenty-seven hundred kinds, from the four-inch thread snake to the thirty-two-foot reticulated python. On cool days, many snakes like to warm their cold blood in the sun; when temperatures are high, they seek shade. They are most active when temperatures are moderate.

Jim Hamilton once had a nasty brush with both raccoons and skunks all in one night. "We were camped in Maine's Acadia National Park," he says. "I drank a bit too much wine around the campfire, and sometime in the middle of the night, our Afghan hound, Maggie, dived into our tent, barking and madly rubbing her eyes on our sleeping bags. My wife, Sheila, who was pregnant at the time, shouted that Maggie had been sprayed by a skunk. Maggie's eyes were burning, my head was splitting, and in the dark and confusion, I tried to shove her outside through the tent window. When I finally got Maggie outside, I tied her to the closest tree. In a couple of minutes, she was barking again. I'd tied her to a tree that had two baby raccoons in its branches. Momma raccoon was nearby freaking out. Between the dog and the skunk and the raccoons and the wine, there wasn't much sleep that night."

Diamondback rattlesnake

Copperhead

Cottonmouth

Coral or harlequin snake

Even a poisonous snake doesn't always inject its venom. The amount of poison entering a victim's bloodstream can vary from none to a potentially lethal dose. Fifteen percent of rattlesnake bites are not poisonous and another fifteen percent are minor.

> When I was nineteen, my hiking partner and I surprised a four-foot rattlesnake on the trail. The snake rattled a warning, but we were upon it before we could react. Even then, the snake sought only escape. Alas, my partner, a macho youth, found a tree limb, beat the snake to a pulp, and cut off its rattle for a trophy.
>
> —S.B.

Like most sensible animals, snakes want no part of man. Except for rattlesnakes, which have an early warning system, most catch your attention only when they are slithering away.

Chances are slim that you'll die at the fangs of a snake. Of the forty-five thousand snakebites reported in the United States every year (most of which are inflicted on snake handlers), only about eight thousand are venomous. Of those, fewer than twenty are fatal. According to Dr. Findlay Russell, professor of toxicology at the University of Arizona, most venomous bites occur in the South and Southwest, including California.

■ Squirrel

You will see squirrels almost everywhere you go. They are diurnal (meaning they work and play during the day) and, unlike most animals, make no attempt to hide from humans. In fact, they seem to delight in showing off. They are primarily tree dwellers, but also spend time on the ground. Except for the arctic ground squirrel, they do not hibernate.

They are distinguished by an oversized, bushy tail that is more than just ornamental. It serves as a blanket in winter, a sunshade in summer, and is used for balance during acrobatics. Squirrels can convey a variety of messages with their tails:

- Rapid jerks are a threatening gesture.

- Rapid waves (looser than jerks) indicate agitation.

- Holding the tail against the back may mean danger has passed.

Squirrels also communicate with growls, gurgles, purrs, and buzzes that people often assume are made by birds. Some sounds have specific meaning:

- A rapid *kuk, kuk, kuk* signals danger. If a predator is actually in pursuit, the squirrel adds a short trill at the end. Still more embellishments are added to identify the attacker, so other squirrels can take appropriate action. If they are warned that the enemy is a hawk, for example, other squirrels know they will be safe in any burrow; if a badger threatens, they must find a burrow with a back door for use as an escape hatch.

- A drawn-out *ku-u-uk*, at two-second intervals, signals less immediate danger.

- A slow *kuk, kuk, kuk* indicates danger has passed.

Like all rodents, squirrels have two pairs of curved incisors, ideal for gnawing on nuts, their favorite food. Those incisors continue to grow five or six inches a year throughout their life. Their habit of grinding their teeth on tree bark, nut shells, and animal bones prevents their looking like saber-tooth squirrels.

Squirrels bury nuts each fall, relying on their excellent sense of smell to retrieve most of them. Because the ones they forget sometimes germinate, squirrels are responsible for planting many trees throughout parks and forests.

Squirrel breeding, usually twice a year, is accompanied by chatter, chases, and fights. Late-winter and early spring litters are usually born in tree hollows; summer young enjoy leafy nests out on tree branches. Males play no role in raising the young, which average three per litter.

Squirrels are well adapted for life in trees. They have sharp claws for climbing and hanging and can turn their paws 180 degrees, so their claws are always in perfect grasping position, even when descending trees headfirst. They have strong hind legs for leaping from branch to branch. One squirrel's leap was measured at sixty feet. Have your children watch the squirrels near your camp and try to gauge their jumping distance.

■ Wolf

On a long list of misunderstood animals, none is more misunderstood than the wolf. Western culture has characterized this animal as a red-eyed, saliva-dripping, mean-spirited menace to millions of children. Children's classics like *Little Red Riding Hood*, *Three Little Pigs*, *The Big Bad Wolf*, and *Beauty and the Beast* are enough to make a lobophobe out of anyone.

Although the wolf is the largest canine predator—at ninety pounds, it's three times as heavy as a coyote—it is a cautious, timid animal around people. Says L. David Mech, an internationally recognized wolf expert and author of *White Wolves of the High Arctic*: "In North America, there is not one documented case in modern times of a healthy wild wolf attacking or killing a human."

Like most animals, wolves have far more to fear from us than we do from them. For the past two centuries, irrational fear and a passion for protecting livestock have fueled an appallingly effective wolf wipe-out. Though it once roamed freely over most of North America, the wolf was nearly extinct outside Alaska and Canada by 1920.

Federal protection has permitted a partial comeback. The gray wolf (Eastern timber wolf), listed as an endangered species, has been seen in Idaho, Montana, Wyoming, North Dakota, Minnesota, Wisconsin, Michigan, and eastern Washington. Many of these sightings have been on public lands, where wolves are protected.

> "Wolves howl more before a storm because their ears hurt. They're sensitive to low pressure," says weather expert Conrad Nelson.

The largest concentration of wolves in the continental United States is in northern Minnesota, where twelve hundred animals roam. Even there, they are rarely seen and pose no threat to campers, though you may want to leave your dog at home during mating season.

It's unlikely you'll see a wolf, but you may be fortunate enough to hear them. Usually in the evening, wolves howl to keep the pack together, to stimulate the urge to hunt, or just because they feel like it.

According to Mech, the call of the wolf can carry two to three miles under ideal conditions. Chances are, that's the closest you'll get to this elusive animal.

Farley Mowat, who wrote the book *Never Cry Wolf*, and actor Timothy Dalton, who worked on the PBS documentary *In the Company of Wolves*, have described wolves in essentially the same terms: playful, intelligent, and loving, with good family values. Dalton concludes, "The wolf is neither to be feared nor hated. It's not dangerous, evil, or malicious. It's simply the wolf, and that's a smart animal trying to make a living under tough conditions."

■ Animal Warning

With the explosion of rabies in the 1990s, there is a greater need than ever to mind the proper relationship between us humans and wild animals.

Rabies is a viral disease transmitted by the saliva of infected animals. It attacks the nervous system, producing a frightening array of symptoms in humans: hallucinations, weakness, thirst, irrational fear and furies, and foaming at the mouth (as well as difficulty swallowing food and water, hence its other name: hydrophobia). Since the virus travels through the body inside nerve tissue, rather than through the bloodstream, the disease triggers no antibodies and can't be detected during incubation. Once it reaches the brain, death is virtually inevitable.

Since 1980, only eighteen people have died of rabies in the United States, and ten of those victims became infected in other countries. But the threat is rising. In July 1992, an eleven-year-old girl became the first New Yorker to die of rabies since 1954. Largely eradicated from pets by vaccination, the virus has reemerged with a vengeance among wild mammals, particularly raccoons, skunks, foxes, and bats. Between 1988 and 1992, reported rabies cases nearly doubled, with raccoons (4,311 cases) easily eclipsing skunks as lead carriers. Dr. Charles Rupprecht, head of the rabies section at the National Centers for Disease Control in Atlanta, calls it "one of the most intensive wildlife rabies outbreaks in history."

One reason raccoons account for half of the reported rabies cases is because they are so adorable. You and your children will not be tempted to feed skunks or bats and you won't get near foxes, but those cute little coons will march right into your camp like a horde of trick-or-treaters, and right into your children's hearts.

Without exception, resist the temptation to feed wild animals. Rabies is harder to spot than many people realize. An infected animal may not appear crazed or menacing; instead, it may seem tame or sick, tempting animal lovers to try to help. Your pets should also observe wildlife from a distance. Get them vaccinated, especially the bounding dog likely to encounter wild animals. Protect garbage and pet food from furry intruders.

If bitten or otherwise exposed (at least two victims got rabies in caves by breathing air contaminated by infected bats), wash the wound immediately with soap and water, then get medical help. The rabies treatment, once an excruciating series of fourteen to twenty-one shots in the abdomen, is now a gentler set of five shots in the arm. Even if you test negative for rabies, you may need a tetanus shot.

■ Wildlife-Watching Tips

Special thanks to *Backpacker* magazine for these tips.

- Leave perfumes and smelly lotions at home. There's a chemical now sold under the name Ghost Scent, which will render you undetectable to even the most discriminating nose. (Use with caution in grizzly country, where you want them to know you're coming.) Contact: DeWitt U.S.A., (800) 735-0666.

- Avoid brightly colored clothes, tents, and packs.

- Find out which animals live in the habitat you'll be exploring. Start with those likely to pass through your camp, such as squirrels, chipmunks, and deer.

- Get a good pair of binoculars and practice until you can focus on your subject before it flies, crawls, or swims away.

- Look for ecotones (areas where two habitats overlap). Ecotones such as forest/meadow edges, stream and lake shores, talus slopes/alpine meadows, and sand dunes/coastal scrub allow you to see animals from two adjacent habitats.

- Be especially alert at dawn and dusk, when many animals are active. Key on grazing grounds and watering holes.

- Except in grizzly country, walk softly. Keep that frying pan from clanging against your pack frame. Now listen to nature.

- Listen with "rabbit ears," a simple technique that improves your hearing. Place your thumbs against the back of each ear and cup your hands so the fingers bend over the tops, maintain a tight seal around the back of your ears, and turn your head from side to side and up and down.

- Be alert to shapes and colors. Pay special attention to horizontal lines, which are uncommon in a forest; they may be an animal. Look for birds as oblong shapes high in trees. Objects that appear to be boulders may be bears or bison.

- Look for tracks and scat. Even if you can't identify the animals that left them, noting animal signs makes you more aware of whom you're sharing the outdoors with. If you want to identify animals from tracks or scat, carry a guide.

- Take your rest stops off the trail. Animals like trails, too, but they will go elsewhere if they sense humans.

- When crossing waterways, pause to look up- and downstream. Rushing water hides human noises, so you may be able to spot animals bathing or drinking.

- If you see something, freeze. You can often prolong the observation, especially if the animal decides you're no threat.

- Pick a campsite far away from well-traveled animal routes. This may seem backward, but laying your sleeping bag down on an animal trail will not increase your chances of seeing wildlife.

- Don't build a fire. Animals avoid light and smoke.

- Make a "track trap" by smoothing out a patch of ground and then checking for tracks later. Make your trap in an area likely to be visited. If you already see tracks, that's a good place to start.

- You can see a variety of wildlife if you're willing to get down on your belly. Insects and arachnids are abundant. Or climb a tree, which increases your field of vision and directs your scent away from animals.

- Strive to be one with nature. Backpacking helps achieve this feeling, especially if you avoid large groups of people.

- Don't interfere in animals' lives. Remember that you are invading *their* space. Above all, do not feed them.

- Be patient. If you want to see an animal that has disappeared into a burrow, such as a marmot, squirrel, mouse, or chipmunk, find a comfortable place to sit and remain quiet. It usually will reappear, curious about you.

We have much we can learn from animals—if we'll just pay attention. For example:

- Animals can foretell stormy weather. Increased activity and duration of feeding among fish, birds, and wild animals may indicate a dropping barometer and the approach of a storm.

- Animals can find water for you. They will sometimes dig "wells" in the gravel near dry creekbeds. You can benefit from this digging, just as other animals and birds have learned to.

- Crickets can tell us the temperature. Male tree crickets chirp faster when the temperature rises, more slowly when the mercury drops. To figure the approximate Fahrenheit temperature, count one cricket's chirps for fifteen seconds, then add forty.

- Elk or deer can make our bed for us. If caught in a sudden storm, search for an elk or deer bed beneath overhanging limbs on the lee side of mature conifers, especially spruce and fir.

Do further research and become a true wildlife maven.

Resources

Books

A Field Guide to Animal Tracks by Olaus J. Murie (Peterson Field Guide Series, Houghton Mifflin)

Never Cry Wolf by Farley Mowat (Dell Publishing)

Cougar: The American Lion by Kevin Hansen (Northland Publishing)

Mammal Tracking in Western America by James Halfpenny (Johnson Books)

Miscellaneous

Scat shirts available from Panagraphics, 1312 North Wahsatch, Colorado Springs, CO 80903; (719) 520-9953

For more information, contact one or more of the following organizations:

Defenders of Wildlife, 1244 19th St. NW, Washington, DC 20036

National Audubon Society, Education Division, Route 1, Box 171, Sharon, CT 06069

National Wildlife Federation, 1412 16th St. NW, Washington, DC 20036

The Nature Conservancy, 1800 N. Kent St., Suite 800, Arlington, VA 22209

The Timberwolf Alliance, c/o Sigurd Olson Environmental Institute, Northland College, Ashland, WI 54806; (715) 682-1223

Chapter Fifteen

BACKPACKING WITH BABIES AND SMALL CHILDREN

Ask your child what he wants for dinner only if he is buying.

—Fran Lebowitz

HAVING a baby is no reason to stop going into the wilderness. All it takes is some special gear and a thorough checklist. Both parents should list the items they think are important, then decide what goes and what stays. Besides special foods, toys, and practical clothes, you may need diapers and bottles, which are bulky. There are also regular items such as insect repellent, sunscreen, and medicine that take on special importance when a baby is along.

■ Diaper Bag

Although you may not need all of these items, your checklist might look like this:

☐ Diapers (cloth or disposable)

☐ Blankey/lovey

- ☐ Damp towelettes without alcohol
- ☐ Baby powder/diaper rash cream
- ☐ Bottles
- ☐ Washcloths
- ☐ Formula
- ☐ Bibs
- ☐ Baby food and juice
- ☐ Garbage bags for used diapers
- ☐ Baby spoons

Let's face it, the monster issue here is diapers—cloth or disposable? Camping with diapers causes environmentalism to run smack into convenience. Both cloth and disposable types are bulky and must be packed out. Both cause environmental problems (disposables create trash; cloths require water and fuel to wash). Cloth diapers are reusable and thus cheaper in the long run. They pack better than disposables and can play other roles—for instance, as towels, bibs, and washcloths. On the other hand, cloths are heavier, less convenient, and less absorbent than state-of-the-art disposables. Also, washing cloth diapers in the wilderness is no small hassle.

Many parents who do take cloth diapers refuse to wash them until they get home. The alternative is using time and precious fuel to heat water, dumping feces and wastewater at least two hundred feet from waterways, then scrubbing diapers in hot, soapy water, rinsing twice, and trying to dry them, perhaps in wet or chilly weather. Our advice: take disposables.

> If you plan to do a wilderness diaper wash, consider carrying a plastic bathtub in which to soak and wash them. Get one that fits in your backpack. Stuff gear in and around it and it won't take much room. You can also use it for bathing baby or soaking your feet.

Whether you carry cloth or disposable diapers, include plenty of plastic bags, big and small, for transporting the dirty diapers. An ammonia-soaked sponge kept in the diaper bag will help control odors.

Food

The nursing infant is the easiest person to feed on a camping trip, as long as you don't lose Mom. Bottles present more of a problem, as the formula and paraphernalia are heavy and bulky, and cleanliness is essential. For a day trip, fill bottles with boiled water at home or camp, then add formula powder to the bottle on the trail.

For camping, the lightest and least bulky method is to carry powdered formula, a couple of special plastic bottles, and plenty of their disposable plastic bag inserts. Because this method demands boiling water in camp, it requires the most time and fuel. An alternative is to carry ready-to-drink bottles. This is much less work, but you must deal with the weight, bulk, and expense of all those bottles.

Other options fall between those two extremes. One possibility for short trips is to reduce the amount of formula the baby gets. This won't be a problem as long as she gets lots of fluids and other healthful foods. If you rely heavily on juices, provide a variety of flavors.

Most bottles you make up in camp will be clean but not sterile. Bacteria love warm formula; don't mix it until feeding time. If you are worried about keeping formula fresh, bring "terminally" sterilized bottles from home. This involves cooking filled, loosely capped bottles in a sterilizer for twenty minutes. After the bottles have cooled in the sterilizer, the caps are tightened. These bottles can be stored without refrigeration, for you have, in effect, canned the milk.

> When you pack the little nipper's meals, include her plastic Peter Rabbit bowl and spoon, her Aladdin bib, and her Winnie-the-Pooh washcloth.

The baby's solid foods in camp can be the same as she gets at home. Cereals can be stored in plastic bags; juices in plastic bottles. Store-bought baby foods should not be opened until ready to use. Pack them so the glass jars don't bang against one another.

There is a wide range of dried baby foods—cereals, fruits, dinners, and desserts. With snap-on lids, you reconstitute only the amount you need, saving the rest.

Take the same precautions camping that you would at home. Beware of inappropriate foods. According to surveys from Johns Hopkins University, the following foods were most likely to be involved in the fatal choking of children under five.

- Peanut butter/peanut butter sandwiches
- Grapes
- Hard cookies/biscuits
- Round candy
- Peanuts
- Apple chunks/slices
- Meat chunks/slices
- Raw carrots
- Hot dogs/sausages
- Popcorn

■ Clothing

☐ Booties

☐ Socks

☐ Hats

☐ Sweater

☐ Hooded sweatshirt

☐ Rain jacket/poncho

☐ Jumpsuit

☐ Mittens (they're warmer than gloves but reduce dexterity)

When evaluating clothing needs, remember that babies are not just miniature adults; they have their own special needs. They are especially at risk during their first year when they have less insulating fat, a smaller reservoir of heat, no clue about cold, and an inability to communicate specific discomfort. If they are being carried, they also have less opportunity to produce heat.

Dress babies and toddlers in warm, nonbreathable layers and monitor their condition for signs of cold or overheating. Check telltale extremities like nose, ears, toes, and fingers. Footed sleepers, hooded sweatshirts, and balaclavas all warm cold extremities. One-piece baby bags cover most of the body and won't ride up in a kid carrier.

Layering works for the hands, too. A synthetic, moisture-wicking liner beneath wool gloves or mittens gives added protection. The world's best mittens won't be any good if they're lost or dropped in a puddle. Some parents fasten them to the jacket sleeve with clips, buckles, or Velcro. Or you can use the traditional method of making sure mittens stay attached to a coat: Thread yarn or string through the sleeves and across the back of your young one's garment, then tie a mitten to each end.

You can adapt adult clothing for babies. Adult wool socks, for example, can be pulled up past the knees over a young child's shoes and pants; use safety pins to keep them in place. Bandannas can provide much-needed sun protection. Adult ponchos can be trimmed to fit smaller bodies.

Rainwear worn by children who are not walking does not have to be breathable. On the other hand, kids three and older tend to be sprinters energetic in short bursts, which creates perspiration and a need for an inner moisture-wicking layer of clothing. Once babies are out of diapers, they will need easy-on-and-off clothing for toileting.

Like adults, children lose a disproportionate amount of body heat through their uncovered head and neck. Have them wear hats and hoods to reduce heat loss and protect skin and eyes from the sun.

■ For Exploring Nature

- ☐ Small pack
- ☐ Notebook/pencil/ crayons
- ☐ Magnifying glass
- ☐ String
- ☐ Lightweight flashlight
- ☐ Red cellophane

☐ Kitchen strainer   ☐ Rubber bands

☐ Trowel

If you race through nature, it will be little more than a blur to young children. If you stop and investigate some of the micromysteries of life, you will share some spectacular discoveries with your children.

Bring paper and crayons. Most children will enjoy doing interpretive drawings of nature. A kitchen strainer is handy for sifting through dirt, sand, and even water. A plastic trowel is a search-and-don't-destroy tool. You can turn over scat, construct a makeshift pond for a wriggling tadpole, move stubborn rocks, dig up wild onions, and perform myriad other tasks. String can be used for bundling vegetation and as a measuring device. Attach red cellophane to the lens of your flashlight to search for animals at night. Mirrors and magnifying glasses are fun and educational for young children.

■ Carrying a Baby

More than one clever parent of an infant has rigged a sling out of a sweater or towel and hiked with a baby cradled against the front of his or her body. For bigger kids and longer hikes, however, the baby will have to ride on your back.

A quality child carrier will fit and ride like a backpack. It will have a hip belt for you and safety straps for the baby. It will be so comfortable that sometimes you may have to remind yourself that there's a child back there, not gear. There is good reason to stay alert. To avoid problems:

- Duck when you walk beneath low branches.

- If you bend over to pick something up, bend at the knees, not the waist.

- If you sit down, don't crush the baby's little feet.

Photos by Rick Ridgeway

- Check the baby frequently for diaper needs and for signs of chafing where her skin might be rubbing against the pack.

- Periodically, help her change positions to avoid circulation problems.

- Stay off steep snow slopes with a baby on board. In fact, stay away from any place where you might fall.

- When the baby falls asleep (riding is soporific), cushion her head with a shirt or towel.

- Reduce facial glare by wearing dark clothing and wrapping the shiny parts of the baby carrier with black tape or bandannas. Don't forget sunglasses and sunblock.

- Stuff something—a pillow, towel, diaper, or magazine—between the baby and the back of the carrier for support and insulation.

- Most child carriers have an extra metal bar that swings out to allow the pack to stand alone as a seat. It's convenient in camp for feeding and keeping track of a baby, but beware of the contraption tipping over.

- The adult not carrying a child will probably be burdened with a heavier load than usual. Take advantage of the compartments available on the child carrier.

■ Innovations

Photo by John Kelly

From Kelty comes an elite child carrier called Kelty K.I.D.S. With an ergonomic frame and mountaineering suspension, it is the Cadillac of kid carriers. Additional features include no-pinch hinges, easily adjustable shoulder straps, an overhead shade, and an auto-deploy kickstand. One adjustable size fits tiny torsos fourteen to twenty-one inches. Total weight: five pounds, three ounces.

Chapter Sixteen

WILDERNESS ETHICS

*If the Aborigine drafted an IQ test,
all of Western civilization would presumably flunk it.*

—Stanley Garn

■ On the Trail

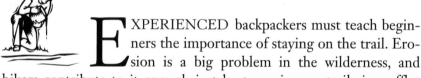

EXPERIENCED backpackers must teach beginners the importance of staying on the trail. Erosion is a big problem in the wilderness, and hikers contribute to it enough just by tromping on trails in waffle-soled boots.

Impress upon children and others the need to avoid creating new trails next to old ones. Not only should hikers stay on the path, they should stay near the middle to keep from caving in the sides. When chatting with people you meet on the trail, move off-trail to avoid breaking down the edges and widening the path. Instead of skirting trail mud, walk through it and clean your boots later. Good-fitting gaiters will keep mud out of socks.

The most common trail abuse is

Olympic National Park officials are considering a unique solution to overuse of trails: erasing them from maps. Although no trails will actually be closed or destroyed, mapmakers and guidebook authors will be persuaded to delete all references to them. The goal: to protect wilderness resources and curb safety problems on popular but undermaintained trails.

When hiking in a group, allow a comfortable distance—at least two paces—between you and the hiker in front of you. Tailgating on the trail is just as annoying as it is on the road and just as pointless. If you overtake slower hikers who don't move over, ask politely if you may pass.

cutting switchbacks, the S-curves that enable a hiker to ascend or descend a more gradual grade. Shortening the route kills vegetation and forms a new path. With no vegetation, the topsoil soon washes away, forming a gully, a perfect sluice for storm water. Nature has little chance to reclaim the land.

For the same reasons, when you see an unauthorized shortcut, throw brush or logs across it, blocking access to other hikers.

In Camp

The perfect campsite isn't made, it's discovered. Trenching, cutting branches, and leveling or removing vegetation are frowned upon. Look for a fairly level spot with good drainage. Try to select established campsites. Always camp out of sight of trails and other people.

More and more, state and national parks are demanding that campers set up at least two hundred feet from lakes and streams. In the Yosemite backcountry, for example, the park service has dismantled campsites they deemed too threatening to the local water source.

Once you settle on a site, strive for "no-trace camping." When clearing the ground for the sleeping area—a first-rate chore for kids—don't sweep it with your foot. Get down on all fours and remove body-stabbing sticks, pine cones, and rocks; leave the leaves and needles for cushioning. In the morning, after you pack up and move on, the

Here are seven important questions to ask before you set up camp:

• Am I damaging the ground cover?
• Will I spoil the view for others?
• Am I blocking animal traffic?
• Where's the water?
• Do I need a tent?
• Is a fire really necessary?
• Where's the bathroom?

only evidence that you slept there should be some matted leaves, which will fluff up in a few hours.

Cut no living boughs for bedding, tent stakes, or firewood. If you lose stakes, tie guy lines around heavy rocks. Don't dig trenches around your tents—they don't work anyway.

Take nothing that belongs to the land; leave nothing that belongs to you. Even biodegradable matter takes years to biodegrade, and in the meantime others have to gaze upon your garbage. To compensate for the boorish brigade that doesn't see it that way, pick up after your neighbors.

■ Animal Relations

One of your first camp chores should be animal-proofing your food. This is an ethical, as well as a practical, issue, as animals fed by humans, whether intentionally or not, become conditioned to human food and increasingly dependent on their handouts. Feed only your own species.

Food-conditioned animals can be dangerous. Once a bear makes the mental link between food and its human source, it's nearly impossible to break the connection. Result: persistent campground raids. Food conditioning can also thwart an animal's natural inclinations. Normally reclusive and nocturnal black bears in Great Smoky Mountains National Park have become diurnal in order to take advantage of midday picnics.

If you are car camping or in an area with lots of bears, you might find bear-proof boxes, steel hanging cables, or slippery poles with hanging hooks. If you're car camping in bear country, with none of those amenities, store food in ice chests in your trunk. If you're still worried, slather stove fuel around the trunk lid. No trunk and not enough ice chests? Cover the food so the bears can't see it. If you're backpacking and lack any

> Don't bury food scraps. Pack out all leftovers, even fish entrails. Burying food near camp is an invitation to animals and a potential danger to the unsuspecting campers who follow.

man-made bear defenses, you must counterbalance your food in a tree.

First, gather together all food, toothpastes, lotions, shampoos, vitamins, and anything else an animal might mistake for food. Divide the lot into two stuff sacks or garbage bags, roughly even in weight. Open all the pockets of your pack and do a final search. Leave the pockets open. That way, rodents can investigate without having to chew through the pack.

When you are sure you have gathered all bear edibles, begin searching for the perfect limb. It will be a live, sturdy branch, at least ten feet long, fifteen to twenty feet off the ground, and well away from other limbs. It should be no more than four inches in diameter and narrow to no more than one inch at its end.

Tie one end of a rope around a baseball-size rock and toss it over the limb, at least eight feet from the tree trunk. Did you hang on to the other end of the rope? If not, try again. Can you reach both ends of the rope? If not, try again.

Tie one end of the rope to the first sack. Pull on the other end of the rope until the first sack hangs near the limb. Now reach up as high as you can on the rope and tie off the second sack. Tie a loop in the leftover rope near the lip of the sack; that will allow you to reach up with a stick, hook the loop, and pull down the bag. You can also use a stick to push one bag up, thereby lowering the other one. When you're done, push the lower bag high enough so that both sacks hang evenly. Your food sacks should be at least twelve feet off the ground, eight feet from the tree trunk, and five feet below the limb. If not, do it over.

Of course, bears aren't the only varmints who are a threat to your food. In

Recently, a husband and wife, Dan and Jan O'Brien, had two delinquent five-hundred-pound bears rip through their Lake Tahoe camp in the middle of the night. Even though all their food was stored safely in the car, the bears vandalized their camp, then did it again an hour later. During their second visit, with the couple cowering in their tent and the bears sniffing and snorting outside, Jan remembered she had five Hershey's Kisses in her purse in the tent. "Although the bears eventually went away, it was nerve-wracking," Dan said.

the Appalachian Trail shelters, mice are notorious for pillaging food bags. If you saved that tuna can in which you made a fire starter, you can use it to thwart the little rascals. Bake the empty can in the fire or over a stove burner to remove the fishy odor, then poke a hole in its bottom with your Swiss Army knife. Tie a knot halfway down from your food bag, and thread the rope through the hole in the can before hanging the bag. They won't be able to get past the inverted can.

■ Sanitation

Another important camping chore is choosing the location of the "toilet." In established campgrounds and high-use backcountry areas, it will be obvious—either an outhouse or a conventional cellblock model with indoor plumbing.

Latrines, with their dark, smelly holes that seem bottomless, can be unpleasant for adults and frightening for children. One researcher found that two-thirds of all visitors to heavily used Desolation Wilderness, near Lake Tahoe, shunned outhouses.

Some would say there are sound environmental reasons for rejecting latrines. They concentrate human waste; if not properly located, they can pollute water; they are a possible source of insect contamination; they create a large area of disturbed soil (from both the hole itself and the compacted soil due to foot traffic); and waste takes a long time to decompose, increasing the chance that animals will dig it up and scatter the remains. Still, latrines may be the best choice in fragile ecosystems with a limited number of disposal sites, or for large groups on long stays.

In most backcountry areas, the location of the toilet is left to you. There is no latrine, no hole in the ground, no rule book.

There are two recommended means of human waste disposal. Your choice should depend on prevailing conditions.

1. In low-use areas, where risk of discovery is minimal, surface disposal of feces is recommended. Choose a dry, open exposure, above the spring high-water

line, unlikely to be visited by others. Scatter feces with a stick to maximize exposure to sun and air.

2. In more popular areas, bury waste in catholes.

In either case, pack out your used toilet paper in plastic bags.

To give feces a decent burial, choose a fairly level spot well away from camp and waterways, above the spring high-water line, and unlikely to be visited by others. When traveling in a family-size group, it is usually best to disperse everyone's waste, not concentrate it.

To dig the perfect cathole, use a stick or a lightweight backpacking trowel to excavate to a depth of no more than six to eight inches. That's home to the microorganisms that most effectively break down excrement. When you've finished what you came to do, take a stick and mix soil with the feces for quicker decomposition. Then cover with a couple of inches of topsoil and camouflage the surface.

The decomposition rate of buried fecal matter varies widely, depending on soil type, texture, acidity (pH), moisture content, slope of terrain, exposure, insect population, and temperature. Under the *best* conditions, human excrement can take more than a year to vanish. In desert conditions, it can take a lifetime or longer.

When disposing of human waste, keep in mind our three main objectives: minimizing the chance of water pollution, minimizing the chance of any human or animal finding the waste, maximizing the chance of rapid decomposition. As Kathleen Meyer writes in *How to Shit in the Woods*, "The objective in digging a hole is to inhibit the passing of disease-causing organisms by humans or animals or storm runoff into nearby surface waters and by flying insects back to food areas."

Because urine evaporates quickly and is relatively clean, it's not nearly the environmental and health hazard that solid waste is. Avoid urinating on sensitive flora and don't frequent one place, lest it begin to smell like an alleyway. In Grand Canyon National Park, the park service instructs people to urinate directly into the river or on the wet sand at the water's edge, and to avoid urinating on rocks and gravel, where the odor lingers.

For years we were told to bury toilet paper. Turns out, though, the stuff is slow to decompose. Then we were told to burn it. But that started the occasional forest fire, such as the 1985 blaze in Washington State. A group of campers, trying to practice minimum-impact camping, burned their toilet paper and along with it a half million dollars' worth of trees.

So now you can pack it out or use a natural alternative. If you choose the first, make available a plastic collection bag with a disinfectant-soaked sponge in it. Place it in a discreet location and notify everyone of its purpose. You can also station the toilet paper and trowel there.

There are many natural alternatives. The first and simplest is to wipe with hand and water, the method favored by billions of people worldwide. Take a cup of water to the toilet, pour small amounts on your fingertips, and cleanse yourself. Afterward, wash your hands with soap and water.

Or you can use leaves, bark, cones, or rocks. Author Kathleen Meyer offers advice on alternatives: "There are many items suitable for substitute toilet paper, and the choice of living plants should only be a last resort. If you pick leaves at all, be especially mindful. Always select dead grasses and leaves over live ones. Don't pick wildflowers or rare species. Don't pick in parks or other restricted areas. Don't pull anything up by the roots. Don't rob large clumps or strip an entire branch. Carefully pick a leaf here, a leaf there—so no one, not even the plant (especially the plant), will know that you have been there."

Look for large, soft leaves. Before picking, examine the leaf carefully. Avoid the sticky, the scabrous (having a rasplike surface), and the prickly. Be absolutely certain you do not use poison oak, ivy, or sumac. Stay away from fragile mosses, reeds, bamboo, and sharp grasses that can cause wounds resembling paper cuts. Pine needles will work, as long as you take the time to line them all up in the same direction. And some people swear by pine cones, not new spiny ones, but old, spongy ones. You can also try sheets of smooth, peeling bark, polished driftwood, seashells, feathers, and smooth, sun-baked stones.

Every means of waste disposal in the backcountry has problems, but that is no excuse for carelessness. It is critical to avoid further contamination of wilderness waterways.

The flush toilet is the basis of Western civilization.
—Alan Coult

■ Cooking

If you camp somewhere that permits fires, show restraint (some areas permit fires, but prohibit wood gathering). If you have to roam far and wide to find fallen wood, it's a sure sign the area is overused. If so, don't build a fire. Decaying wood is essential to healthy forests.

Even if you can build a fire, you should cook over a stove. It conserves wood, keeps your pots from getting black, and enables you to control a flame.

■ Washing

I'd rather be dumb and clean than smart and dirty, anytime.
—Dr. Norman Vincent Peale

To use soap or not—ah, that is the question. Some backpackers are devout no-soapers, relying instead on sand for the dishes and daily, brief dips in mountain lakes or streams to cleanse. Soapless dips seem sufficient in the mountains because nature's dirt seems downright benign compared to city dirt and because mountain lakes are quite bracing, making you feel cleaner than you really are.

If you must take soap, use it sparingly and carry a biodegradable, nonphosphate type. Even with the right soap, never put it or toothpaste into a water source. Both can upset the delicate balance of life in rivers and lakes.

Consider using soap on hands only after toileting and not at all on dishes or clothes. Scour pots with sand, rocks, or a pine cone. Do the dishes immediately after eating and before residue dries.

Rinse out those dirty socks and dusty trail clothes in soapless water away from the lake or stream. Besides its polluting effect, soap is difficult to remove from clothing without plenty of warm water, and residual soap can cause a rash.

Whether or not you insist on using soap, carry washing water in cooking pots or water jugs at least two hundred feet from its source (and from any campsite) and wash there. This will allow the waste-water to filter through the soil and break down before seeping back into the water supply.

You can easily prepare no-dishwashing meals: Select foods that can be reconstituted with water. Grocery stores are filled with them, from potatoes to powdered milk. Repackage meals in quart-size self-sealing plastic bags. Carry a quart-size plastic cup or bowl. At meal-time, boil water and pour it into the bag supported in the bowl. Most plastic bags are rated to 170 degrees Fahrenheit, but if supported they will hold boiling water. Stir the contents, zip the bag closed, and let sit for a few minutes. Cleanup consists of rinsing the spoon and drop-ping the used bag in the trash bag. Do the same with freeze-dried dinners. Because some of them take longer than five minutes to re-constitute, run them through a blender before you leave home. Smaller pieces will soak up water faster and reduce waiting time.

■ Human Relations

Even though you are now highly educated on wilderness ethics, you are bound to encounter other hikers still wallowing in ignorance. Say you happen upon someone feeding Twinkies to deer or camping ten feet from an otherwise pristine mountain lake. Do you speak up? Many will say nothing, preferring to avoid a confrontation. Even seasoned wilderness officials are taught to use their best judgment when approaching wayward backpackers.

Photo by Rick Ridgeway

If you do decide to act on your principles, try to educate rather than alienate. Some people will be defensive, no matter what you do or say, but strive to be as respectful as possible. Some suggestions:

- Give people the benefit of the doubt. Remember that everyone makes mistakes.

- As you approach a group, pick out one person to speak to; it's easier than dealing with a crowd.

- Engage in some friendly chitchat before guiding the conversation toward "the changes that can be set in motion by a series of seemingly innocent acts."

- Be alert to body language and tone of voice—they can be the difference between honey and vinegar. Speak softly, avoid blame, and stand shoulder-to-shoulder rather than face-to-face.

- Deemphasize rules and regulations and rely instead on "the authority of the resource," pointing out how certain actions affect the balance of nature. You might remind them of John Muir's remark: "Everything in nature is hitched to everything else."

- Back off if the situation becomes too acrimonious. Note the time and location of the incident, as well as a physical description of the offenders, and report it to the appropriate land management agency.

- Continue to influence others by your good example.

When trying to get along with other backpackers, consider the following etiquette tips:

- Respect the value of silence. When people talk about "getting away from it all," human sound is high on the list.

- Respect others' need for space. Try to avoid setting up camp within sight or sound of someone else.

Checkers anyone?

Photo by Carl Siechert

- Let others know you're coming. Make a friendly noise fifteen or twenty feet away, before you're close enough to startle them.

- Know who has the right of way. It's courteous for the downhill hiker to pull off for the uphill hiker, who will have a tougher time breaking stride. Hikers should yield to horses, and bicycles and motorized vehicles should yield to both hikers and horses. Exception: if a biker is climbing uphill, it's easier for the oncoming hiker to step aside.

- Keep groups small. Research suggests that people have an easier time with a large number of small groups than with a small number of large groups.

- Be prepared to share shelters. The shelters found on the AT and other trails are public places, available on a first-come, first-served basis. Avoid rowdiness, curb your dog, and pitch a tent elsewhere if you snore.

- Always consider impact.

■ Rescue

Recently *Backpacker* magazine asked its readers whether back-country travelers should have to pay for rescue costs they incur. In an admittedly unscientific survey, 73 percent said yes. No matter how you feel, there are good points to be made by both sides.

Those in favor tended to focus on the issue of responsibility. One caller said, "I've been on rescues, and just about any one of them could've been prevented by either packing enough clothes or not going into a dangerous area, or just being smart about what you're doing and knowing your limits."

Accordingly, many voters on both sides agreed that rescuees should be assessed only in cases of "gross negligence" or "unusual stupidity." The question, then, becomes how to determine exactly when negligence becomes gross. Such discussions usually lure lawyers into the mix.

Several of those voting "yes" resorted to urban metaphors: "If my car breaks down, I have to pay for a tow." Or: "If you're hurt in a city, whether it was because of your own stupidity or not, you're still charged for the ambulance ride."

Some suggested paying for rescue with an insurance premium or a small up-front fee. Colorado residents cited their state's practice of contributing a portion of fees from hunting and fishing licenses to a state rescue fund. One caller suggested that those being rescued repay the appropriate public agency in volunteer work.

Callers opposing payment often referred to other services the government provides for free. One man said, "If the Department of Interior can subsidize logging, cattle grazing, and mining interests, then the mere pittance of $3 million (spent by the NPS annually on rescue) is nothing."

One man, a search and rescue volunteer, worried that hikers wouldn't go for help because of the potential cost. Another compared it to the New York City Police Department charging tourists mugged in high-crime areas.

Though the basic message of those opposed seemed to be that "bad things can happen to good people," they too were mindful of personal responsibility. One caller suggested "no-rescue zones, where people can go and know that they won't be rescued." And Adam Dresser of Arcadia, California, offered what might be called a Jeremiah Johnson approach to rescue: "Wilderness means total self-reliance," he said. "When I go into the backcountry, I defy rescues by hiking in remote, unpopulated areas and being vague about where I'm going. Then I know I'm on my own."

The following true stories all touch on at least one ethical issue. Can you spot them?

Peter Waite and his future wife, Lauren, were nearing their goal of climbing all forty-six peaks in New York state and New England. They lacked only East Dix in the Adirondack High Peaks region to qualify for membership in the 46ers Club.

Leaving Burlington, Vermont, early one morning, they drove to New York, arriving midafternoon at a spot not far from Keen and Keen Valley, the access point of the North Fork of the Bouquet River. The trail begins at an unmarked but distinctive hunters' trail, and continues through some wonderful hardwood and open areas on its way to the Dix Range—a beautiful four-mile hike. By six in the evening, having reached the South Fork of the Bouquet, they chose a campsite.

Peter and Lauren left at about eight-thirty the next morning in a miserable drizzle, hiking through tangles of dense shrubbery before reaching the summit about two hours later. They rested for about thirty minutes before returning to camp, getting there about noon. As they ate lunch, a couple of gunshots shattered the serenity like broken glass. Shrugging their shoulders, they dismissed it as target shooting.

On their way back to the car, they suddenly spotted in the distance two men wearing bright red Day-Glo clothing, carrying guns. A jolt of fear ran through them, sending rivulets of sweat running down their faces. Deer season! In Vermont, it wouldn't start for another two weeks. In dismay, they looked down at their clothing—all browns and grays. Distressingly deerlike. They dug into their packs to find anything colorful they might wear. "At least our packs are red," Peter said hopefully.

Still three and a half miles from safety, they began to sing at the top of their lungs. Hurrying down the trail, they saw dozens of hunters. Some were up in trees, others sat right in the middle of the trail. Kids not much bigger than their rifles were just itching for a reason to shoot. After safely reaching their car, Peter and Lauren hightailed it out of the area.

It was a scary but beautiful trip. The following year—before the start of hunting season—the couple returned to Dix and Peter proposed to Lauren on the summit. Later, Peter told his story to Dick Kelty, adding that "we might not be alive today if not for Dick's willingness to make red packbags."

Dick's response was, "Hmmm, I wonder how many we lost because they were wearing green packs."

Rod, Dave, and Lynn, all experienced backpackers, were planning a four-day trip to Dream Lake, an aptly named alpine lake in the Wind River Mountains of Wyoming. Twelve people were invited, including Debbie, who had never hiked before and who owned no equipment. This was soon remedied by friends, who lent her everything she needed. The more experienced hikers took charge of buying and packaging all the food for everyone. The packages would be distributed at the trailhead.

The group headed west out of Salt Lake City toward Pinedale, Wyoming, on a Thursday afternoon, reaching Scab Creek trailhead four and a half hours later. They slept overnight in the campground, and in the morning gathered around for the distribution of food packages. Debbie's pack was crammed full, she claimed, leaving no room for anything else. Everyone looked surprised, but they just shrugged their shoulders and split up her share.

The first mile of the trail was very steep and challenging, and Debbie was not doing well. "My feet hurt, I can't get my breath, my shoulders ache," she moaned. Lynn tried to help her by adjusting her shoulder straps and waist band, but nothing seemed to help. She continued to complain, lagging far behind everyone else.

By about three that afternoon, they reached the South Fork of Boulder Creek. They walked along the edge of the deep, swiftly running creek, looking for a place to cross. Finally they found a spot where they could jump from rock to rock, thus keeping their boots dry. The jumps were a bit tricky with forty- or fifty-pound packs on their backs, so they formed a chain, passing the packs hand-to-hand. Dave grinned at Lynn when he handed him Debbie's pack. It was so light. With one hand, Lynn tossed it over Rod's head to an unsuspecting Albert, who screamed and ducked, letting the pack fall on the grass. When he picked it up, he just shook his head.

As they hiked along, they speculated on how such a stuffed pack could be so light. When they arrived at Dream Lake, they watched with interest as Debbie unpacked. Out came three items: an electric toothbrush, a makeup case with mirror, and the largest feather pillow they had ever seen. Needless to say, Debbie wasn't invited on the next trip.

David Klemes and two of his friends decided to drive to the Fort Apache Indian Reservation in Arizona and hike up Cibicue Creek. They'd heard about a beautiful three-mile hike to a waterfall.

The hike begins in a canyon, and the temperature there was in the nineties. There is no trail, so they had to hike along the creek bed. They carried no water—only the means to purify it. At first it was a nice, relaxing hike through beautiful scenery. There was even cool water to swim in when it got too hot. They soon learned, however, why the hike was not recommended for beginners. They reached a spot where the canyon was so narrow that they had to put hands and feet on both sides of the steep canyon walls and shuffle along as best they could with the water rushing beneath them. Later they had to do some rock climbing. It was more scrambling than technical, but perhaps too difficult for the average hiker.

It was a thrilling experience, but it occurred to them that it would be undesirable to be there during a flash flood. Smart hikers would check on the possibility of rain upstream before attempting this route.

The three friends met very few people, but twice came upon people hiking naked. They wore only backpacks, boots, and big smiles. "We didn't ask," said David, "but we hoped they were wearing sunscreen."

Born in Kenya of Scottish parents, Ian Allan was about to fulfill a long-held dream—to walk east from the top of Kilimanjaro to the Indian Ocean, a trek of about three hundred miles. Allan, who for twenty years has been the only man allowed to lead walking safaris in Kenya, was well qualified to lead this walk.

Ian invited his longtime friend Rick Ridgeway, the noted climber and author, and Michael Crooke, general manager of Kelty Pack, to join him in this momentous event. For those who would climb the mountain, it would be a three-week trip. Crooke, who could only spare ten days, would meet everyone at the bottom of the mountain after their climb, and hike about two hundred miles. Sponsors for the trip were Venture Films and Kelty.

The main group climbed Kilimanjaro from the Tanzania side. After descending the mountain, they met Crooke and then crossed the border into Kenya. Following the water drainages into Tsavo National Park, which is as large as Rhode Island, they entered a world of totally unspoiled nature. "We wanted to see this wild country just like people would have seen it sixty years ago—by walking," said Rick. "It was a thrill seeing all the animals in their natural habitat." Ian shot dozens of animals—with his camera.

They saw nary a dwelling on the whole trip, but there were plenty of animals, some of which were hostile. One day they stumbled across a lion and its kill—a big buffalo. They watched in awe as he marked out his territory and guarded his kill. "We were seriously charged by elephants, rhinoceroses, and water buffalo, and at night roaring lions circled our camp," said Michael. "Even while walking, we had to be alert for animals charging us from out of nowhere. Crocodiles were a worry, and lions had killed 130 people in this one area. I really felt a part of the food chain in Africa."

At the end of each day, after they had hiked twenty to thirty miles, the tired group reached a prearranged site where the safari company had set up tents and had a meal ready for them. It was a most welcome sight.

Twin brothers, Lou and Jim Whittaker, along with Pete Schoering and John Day, all avid climbers, had just made a record-setting three-day climb of Mount McKinley. But the speed of their climb exacted a price. Unaware that they had become punchy from oxygen deprivation, they made a mistake on the way down at about 17,800 feet, causing all four climbers to fall five hundred feet.

The Whittakers were lucky and had no serious injury, but Day broke both legs, and Schoering sustained a concussion and a frostbitten hand. The seriousness of the situation was exacerbated by the below-zero temperature. After the men endured a three-day bivouac at 17,300 feet, a helicopter arrived and lifted the two injured men out, at that time the highest rescue in aviation history.

Lou and Jim, knowing that a rescue team was on its way up the west buttress to help them down, looked through Pete's and John's packs to determine which of their gear should be taken down for them. They packed up the stuff and started down toward the rescue team, using the fixed rope they had previously attached at the top of the buttress.

The going was rough, and the brothers doubted that in their condition they would be able to carry the heavy loads very far. At 16,400 feet, they were joined by the rescue team, and suddenly the brothers had an idea. After asking if anyone was below them on the mountain, they faced the steep slope and slipped out of their packs, which dropped like stones, bounced two or three times, and then disappeared into the clouds, eventually landing over one thousand feet below.

When Lou and Jim reached the bottom of the rope, they walked over to the packs, fully expecting to find a pile of broken gear. They were astounded to find that their packs had not only survived but had suffered no damage. "Those Kelty Packs kept their integrity," said Lou. They picked up the packs, put them on, and started walking again. After two days of enduring severe storms, they finally got off the mountain.

Although John lost some mobility in his legs, and Pete part of his fingers due to frostbite, the experience didn't deter any of them from climbing again. In 1963 Jim distinguished himself as the first American to conquer Mount Everest, and today Lou runs the largest guide service on Mount McKinley. But the speed climbs are in the past. Lou tells his customers to expect the climb to take two or three weeks.

When Dick Kelty heard this story, he said, "I don't advocate transporting your packs that way. But if you can throw it, why carry it?"

■ Resources

Contact the National Outdoor Leadership School (NOLS) for its Leave No Trace guidelines: 288 Main St., Lander, WY 82520-3140; (800) 332-4100; http://www.lnt.org/

RESOURCES

Magazines

Outside Box 54729, Boulder, CO 80322-4729; (800) 678-1131 (in Colorado: 303-447-9330)

Backpacker P.O. Box 7590, Red Oak, IA 51591-0590; (800) 666-3434. On-line: Keyword: "backpacker" on American Online or at www.backpacker.com

Organizations

For more information about bird-watching, contact the American Birding Association, P.O. Box 4335, Austin, TX 78765; or the National Audubon Society, 950 Third Ave., New York, NY 10022

If you'd like to help support the 6,356-mile, coast-to-coast Discovery Trail, you can become a member of the American Discovery Trail Society, formed in April 1996 to manage and support the trail. For more information, including membership options, contact: American Discovery Trail Society, P.O. Box 729, Orinda, CA 94563; (510) 283-6800; E-mail: ADTSociety@aol.com

Contact the American Hiking Society and ask about the Volunteer Vacations Program, which has sent trail workers to national and state parks, national forests, national monuments, and Bureau of Land Management territory. American Hiking Society, P.O. Box 20160, Washington, DC 20041-2160; (703) 255-9308; Fax: (703) 255-9304

Rails to Trails Conservancy, 1400 16th St., N.W., Suite 300, Washington DC 20036; (202) 939-3425

Pacific Crest Trail Association, 5235 Elkhorn Blvd., Suite 256, Sacramento, CA 95842; (800) 817-2243

Appalachian Trail Conference, P.O. Box 807, Harpers Ferry, WV 25425; (304) 535-6331

Conservation Groups

Defenders of Wildlife publishes updates on pending legislation: Activist Network, 1101 14th St. NW, #1400, Washington, DC 20005; (202) 682-9400; Website: http://www.defenders.org

League of Conservation Voters tracks candidates through its National Environmental Scorecard: 1717 L St. NW, Suite 750, Washington, DC 20036; (202) 785-8683; http://www.lcv.org

National Resources Defense Council provides legislative updates on its Web site. For those without access to the World Wide Web, contact Public Education Department, 40 W. 20th St., New York, NY 10011; (212) 727-2700; http://www.nrdc.org

National Wildlife Federation, 1400 16th St. NW, Washington, DC 20036-2266

Sierra Club is involved in a wide array of environmental activism: 85 Second St., 2nd floor, San Francisco, CA 94105-3441; (415) 977-5500; http://www.sierraclub.org

The Wilderness Society endeavors to protects America's wild-
lands: 900 17th St. NW, Washington, DC 20006-2596;
(202) 833-2300

Maps

United States Geologic Survey, Box 25286, Federal Center,
Denver, CO 80225; (800) 435-7627. USGS maps are available for anywhere in the country, though some haven't
been updated in thirty years.

Trails Illustrated, P.O. Box 4357, Evergreen, CO 80439;
(800) 962-1643. Web site: http://www.aescon.com/trails.
Trails Illustrated topo maps, of national parks throughout
the United States, and recreation areas in the Southwest,
are waterproof and tearproof.

Latitude 40 combines USGS accuracy with local wisdom to
create easy-to-use, waterproof, and tearproof topos. For
more information, call 303-258-7909.

Parks

Grand Canyon National Park, P.O. Box 129, Grand Canyon,
AZ 86023; (520) 638-7888

Great Smoky Mountains National Park, Gatlinburg, TN
37738; (423) 436-1200

Olympic National Park, 600 E. Park Ave., Port Angeles, WA
98362; (360) 452-4501

Shenandoah National Park, 3655 U.S. Hwy. 211 E, Luray,
VA 22835-9036; (540) 999-3500

Wind Cave National Park, RR 1, Box 190-WCNP, Hot
Springs, SD 57747-9430; (605) 745-4600

Yellowstone National Park, P.O. Box 168, Yellowstone National Park, WY 82190; (307) 344-7381

Yosemite National Park, P.O. Box 577, Yosemite, CA 95389; (209) 372-0200

INDEX

Italicized page numbers indicate illustrations; those in boldface indicate tables

ROUGH GUIDES...
SMOOTH TRAVEL

More than 200 travel guides from Amsterdam to Zimbabwe and everywhere in between

ROUGH GUIDES

"The antidote to unhip guidebooks"

—Detroit Free Press

www.roughguides.com   **At bookstores everywhere**

Distributed by Penguin Putnam, Inc.